THE UNIVERSITY OF WINCHESTER

Martial Rose Library
Tel: 01962 827306

To be returned on or before the day marked above, subject to recall.

The Theatres of War

The Theatres of War
Performance, Politics, and Society, 1793–1815

GILLIAN RUSSELL

CLARENDON PRESS · OXFORD

This book has been printed digitally and produced in a standard specification
in order to ensure its continuing availability

OXFORD
UNIVERSITY PRESS

Great Clarendon Street, Oxford OX2 6DP

Oxford University Press is a department of the University of Oxford.
It furthers the University's objective of excellence in research, scholarship,
and education by publishing worldwide in

Oxford New York

Auckland Cape Town Dar es Salaam Hong Kong Karachi
Kuala Lumpur Madrid Melbourne Mexico City Nairobi
New Delhi Shanghai Taipei Toronto
With offices in
Argentina Austria Brazil Chile Czech Republic France Greece
Guatemala Hungary Italy Japan South Korea Poland Portugal
Singapore Switzerland Thailand Turkey Ukraine Vietnam

Oxford is a registered trade mark of Oxford University Press
in the UK and in certain other countries
Published in the United States

ISBN 978-0-19-812263-0

Printed and bound in Great Britain by CPI Antony Rowe,
Chippenham and Eastbourne

Cover illustration: [J.S.], *Noddle-Island, Or How, Are We Decieved* [sic],
pub. M. Darly, 1776. By permission of the British Museum

*To Ada,
Colin, and Philip*

Acknowledgements

In 1969, when the British army was being welcomed by both Catholics and Protestants to Northern Ireland, my family invited a group of soldiers on security patrol to join us for a cup of tea. I have vivid memories of those soldiers reminiscing about Aden as they sat squeezed together on our sofa, their guns stacked in a pile in the centre of the living room. During the course of writing this book, which is concerned with military–civilian encounters in another place and era, I realized how much it derived from early experience of a community at war. The book has, however, been produced in a very different environment from that of Northern Ireland—Australia—and I would like to acknowledge the institutional, intellectual, and personal support I have received here. The project was aided by grants from the Faculties Research Fund of the Australian National University and the Australian Research Council; in 1993 a grant from the Staff Development Fund gave me time to complete the manuscript. I would also like to thank my colleagues at the ANU—Jon Mee, Iain Wright, Ian Higgins, and in particular, Iain McCalman, whose work has informed this book in more ways than he probably knows.

From Sydney, Deirdre Coleman gave wonderful boosts to my morale when they were most needed. Simon Penny directed me to the work of Paul Virilio, for which I am grateful. Thanks also to Susan Fraser for assistance in researching Chapter 8, to Glen Rose and Janet Lawrence for help in final preparations, and to Gerwin Strobl for support in London. I am also grateful to Andrew Lockett, whose interest in the project at an early stage was a significant factor in its coming to fruition. Thanks also to Susan Wiseman, for providing encouragement, as well as coffee and a roof, at the very beginning of my research. Benjamin Penny has talked the book through with me at every stage—my overriding debt is to him.

Contents

List of Illustrations

Abbreviations

DW Richard Brinsley Sheridan, *Dramatic Works of Richard Brinsley Sheridan*, ed. Cecil Price (2 vols.; Oxford, 1973), ii.
WP Tate Wilkinson, *The Wandering Patentee* (4 vols.; York, 1795).

I

Introduction:
War and Late Georgian Society

In February 1793 the French National Convention declared war on Britain, a war which was to continue, apart from the brief respite of the Peace of Amiens in 1801–3, until Wellington's victory at the Battle of Waterloo in 1815. It was a war conducted on a global scale, engaging most of Europe and fought in a number of 'theatres', including Russia, the Mediterranean, and the West Indies. As C. A. Bayly has pointed out, the British victory over France in 1815 signified a tremendous recovery in the country's fortunes after the nadir of the loss of the American colonies in 1783. In the period between 1793 and 1820 the armed forces of Britain trebled in size and British rule was extended to cover 26 per cent of the world's population.[1] Curiously, however, the social and cultural ramifications within Britain of a global conflict of such magnitude have been largely neglected. Linda Colley has noted how 'extraordinarily little' we know about the response of most British people to what was only one of a long series of wars throughout the eighteenth century. She suggests that this ignorance is due to the long-standing assumption by political and military historians that war was the game of parliamentarians, bureaucrats, and generals, conducted outside Britain and of little interest to the majority of the population.[2] Recent general surveys of eighteenth-century society reflect this view: Roy Porter's *English Society in the Eighteenth Century* devotes very little space to the army and navy while the category of 'Albion's People', the title of John Rule's recent book, does not seem to include those who fought in its name. Rule considers war only in so far as it impinged on crime levels.[3] The idea of war as occurring outside the ambit of most people's lives in the eighteenth century is a mistaken one:

---

[1] C. A. Bayly, *Imperial Meridian: The British Empire and the World 1780–1830* (London, 1989), 3.

[2] Linda Colley, *Britons: Forging the Nation 1707–1837* (New Haven, Conn., 1992), 3.

[3] Roy Porter, *English Society in the Eighteenth Century* (Harmondsworth, 1982); John Rule, *Albion's People: English Society, 1714–1815* (London, 1992). The standard work on the social history of Revolutionary and Napoleonic Wars remains Clive Emsley's *British Society and the French Wars, 1793–1815* (London, 1979).

for one thing, a considerable section of the population experienced military service, if not directly as participants, then indirectly as the relatives and dependants of soldiers and sailors. In the Revolutionary and Napoleonic Wars one tenth of the male population saw some military service, while 400,000 volunteers signed up to defend Britain against the French threat in 1803–4, amounting to what one historian has described as the 'greatest popular movement in Georgian Britain'.[4]

If social and political historians have been slow to acknowledge the presence of the soldier and sailor in Georgian life, then the response of literary studies has been even more negligible. Two important anthologies of poetry—Betty T. Bennett's *British War Poetry in the Age of Romanticism* (1976) and Roger Lonsdale's *New Oxford Book of Eighteenth Century Verse* (1984)—have revealed the extent to which all kinds of writers were engaging with the subject of war and the status of the soldier and sailor in contemporary society but, so far, their findings have largely been ignored.[5] The impact of the Revolutionary and Napoleonic Wars on the work of British Romanticism's 'Big Six'—Blake, Wordsworth, Coleridge, Byron, Shelley, and Keats—remains one of the few uncharted territories for canonical Romantic studies, and while the turn to cultural history and New Historicism has led to some preliminary work in this area, much more is still to be done.[6] In particular, the significance of war as a cultural, and not just a social or economic phenomenon needs to be fully explored and contextualized.

The neglect of the subject of war by both literary studies and, to a lesser extent, social history, can be partly explained by the view of military history as the (predominantly male) preserve of militarists—ex-brigadiers in tweed jackets or graduates of West Point and Vietnam. However misconceived and prejudicial, this identification represents an invisible barrier, ensuring that military history has remained unaffected by the interdisciplinary change sweeping the humanities as a whole in recent years. It has also allowed literary studies and social history to be incurious about the subject of war, as if in approaching it one was somehow politi-

---

[4] J. E. Cookson, 'The English Volunteer Movement of the French Wars, 1793–1815: Some Contexts', *The Historical Journal*, 32 (1989), 867.

[5] Betty T. Bennett (ed.), *British War Poetry in the Age of Romanticism: 1793–1815* (New York, 1976); Roger Lonsdale (ed.), *The New Oxford Book of Eighteenth Century Verse* (Oxford, 1984).

[6] See Nicholas Roe, *Wordsworth and Coleridge: The Radical Years* (Oxford, 1988) and Alan Liu, *Wordsworth, the Sense of History* (Stanford, Calif., 1989). For a study of the relationship between war and eighteenth-century fiction see David McNeil, *The Grotesque Depiction of War and the Military in Eighteenth-Century Fiction* (Newark, NJ, 1990).

cally compromised. One of the aims of this book is to reclaim military history for eighteenth-century cultural studies, mainly because war is as much a cultural event as it is a matter of government policy or the grand strategy of generals and admirals. The mediation of war—whether in the form of plays, poems and novels, acts of public commemoration or, as I shall argue later, the behaviour of audiences in the theatre—is crucial to its perpetuation. The impact of the French wars was not just a matter of food crises or rising crime rates, important though they were: it was also a matter of how the wars affected and altered the textures of feeling, thought, and behaviour at this period and, in particular, how men and women perceived themselves as actors in the theatres of war.

War and Patriotism

This culture of war was profoundly affected by the fact that the Revolutionary and Napoleonic Wars were different in character from previous conflicts between Britain and France. Throughout the eighteenth century Britain had been engaged in a series of armed disputes with France and her allies—the War of the Spanish Succession (1702–13), the War of Jenkins's Ear and the Austrian Succession (1739–48), the Seven Years War (1756–63), and the American War of Independence (1775–83). These conflicts were part of the long struggle between Britain and France for global hegemony. Linda Colley has argued that they were also crucial in the shaping of British national identity in so far as war functioned as a crucible in which 'manly' British values could be tested against the effeminate Gallic 'other'.[7] In 1793, however, the nature of the enemy had changed: the British people found themselves confronting not the old absolutist France but the Revolutionary *patria*. Influenced by the American War of Independence, the French Revolution mobilized the nation as a whole—men, women, children, and the old—in order 'to preach the unity of the republic and the hatred of kings'.[8] This was a challenge to the ideology of absolutist war in that soldiers had been previously accustomed to fight on behalf of kings and not against them. Most eighteenth-century wars had been conducted on a limited scale by professional armies, led by representatives of aristocratic élites and often augmented by foreign mercenaries. The French Revolution altered this

---

[7] Colley, *Britons*, esp. 87–90. See also Gerald Newman, *The Rise of English Nationalism: A Cultural History, 1740–1830* (New York, 1987), esp. 74–7, 189–91.

[8] From the decree of the *levée en masse*, Aug. 1793, quoted Emsley, *British Society*, 3.

by introducing the concept of a citizen army fighting for the security of the nation and for ideological principles. Military struggle became an intrinsic part of the propagation of the Revolution and a key to its survival. The bearing of arms was represented as a basic right and duty of citizenship to the extent that to be a citizen was to be a soldier of the Revolution and vice versa.

Alan Forrest and others have pointed out that the ideology of the nation-at-arms as promulgated by the *levée en masse* of 1793 was not so thoroughgoing in practice. Certain regions of France and some sections of the community as a whole remained resistant to the call to arms, preferring to maintain their families and their farms rather than fight for the Revolution, while significant elements of the pre-Revolutionary army of the line remained intact.[9] Moreover, in many respects, the Revolutionary governments of the 1790s were influenced by the same considerations of foreign policy that had dominated relations between France and Britain before 1789, the same suspicions of British motives, the same desire to assert and extend French hegemony. The ideology of a 'people's war' was nevertheless a potent one, as indicated by the British government's promotion of its own *levée en masse*, the second phase of the Volunteer Movement in 1803–4. War with Revolutionary France also compelled the British government and people to re-examine fundamental questions of patriotic identity: what did it mean to fight for 'king and country' in a war which was, at base, a struggle over these very concepts?

For most of the eighteenth century patriotism had been identified with oppositional figures such as John Wilkes. It was an urban phenomenon, characterized by a militant protestantism, xenophobia, imperialist enthusiasm, and above all, bellicosity. In the 'Epistle to Bathurst', Alexander Pope caricatures a typical patriot of the day as an avid supporter of war, who would sell his birthright in order to defend his country:

> The woods recede around the naked seat,
> The Sylvans groan—no matter—for the Fleet:
> Next goes his Wool—to clothe our valiant bands,
> Last, for his Country's love, he sells his Lands.
> To town he comes, completes the nation's hope,
> And heads the bold Train-bands, and burns a Pope.[10]

[9] Alan I. Forrest, *Conscripts and Deserters: The Army and French Society during the Revolution and Empire* (New York, 1989) and *The Soldiers of the French Revolution* (Durham, NC, 1990).

[10] John Butt, Maynard Mack, *et al.*, *The Twickenham Edition of the Poems of Alexander Pope*, iii, part 2, ed. F. W. Bateson (London, 1951), 107–8, ll. 209–14.

There was a powerful element of commercial self-interest in radical patriotism: the strongest supporters of British rights were those who had most to gain from the acquisition of French and Spanish colonies. At the same time, claims to patriotic virtue could be used to further the demands of these groups for access to local and national decision making. Throughout the eighteenth century, therefore, the struggle to define 'true' patriotism and its 'natural' defenders had an important political dimension.

In the 1770s, however, the identity of the patriot began to change. As Linda Colley has argued, elements of the governing élite and, in particular, George III, actively sought to reclaim patriotism from the radicals. This process of redefinition was a complex one, involving, on the one hand, an elaboration of the mystique of kingship by means of a revived honours system and an increasingly sophisticated level of public ceremonial and, on the other, an attempt to humanize the King by representing him as an uxorious family man, a farmer, and particularly after his bouts of illness, physically vulnerable.[11] The 'Farmer George' image became a target for criticism, especially in the form of print caricature, but as Vincent Carretta has argued, such satire was ultimately a factor in the resilience of the British monarchy after 1789: 'domestication of the regal image brought the viewer up to the king's level as much as it brought the king down to his subject's.'[12] George III was increasingly perceived as the 'father' of the nation, paternally devoted to his subjects who were in turn encouraged to offer him their affection and respect. The ideological impact of this was threefold: it tended to place the King in a position above politics, thus rendering him increasingly invulnerable; it established affection for the monarch as a crucial test of British identity—it had not always been so—and finally, it attempted to remove patriotism from the realm of the political. Patriotism, or 'loyalty' as many supporters of the King and constitution preferred to call it, became a matter of 'natural' obligation transcending allegiances of party, class, and ethnicity. This construction of patriotic identity could be highly

[11] Colley, *Britons*. See also her articles 'Whose Nation? Class and National Consciousness in Britain 1750–1830', *Past and Present*, 113 (1986), 97–117; 'The Apotheosis of George III: Loyalty, Royalty and the British Nation 1760–1820', *Past and Present*, 102 (1984), 94–129. See also Hugh Cunningham, 'The Language of Patriotism, 1750–1914', *History Workshop*, 12 (1981), 8–33 and David Eastwood, 'Robert Southey and the Meanings of Patriotism', *Journal of British Studies*, 31 (1992), 265–87.

[12] Vincent Carretta, *George III and the Satirists from Hogarth to Byron* (Athens, Ga., 1990), 297.

effective politically and militarily, in that it allowed individuals to retain local ties while at the same time securing the fiction of a transcendent loyalty to Britain and the King. The soldiers and sailors fighting in the French wars may have felt themselves to be Irish, Highland Scots, or Welsh, but they were above all 'British', defending their king and country. By this I do not mean to suggest that the category of 'Briton' was always a stable one. On the contrary, precisely because of their relationship to other forms of identity—ethnic, localized, class or gender based—and because of their intensely politicized role in Georgian society, the meanings of Britishness were always contingent and provisional. Like many other aspects of eighteenth-century subjectivity, being British could be a theatrical performance, open to a variety of interpretations by its actors.

For its part, radical patriotism also underwent a profound change in the late Georgian period, beginning with the American War of Independence. Linda Colley has argued that Wilkite support for the colonists eventually allowed the government to seize the patriotic high ground, a position that became even stronger after Britain's traditional enemies, France and Spain, joined the conflict on the side of the Americans.[13] In the realignment of radical patriotism that followed, its traditional pro-war stance was the major casualty. Radical opposition was increasingly couched in terms of a critique of war and not, as previously, an attack on the government for being insufficiently bellicose. This change was due to a number of factors: the internationalism of the Enlightenment which countered chauvinism and xenophobia and tended to condemn war as a barbaric practice, the pacifism of dissent, and most importantly, the ideological dimension of the French wars—the fact that this time the enemy was different and, moreover, that it was an enemy proclaiming many of the goals that the radicals themselves espoused. Anti-war radicals claimed that war was being used by Pitt to defeat not only the French Revolution but also the enemies of the government at home: war was thus a means of entrenching the bulwarks of 'Old Corruption'—ministerial power, a luxurious and vicious aristocracy, and a self-serving Anglican establishment. The true patriot was one who would defend the proper liberties of Englishmen against the encroachments of Pitt and his military machine: war could be represented not as a glorious crusade in defence of British values but as Britain held captive by its own corrupt guardians.

[13] Linda Colley, 'Radical Patriotism in Eighteenth-Century England' in *Patriotism: the Making and Unmaking of British National Identity*, ed. Raphael Samuel (3 vols.; London, 1989), i. 169–87.

The Army and the Navy

Within these competing discourses of patriotism, the issue of the French wars and the figures of soldier and sailor are of crucial importance. I now want to contextualize the themes of this book by considering public perceptions of the army and navy in the late Georgian period.

Throughout the eighteenth century public opinion had tended to favour the navy above the army. The fleet was not only the defender of the British Isles in time of war but also essential to the commercial life-blood of the nation, the key to the maintenance and extension of the British *imperium*. For these reasons, the navy took priority in government spending, absorbing a great deal of the country's income and in turn stimulating local and national economies. The most innovative industrial centres, in terms of both technological advance and the organization of the workforce, were not the mill towns of the north but the naval dockyards at Portsmouth, Plymouth, Deptford, Woolwich, Chatham, and Sheerness. Even before 1793 there were more men serving on the high seas during wartime than the populations of either Bristol or Norwich: by 1815 the navy had increased to a total of 179,000 men.[14]

In contrast to the army, the navy was perceived as being more open to men of talent; it was possible for someone of comparatively low birth to rise in the ranks, occasionally to the highest level. The most famous sailor-hero of the period, Horatio Nelson, was the son of a parson, as were the brothers of Jane Austen, who made significant careers for themselves during the French wars.[15] Captain Wentworth in Austen's *Persuasion* (1818) is initially rejected by Anne Elliot's family on the grounds of his lack of wealth or connections: the challenge which his naval success represents to a civilian world in which the privileges of birth and rank are still entrenched is indicative of a more widespread perception of the navy as offering an alternative, more meritocratic social model. Victorious admirals were often accorded the status of folk heroes, mainly because they were perceived as being more honest and trustworthy than corrupt and self-serving politicians. In the 1740s, for example, Edward Vernon was able to forge a political career largely on the basis of a disgust for the Walpole ministry and because, as a naval man, he was seen as embodying

---

[14] John Brewer, *The Sinews of Power: War, Money and the English State, 1688–1783* (London, 1989), 36–7; Bayly, *Imperial Meridian*, 3.

[15] See J. H. Hubback and Edith C. Hubback, *Jane Austen's Sailor Brothers: Being the Adventures of Sir Francis Austen G.C.B., Admiral of the Fleet and Rear-Admiral Charles Austen* (London, 1906).

British virtues, uncontaminated by the claims of party or rank. Nelson was to play a similar role in the Revolutionary and Napoleonic wars, becoming a hero to all shades of political opinion which, as we shall see later, struggled to appropriate his patriotic name.[16] Even before his death, a significant Nelson cult had developed. He was mobbed wherever he went, his progresses through the country in 1802 establishing a quasi-regal status that rivalled the popularity of George III.

For the ordinary seaman, life on board a man-of-war could be grim—pay was notoriously inadequate, food was poor, and the casualty rates at times of both peace and war were high. If the ship was commanded by a particularly stern disciplinarian, the seaman could expect regular floggings. The practice of 'flogging through the fleet', whereby the offender was taken from ship to ship to be punished, escorted by a flotilla of armed boats and a band playing the 'Rogue's March', prevailed throughout the period of the French wars. Whereas the campaign against the flogging of soldiers met with limited success, it was felt that it should not be extended to naval punishments, because of the particular need to enforce discipline in the fleet.[17] Not surprisingly, the navy was not the first career choice of men of the lower class. Many joined the fleet out of desperation, others to escape poverty, debt, or gaol. It is clear that both the army and the navy functioned as a means of cleansing society of its more undesirable elements. Douglas Hay has argued that there was a considerable increase in crime levels and general anxiety about crime during peacetime, not only because of the return of soldiers and sailors to society but also because war was no longer available as a means of social regulation: 'the crisis of demobilization . . . was not a passing spasm absorbed in a year or so, but rather a constant peacetime condition. Put another way, war was an invaluable device for the removal of the idle, and hence dangerous, poor.'[18] For this reason and others, sailors were often perceived as dangerously aberrant. Their naval costume, shipboard language, and manner distinguished them from the civilian community, while the

[16] See Kathleen Wilson, 'Empire, Trade and Popular Politics in Mid-Hanoverian Britain: the Case of Admiral Vernon', *Past and Present*, 121 (1988), 74–109; Gerald Jordan and Nicholas Rogers, 'Admirals as Heroes: Patriotism and Liberty in Hanoverian England', *Journal of British Studies*, 28 (1989), 201–24, and Gerald Jordan, 'Admiral Nelson as Popular Hero: The Nation and the Navy, 1795–1805' in *New Aspects of Naval History: Selected Papers from the 5th Naval History Symposium*, ed. The Department of History US Naval Academy (Baltimore, Md., 1985), 109–19.

[17] J. R. Dinwiddy, 'The Early Nineteenth-Century Campaign against Flogging in the Army', *English Historical Review*, 97 (1982), 309.

[18] Douglas Hay, 'War, Dearth and Theft in the Eighteenth Century: The Record of the English Courts', *Past and Present*, 95 (1982), 141.

tensions of life on board ship were often relieved by disorderly behaviour on shore. For Leigh Hunt, the sailor on leave was like 'a conqueror taking possession. He has been debarred so long, that he is resolved to have that matter out with the inhabitants.' His 'otherness' manifested itself in the very details of his physicality:

he goes treading in a sort of heavy light way, half waggoner and half dancing-master, his shoulders rolling, and his feet touching and going; the same way, in short, in which he keeps himself prepared for all the rolling chances of the vessel, when on deck. There is always, to us, this appearance of lightness of foot and heavy strength of upper works, in a sailor.[19]

Hunt's comment indicates the extent to which sailors were perceived as a distinctive subcultural group in Georgian society, as strange as the shark's teeth or shells that they carried with them as mementoes of their voyages.

The magnitude of the war effort between 1793 and 1815 meant that the government's use of the press-gang to recruit men for the navy became more widespread. Naval impressment aroused considerable opposition, not only because families and communities did not want to lose their young men, for emotional as well as economic reasons, but also because the practice was regarded as an act of tyranny, an assault on the freedoms of Englishmen. Press-gangs were hounded out of coastal towns and villages, and naval recruiting offices burned down. Plymouth dockyard workers used their industrial muscle and went on strike when one of their number was taken for the fleet, while in 1794 it was reported that over sixty merchant vessels were lying idle in the Thames for want of sailors to man them.[20] In spite of this, the press-gangs were still unable to keep up with the demands of the navy and in 1795 the government compelled local authorities to provide men for the fleet by means of the Quota Acts. Bounties and reduced sentences were given to debtors and petty offenders, a measure which led to the influx of better educated and often radicalized elements into the navy. This, combined with the government's policy of using the navy as a dumping-ground for Irish rebels—between 1793 and 1796 an estimated 15,000 Defenders and United Irishmen were dispatched to the fleet—created the conditions which led to the naval mutinies of 1797. While a significant element of the mutineers' grievances related to poor working conditions in the navy—bad pay, poor food, and overweening and brutal officers—they were also motivated by disaffection for the government and the war.[21] The mutinies represented one of the

---

[19] *Indicator*, 1 (1820), 177, 179.   [20] Emsley, *British Society*, 32.
[21] Roger Wells, *Insurrection: The British Experience 1795–1803* (Gloucester, 1983), 82.

most serious crises of the French wars, in that they not only threatened British security for a period but also undermined public confidence in the loyalty of the ordinary sailor. Eventually the mutinies collapsed and ring-leaders such as Richard Parker were hanged, but the events of May and June 1797 remained a lingering nightmare for government, a reminder of how dependent the country was on its armed forces.

The priority of the navy in military expenditure reflected its high prestige throughout the eighteenth century as promoter and defender of Britain's imperial interests. The political and social status of the army was less assured for a number of reasons. Standing armies were tradition-ally regarded as the tools of tyranny and both Whig and Tory govern-ments were reluctant to increase the military establishment in case they gave the impression that the liberties of Englishmen were under threat. Government ambivalence towards the army was also influenced by the fear of a politically independent officer class that can be traced back to the Civil War. In spite of these reservations, however, the authorities still found the army indispensable for the maintenance of public order. The militia acted as an unofficial police force throughout the eighteenth century, its main tasks being the prevention of smuggling and the sup-pression of riot. Its reputation was such that even rumours of the calling out of troops were enough to quell a disturbance. Civilian injuries and fatalities were not uncommon: an estimated 285 people were killed in the most serious disturbance of the late eighteenth century, the Gordon Ri-ots.[22] Throughout the period of the Revolutionary and Napoleonic Wars, the army was used extensively by the government to maintain public order. In 1812, as a result of the Luddite disturbances, 12,000 soldiers were sent to Lancashire and Yorkshire, amounting to more than the force which Sir Arthur Wellesley had brought with him to the Peninsula in 1808.[23]

Inevitably the army was reviled in many quarters as an instrument of oppression. When he was serving as part of the anti-Luddite forces in 1812, Alexander Alexander was verbally attacked by a man at an inn:

what are you but a slave yourself to them [the government], a poor pitiful scoun-drel, who has sold himself for a shilling a day; body and mind, you cannot have a will of your own, or do one thing but what you are bid, and must go to be shot at like a cock at Shrovetide; there is not a spark of spirit in thy body.[24]

[22] Brewer, *Sinews*, 53.   [23] Emsley, *British Society*, 158.
[24] Alexander Alexander, *The Life of Alexander Alexander*, ed. John Howell (2 vols.; Edinburgh, 1830), i. 215.

There was considerable resistance to recruitment for the army which, like the navy, was popularly identified with the dregs of society—Wellington at one time described the ordinary soldiers who had fought for him in the Peninsula as 'the scum of the earth'.[25] In 1794 houses used by the army for crimping—the military equivalent of impressment—were attacked by rioters in London.[26] When the government tried to expand the militia through a ballot system in 1796–7 there were widespread riots in the countryside. Even at the height of the invasion crisis in 1803 when the very survival of Britain seemed in doubt, many men expressed a reluctance to commit themselves to military service.[27] Moreover, some elements of the army had showed themselves to be susceptible to the anti-war arguments of the radicals. When the militia were called upon to fire on food rioters in 1795, some soldiers refused to obey orders. In towns throughout the country soldiers were being given handbills urging them to resist their superior officers and identify with the cause of the people.[28] A number of guardsmen were involved in the Despard conspiracy of 1802, while many radicals and ultra radicals, including William Cobbett, Robert Wedderburn, Arthur Thistlewood, and Despard himself, were ex-soldiers and naval men.[29] Whatever the actual extent of political disaffection within the army, it is clear that the government was sufficiently worried to act against the possibility of mass mutiny. Its response was to increase the number of barracks in Britain in an attempt to separate the military from the civilian population and also to ensure effective policing of radical towns such as Sheffield and Norwich. Before 1792 there were only 17 permanent infantry barracks in England, but by 1805 a total of 168 had been built with a capacity for 133,000 men. It is important to stress that the barrack-building programme began before the war with Revolutionary France. It was as much a response to the domestic political situation as it was to the demands of a foreign war.[30]

[25] Quoted Dinwiddy, 'Flogging', 320.

[26] John Stevenson, 'The London "Crimp" Riots of 1794', *International Review of Social History*, 16 (1971), 40–58.

[27] Colley, *Britons*, 291.

[28] Clive Emsley, 'Political Disaffection and the British Army in 1792', *Bulletin of the Institute of Historical Research*, 48 (1975), 232–4.

[29] For Cobbett's military background see: William Cobbett, *The Autobiography of William Cobbett: The Progress of a Plough-Boy to a Seat in Parliament*, ed. William Reitzel (London, 1967), 24–54. For Wedderburn's see Iain McCalman, *Radical Underworld: Prophets, Revolutionaries and Pornographers in London, 1795–1840* (Cambridge, 1988), 51–5 and Iain McCalman (ed.), *The Horrors of Slavery and Other Writings by Robert Wedderburn* (Edinburgh, 1991).

[30] Clive Emsley, 'The Military and Popular Disorder in England 1790–1801', *Journal of the Society for Army Historical Research*, 61 (1983), 17.

The barracks became targets for radical opposition to the war and to 'Old Corruption' in general. John Thelwall, and later William Cobbett, used Blackstone's *Commentaries* to argue that barracks were unconstitutional, an infringement on the liberties of Englishmen.[31] According to 'Albanicus', writing in 1793, Blackstone's advice that soldiers should live in close proximity to civilians was being flouted by 'those military Bastiles':

It is evident, therefore, this is a dark and daring attempt against our own liberties; that it is intended to estrange the minds of the Soldiers from the interests of the people; and by keeping them together as a distinct class of men, to endeavour to weaken their affections, and to make them forget they are citizens.[32]

This passage typifies the construction of the soldier within radical discourse as the tool of the government, whose affections naturally lie with the people and not the state. For Thomas Paine, the condition of soldiers was a 'double oppression', 'shunned by the citizen on apprehension of their being enemies to liberty, and too often insulted by those who commanded them'.[33] There was a strong emotional appeal in these arguments, not only to the soldiers themselves, who were encouraged to remember who they really were, but also to the civilian population at large. Pamphlet literature represented the soldier as deserving the pity of the general population, not their revulsion. 'Regard not *Common Soldiers*, as they are humiliatingly termed, with an eye of suspicion', advised Old Hubert in *The Village Association*, 'on the contrary, wherever you meet with them, pity and succour them.'[34] This construction of the soldier as an object of pity extended to representing him as a slave, someone who had sold his soul to the government and had no autonomy or control over his existence. The man who attacked Alexander Alexander for being a slave, 'a poor pitiful scoundrel', was presumably familiar with such arguments. 'Albanicus' argued that in the same way as the English people had agitated to relieve the suffering of their 'sable brethren, the unhappy Negroes', so it was appropriate to challenge the equally oppressive slavery of the soldiers. In 1792 William Wilberforce was attacked in a caricature for

[31] John Thelwall, *Tribune*, 2 (1796), 100; *Cobbett's Weekly Political Register*, 9 May 1812.
[32] Albanicus, *Letters on the Impolicy of a Standing Army, in Time of Peace* (London, 1793), 63.
[33] Thomas Paine, *The Writings and Speeches of Thomas Paine*, ed. Moncure Daniel Conway (4 vols.; London, 1894–6), ii. 513.
[34] Old Hubert [James Parkinson], *The Village Association or The Politics of Edley* (London, 1793), 7.

championing the cause of abolitionism while ignoring the plight of the soldier and sailor.[35]

The most powerful sign of the soldier's oppressed status which could be used to reinforce the analogy between his condition and that of the black slave was the practice of flogging. A campaign against this form of punishment, led by the radical Whig baronet Sir Francis Burdett, gained impetus in the early nineteenth century and was an important element in the radical attack on the government's war policy. Indeed, the revival of radicalism after 1809 can be linked to the way in which Burdett, Cobbett, and others seized on military-related issues such as flogging, the extension of the barrack system, the use of mercenaries, the deployment of the army as an internal police force and, in particular, the corrupt practices of the military establishment and those contractors who were profiteering from the war. The Mary Anne Clarke affair of 1809, whereby the Duke of York was revealed to have been dealing corruptly in commissions, furthered the radical critique of war as a prop of monarchical and ministerial privilege.[36] Such controversies became part of the continuing struggle for the meaning of patriotism. Cobbett and Burdett were able to attack the government and the military establishment for betraying the interests of those who were fighting for them and, in the case of flogging, for subjecting these soldiers to cruel and inhuman treatment. By championing the rights of the soldier, radicalism was able to strike back at the depoliticization of patriotism by the monarchy and its supporters, portraying itself as more truly 'British' than those who were directing the war.

Another important aspect of the militarization of British society during the Revolutionary and Napoleonic Wars was the development of the Volunteer Movement. The Volunteers were a force of men organized at a local level with the purpose of defending Britain against a French invasion. Their main function, however, was a political one: the Volunteer Movement was part of the attempt to appropriate patriotism in the name of king and country, mobilizing those elements of society—the urban professional, the prosperous artisan—who might otherwise have gravitated towards radicalism.[37] Its appeal was based largely on the theatricality

---

[35] Albanicus, *Letters*, 61; Dinwiddy, 'Flogging', 328.

[36] For the Mary Anne Clarke affair see J. Ann Hone, *For the Cause of Truth: Radicalism in London 1796–1821* (Oxford, 1982), 170, 177–8, and M. Dorothy George, *English Political Caricature 1793–1832: a Study of Opinion and Propaganda* (2 vols.; Oxford, 1959), i. 116–21.

[37] Cookson, 'Volunteer Movement', Colley, *Britons*, 283–319. See also J. R. Western, 'The Volunteer Movement as an Anti-Revolutionary Force, 1793–1801', *English Historical Review*, 71 (1956), 603–14; Ian F. W. Beckett, *The Amateur Military Tradition, 1558–1945* (Manchester, 1991), 71–89.

of the military—the attractions of a fine uniform, the excitement of manœuvres or a sham fight when there was no danger of being killed or injured, the opportunities for male exhibitionism and camaraderie culminating in the conviviality of the alehouse or the theatre. While military historians have in the past been dismissive of these aspects of volunteering, they were politically significant in so far as they broke down the boundaries between the military and the general population, making it feasible for all men to 'play' at being soldiers. Military pageantry also functioned as a way of affirming the self-worth of the volunteer in the eyes of the community, thus reinforcing a sense of his place within the nation as a whole. Across the country volunteering took the form of civic celebration—parading, commemorative dinners, the presentation of colours, and grand military fêtes such as that which took place at Leeds in 1795, attracting 60,000 people.[38] Such demonstrations represented an attempt to appropriate public space in the name of king and country: they had the effect of repeatedly confronting the British people with issues of communal and national identity—what it meant to be British, to resist the French, and above all, what it meant to be a soldier.

However, as Linda Colley and J. E. Cookson have pointed out, volunteering also had the potential to undermine the authority of what it was ostensibly defending.[39] As a result of the crisis of 1803–4, the government was compelled to broaden the ranks of the volunteers which became much less exclusively middle–class and more plebeian in character.[40] But in emulating the French nation-at-arms, as implied by the naming of the recruiting measure of 1803, the Levy-en-masse Act, the British government was also in danger of importing Revolutionary ideology. It was always possible that the British volunteer might identify soldiering with the rights of citizenship, and that the pikes, which were widely distributed in the crisis years of 1803–4, might resume their previously stigmatized association with revolution. Consequently, the government quickly moved to disband the army of citizen soldiers as the danger of a French invasion receded after 1804.

The Volunteers illustrated the potency of soldiering as an expression of patriotic identity. The government was anxious to promote loyalty to the

---

[38] Cookson, 'Volunteer Movement', 877.

[39] Colley, 'Whose Nation?' and *Britons*; Cookson, 'Volunteer Movement'.

[40] For the changing social composition of the Volunteer Movement see Ann Hudson, 'Volunteer Soldiers in Sussex during the Revolutionary and Napoleonic Wars, 1793–1815', *Sussex Archaeological Collections*, 122 (1984), 165–81, and J. E. Cookson, 'The Rise and Fall of the Sutton Volunteers, 1803–4', *Historical Research*, 64 (1991), 46–53.

crown and the constitution by means of the Volunteer Movement, but at the same time it did not want military activity to lead to a legitimation of political aspirations that might destabilize the existing order. As we have seen, figures such as Thelwall, Cobbett, and Burdett were concerned to maintain the oppositional and libertarian dimensions of patriotism, locating 'true' patriotic feeling with the defence of rights rather than privileges. Within these competing discourses of patriotism the configuration of the soldier and sailor was crucial. Both radical and loyalist patriotisms struggled to appropriate the political and cultural meanings of the armed forces at this period. For loyalism, this entailed the construction of the army and navy on the same ideological lines as the monarchy—as politically disinterested, steadfast in their concern for the welfare of the nation, passive defenders of the state rather than political agents in their own right. To become a soldier or a sailor was thus to exempt oneself from politics and take on the burden of the country's greater good. For its part, radical patriotism was equally concerned to model its own image of the soldier and sailor, to construct them, not as the brutalized agents of the state but as sons and brothers of the larger family of the people who, like prodigals, would be welcomed back into the fold. This contestation for the meanings of the army and navy took place across a range of discourses and cultural practices, one of the most important being the theatre.

Theatre and Theatricality

Until comparatively recently, the predominance of the theatre in the cultural and political life of the late Georgian period has been neglected.[41] Literary critics have either ignored the theatre, on the grounds of the absence of any work of enduring dramatic merit, or they have chosen to consider it in the light of the achievements of canonical figures such as Wordsworth and Coleridge. This tendency has been reinforced by the hitherto narrowly empirical and apolitical biases within theatre history.[42]

[41] An exception is Marc Baer, *Theatre and Disorder in Late Georgian London* (Oxford, 1992). See also Jonathan Bate, *Shakespearean Constitutions: Politics, Theatre, Criticism, 1730–1830* (Oxford, 1989); Paula R. Backsheider, *Spectacular Politics: Theatrical Power and Mass Culture in Early Modern England* (Baltimore, Md., 1993) and Julie A. Carlson, *In the Theatre of Romanticism: Coleridge, Nationalism, Women* (Cambridge, 1994).

[42] This is changing. See Thomas Postlewait and Bruce A. McConachie (eds.), *Interpreting the Theatrical Past: Essays in the Historiography of Performance* (Iowa City, Ia., 1989); Tracy C. Davis, *Actresses as Working Women: Their Social Identity in Victorian Culture* (London, 1991); Sue-Ellen Case and Janelle Reinelt (eds.), *The Performance of Power: Theatrical*

The assumption has been that because the Georgian theatre existed under conditions of strict censorship the drama was politically nullified.[43] In fact, the Georgian theatre was an intensely political place. While the Licensing Act of 1737 may have been efficient in ensuring that explicit political comment never reached the stage, it simultaneously generated the sensitivity which is the concomitant of censorship, ensuring that politics were seen everywhere. Georgian audiences were renowned for their capacity to interpret plays in inventive and unpredictable ways. A standard practice was to take certain phrases or characters out of context and apply them to contemporary events. In his evidence to the 1832 Parliamentary Committee on Dramatic Literature, the playwright Thomas Morton remarked on the tendency for audiences to 'force passages never meant by the author into political meanings. I think constantly I have observed that; and also we all know that a theatre is a place of peculiar excitement; I think their applause is enthusiastic, and their dislikes are violently expressed. I do not know anything more terrible than an enraged audience.' [44] These 'political meanings' could cover the whole spectrum of opinion at the period: audience expression ranged from anti-Gallic prejudice to subversive radicalism, from anti-ministerial factionalism to 'church and king' sentiment. Moreover, the socially encoded hierarchy of box, pit, and gallery tended to encourage the use of the auditorium as a forum for political expression. In 1794, for example, the lower class patrons of the upper gallery of the Sheffield theatre threw printer's ink and bricks and stones at those loyal members of the audience in the pit who had participated in the singing of 'God Save the King'.[45] Such incidents were repeated in the provincial theatres of Britain throughout the 1790s, illustrating the importance of the playhouse as a site for the articulation of social and political tensions.

The significance of the theatre as a political arena was widely recognized. Theatre managers such as Thomas Harris maintained close links with the government—Covent Garden was identified as a Tory house, while Sheridan's long association with Drury Lane marked it as a Whig establishment.[46] The two patent houses were the nexus of the

---

Discourse and Politics (Iowa City, Ia., 1991) and Janelle G. Reinelt and Joseph R. Roach (eds.), *Critical Theory and Performance* (Ann Arbor, Mich., 1992).

[43] L. W. Conolly, *The Censorship of English Drama, 1737–1824* (San Marino, Calif., 1976), 71.

[44] Report from the Select Committee on Dramatic Literature: with the Minutes of Evidence, House of Commons, 2 Aug. 1832, 212.

[45] *Sheffield Courant*, 1 Mar. 1794.

[46] Lucyle Werkmeister, *A Newspaper History of England, 1792–1793* (Lincoln, Nebr., 1967), 42–4.

cultural and political life of the metropolis, places where hack writers, spies, and prostitutes mixed with literati, parliamentarians, and royalty. George III was a frequent visitor to the theatre which retained its importance as a site for the expression of monarchical authority. The day after the royal coach was attacked by the London crowd in October 1795 on the way to the state opening of parliament, George III chose to visit Covent Garden in order to reimpose the significance of the monarchy in his person. Later, in 1800, Drury Lane was the venue for an assassination attempt upon the King by a disturbed ex-soldier, James Hadfield. George III's appearances at both Covent Garden and Drury Lane demonstrated the political significance of the playhouse as a space in which power was rendered visible and theatricalized. In this respect, the Georgian theatre was an old-fashioned institution: its political and cultural importance depended on its continuing to function in much the same way as it had in the early modern period, as a microcosm of society with the monarchy at its apex.

The political potency of the theatre was intensified by the importance of theatricality to Georgian society as a whole. The theatre functioned in a world where performance, display, and spectatorship were essential components of the social mechanism. The formal stage drama interacted with the drama of politics and society in a way which led to the enrichment of the theatre as a metaphor for social relations and, at the same time, intensified the potency of the institutionalized stage. Monarchical authority found expression in the spectacle of coronations and processions, the commemoration of birthdays and funerals, and the ostentation of court occasions. The life of most towns and cities revolved around a complex pattern of social performance—the pageantry of the assize and of local and Westminster elections, the macabre 'show' of public executions, the highly ritualized 'counter theatre' of riot, and the carnivalesque of plebeian events such as fairs and sports. A significant dimension of this theatricality is that of the army and navy. I have already noted the importance of the exhibitionism of military life in explaining the appeal of the Volunteer Movement during the French wars. In a country which had not been invaded by an enemy since 1745, the majority of the population experienced war as theatre—the performance of manœuvres and sham fights, the display, colour, and music of a parade, the elaborate choreography of large scale reviews presided over by the King in much the same way as he commanded Covent Garden or Drury Lane. Some of the reports of these military activities explicitly define them as theatre: for the *Sheffield Courant*, the review of the West Riding Yeomanry and Local Independent Sheffield Volunteers in June 1795 represented the 'grand scene of action, and Theatre of the military exercises . . . The actors, scenery and groupes on the field, exhibited a Coup d'Œil, extremely entertaining, novel, and picturesque'.[47] These 'entertainments' were augmented by a complex pattern of urban ritual and ceremony commemorating the events of the war. Bonfires signalled news of victories, towns were illuminated and decorated with transparencies, public dinners were held, and special performances staged at the theatres. Such rituals were important in publicizing the war and shaping community response to it. Some of them, such as the colour ceremony performed by the Northamptonshire Yeomanry in October 1795 had a distinctly political edge. *The Times* reported how the Colonel, Earl Spencer, 'delivered a most excellent, constitutional, and energetic speech, which met with universal applause, not only from the Gentlemen under arms, but from all the surrounding multitude, who were well wishers to their King and constitution'. After the Earl's speech the yeomanry proceeded to the race-ground 'colours flying, music playing, &c.' where they went through a number of exercises, the day concluding with 'many loyal and constitutional toasts' at the George and Peacock inns.[48] The evening conviviality was an integral part of an event which had used a range of devices—procession, display, music, ceremonial and choreographed exercise—not only to reinforce the standing of the yeomanry within the Northamptonshire community but also to promote loyalism. Two significant points can be made in relation to this: first, that this kind of military activity was an intervention in domestic politics, making it clear to the 'audience' that the yeomanry or volunteers were ready to act on behalf of the King and constitution. Secondly, it serves as a reminder that for many people, war was experienced not as written text—newspaper accounts, pamphlet literature, the broadside, or handbill—but primarily as a communal event. Any assessment of the cultural impact of the French wars has to take this into account. The response to the conflict was played out in the streets, commons, and theatres of Britain, as much as it was in the printed media of the period.

Theatricality was also important to how the military defined and saw itself. André Corvisier has claimed that while societies in Eastern Europe, the most notable example being Prussia, tended to become more military in this period, 'in western Europe we find military social groups *within but distinct* from society as a whole'.[49] Theatricality was important in the negotiation of this relationship: it was the means by which the impli-

---

[47] *Sheffield Courant*, 6 June 1795.   [48] 19 Oct. 1795.
[49] André Corvisier, *Armies and Societies in Europe, 1494–1789*, trans. Abigail T. Siddall (Bloomington, Ind., 1979), 197 (my emphasis).

cations of being 'within but distinct' could be explored, alleviated, or even celebrated. It was of particular importance to those members of the auxiliary forces—the militia, the yeomanry, and especially the volunteers— who never relinquished their identities as gentlemen farmers, urban artisans, or in the case of Volunteer officer Richard Cumberland, playwrights. The idea of military service as a performance was important in enticing these amateur soldiers to join the Volunteers in the first place; the corollary of this was that the role of soldier could be readily discarded and one's civilian identity reasserted.

This aspect of military culture was as important to the officer class as it was to the peasants or artisans of the Volunteers. A professional army was the creation of the nineteenth century and until then an element of amateurism prevailed, even within the ranks of the regulars. A colonel or captain was also a gentleman, anxious to maintain his place within civilian society. Theatricality, in the form of excessive military costuming and generally flamboyant behaviour, was one way for the officer to draw attention to the importance of the military 'within but distinct' from élite society. Conversely, by persisting in gentlemanly behaviour—gaming, amateur theatricals, fine dress, the club, politics—the officer ensured that the army did not become detached from the class whose interests it was defending. The link between the theatre of the battlefield and that of the club or the drawing-room was one of the most significant expressions of the ideology of a war of élites at this period.

There are other ways in which theatricality was important to military practice. Writing in the 1840s of his experience of the French wars, Thomas Jackson described the effective recruiting officer as a performer, someone who could beguile the unsuspecting civilian with his showmanship:

we had to strut about in best coats, and swaggering, sword in hand, drumming our way through the masses, commingled with gazing clodpoles, gingerbread mechanics, and thimble-rig sharpers . . . This sort of life might be said to be pleasant enough, and one might have sung the old corporal's song; but I was glad the revelry was over.[50]

Recruiting was not the only aspect of military life which was indebted to theatre. Discipline in both the army and navy took the form of highly ritualized punishments which had to be acted out before an audience in order to be fully effective. I have already referred to the custom of

[50] Thomas Jackson, *Narrative of the Eventful Life of Thomas Jackson* (Birmingham, 1847), 40.

'flogging through the fleet', a ritual which ensured that the fleet as a whole was made aware of the wrongdoing of one of their fellow sailors. In 1797 two soldiers of the Irish militia who were convicted of United Irish sympathies were executed at the camp at Blair's Warren. The report in *E. Johnson's British Gazette, and Sunday Monitor* described the deaths of the soldiers as 'a most awful spectacle . . . The whole of the execution was conducted with the greatest solemnity: the procession of the troops from Belfast was marked by its regularity and silence.' After the execution 'the troops marched in ordinary time by the bodies, and the ceremony closed by leaving the strongest symptoms of impression on all the spectators.'[51] Such events punctuated an existence for the ordinary soldier or sailor that can be described as a continuously theatricalized encounter with authority: every aspect of his life, from the mundane duty of attending to uniform and kit, to drill, manœuvres, and even recreation were all, to a varying degree, performances, patterns of behaviour defined by military rules. And when the soldier went to war these patterns of theatre became even more accentuated. The limited scale of eighteenth-century warfare lent a certain intimacy to fighting: battles took place in a physical space that could be surveyed by the eye of the commander; the comparatively restricted range of the musket meant that opponents were often in close view of each other; the time taken to reload meant that elaborate manœuvres had to be practised and perfected beforehand in order to maintain continuous fire. The successful general was one who could be simultaneously director and interpreter of the 'theatre of war', reading the signs of battle and moving his men accordingly. In some cases, the drama of battle was performed with a particular intensity. James Anton described one such incident during the battle of Quatre Bras, the day before Waterloo. The last file of Royal Highlanders had formed a square against the enemy and had temporarily checked their charge:

A moment's pause ensued: it was the pause of death. General Pack was on the right angle of the front face of the square, and he lifted his hat towards the French officer, as he was wont to do when returning a salute. I suppose our assailants construed our forbearance as an indication of surrendering; a false idea: not a blow had been struck nor a musket levelled; but when the general raised his hat, it served as a signal, though not a preconcerted one, but entirely accidental . . . Be this as it may, a most destructive fire was opened . . . shrieks and groans of men,

[51] *E. Johnson's British Gazette, and Sunday Monitor*, 28 May 1797.

the neighing of horses, and the discharge of musketry, rent the air, as men and horses mixed together in one heap of indiscriminate slaughter.[52]

Such an incident highlights the theatricality of eighteenth-century warfare. There is the heightened sense of the importance of time—'it was the pause of death', the encoded movements of bodies of men, moving from a file to a defensive square and at the centre, the 'performance' of the General. The fate of both the British and French soldiers was dependent on a normally unimportant act—the lifting of a hat—assuming an exaggerated significance, much in the same way as such a gesture would be accentuated in the theatre. It was the context of General Pack's action which gave it such an intimate, theatrical meaning; a gesture which in normal social intercourse would have been part of the mutual acknowledgement of social peers—the officer class—had in this case become a signal of death.

'The Open Theatre of the World'

The theatricality of military behaviour and indeed that of British society as a whole was profoundly affected by the impact of the French Revolution. The panic induced in the ruling élite by the events in France caused it to reassess its own role within a theatricalized public culture. This is apparent, for example, in the response to Thomas Paine's *Rights of Man*. Apart from using the resources of the print media in order to counter the subversive influences of Paine's book, the supporters of the crown and constitution organized public demonstrations against him. These took the form of a series of mock executions which occurred in towns and villages up and down the country in 1792–3, after Paine had fled England in order to escape prosecution for seditious libel. There is evidence that in some cases people were given money to participate in the burning and shooting of effigies of Paine; at the very least these events were 'allowed' to proceed by tolerant magistrates and local gentry.[53] Some of the mock executions revealed a considerable degree of theatrical sophistication.

[52] James Anton, *Retrospect of a Military Life, During the Most Eventful Periods of the Last War* (Edinburgh, 1841), 195.

[53] See Alfred Owen Aldridge, *Man of Reason: the Life of Thomas Paine* (Philadelphia, Pa., 1959), 182; Robert R. Dozier, *For King, Constitution, and Country: the English Loyalists and the French Revolution* (Lexington, Ky., 1983), 91; Alan Booth, 'Popular Loyalism and Public Violence in the North-West of England, 1790–1800', *Social History*, 8 (1983), 295–313; Gregory Claeys, *Thomas Paine: Social and Political Thought* (Boston, 1989), 144–5.

At Scarborough a sponge was concealed on an effigy and manipulated in order to make it seem that 'Paine' was crying. The poet William Cowper was given an account of a mock execution which suggests that a parson 'officiated' at a ceremony which included visual emblems equating Paine with the biblical serpent.[54] But perhaps the most elaborate 'staging' of Paine's execution occurred at the Yorkshire town of Heckmondwike. A local mill-owner, Benjamin Popplewell, pretended to be Paine in a performance which involved the 'discovery' of the 'arch-sedition monger' reading *Rights of Man* in the suitably satanic setting of a coal-pit. According to a nineteenth-century local historian, he was then led to the marketplace of Heckmondwike and in a flourish typical of the conventions of stage pantomime 'transformed' into a straw effigy which was 'shot amidst tremendous hootings and cries of "Church and King" and "Down with Tom Paine"'.[55]

The mock execution was a long established feature of British political behaviour (and continues to be so, as suggested by the anti-Poll tax demonstrations in 1989–90). While effigy burning could in some cases be politically subversive, in others, such as the example of Paine, it could be used to reinforce the existing social order. The events of 1792–3 represented an attempt by local gentry to harness a form of popular protest, countering the influence of *Rights of Man* at a plebeian level by suggesting a popular rejection of Revolutionary principles. The fact that the mock executions were widely reported in the press at the time may indicate that their audience was also the alarmed middle and upper orders. Numerous accounts of plebeians cheerfully burning and shooting Paine would possibly have assuaged fears of widespread disaffection amongst the lower classes. The fact that these events were allowed and even encouraged to happen suggests a willingness on the part of the ruling élite to participate in a public, theatricalized political culture. However, those who had sponsored the burnings and shootings of Paine's effigy had to be confident that their appropriation of a form of popular protest would not go too far, that the energies which they had released would be restrained within the ritual boundaries of the event. The 'theatre' of the mock executions, as revealed by Benjamin Popplewell's performance at Heckmondwike, was one way of preventing the occasion from going out of bounds by suggesting that it was just an act. Theatricality was relied upon to contain, as much as to permit, licence.

[54] Dozier, *For King*, 91; William Cowper, *The Letters and Prose Writings of William Cowper*, ed. James King and Charles Ryskamp (5 vols.; Oxford, 1979–86), iv. 344–5.
[55] Frank Peel, *Spen Valley: Past and Present* (Heckmondwike, 1893), 307–8.

In the wake of the French Revolution, however, this confidence in the limits of theatricalized political behaviour was called into question. William Cowper objected to the effigy burning of Paine, not only on account of the impropriety of a minister of religion officiating at a 'burlesque execution', but also because he doubted the political wisdom of 'playing with the passions of the multitude' in such a way. 'The wisest thing that government and the friends of government can do', he advised his correspondent Lady Hesketh, 'is to let those crackers sleep if they are disposed to do so. Fired as they may be to day on the right side, you cannot be sure that they will not prove equally combustible on the wrong tomorrow.'[56] Once the people had been inspired to 'act', where would the performance end? As Edmund Burke had suggested in *Reflections on the Revolution in France*, once started, the drama of the Revolution could not be easily contained or controlled. Symbolic acts, such as the King being taken by the people from Versailles to the Tuileries during the 'October Days' of 1789, had effectively 'killed' the sacral status of the monarchy; drama had made politics happen, rather than vice versa. In a particularly resonant analogy for his theatre-going public, Burke compared the French National Assembly to a riotous playhouse in which low fairground actors had usurped the tragedians:

They act like the comedians of a fair before a riotous audience; they act amidst the tumultuous cries of a mixed mob of ferocious men, and of women lost to shame, who, according to their insolent fancies, direct, control, applaud, explode them; and sometimes mix and take their seats amongst them; domineering over them with a strange mixture of servile petulance and proud presumptuous authority. As they have inverted order in all things, the gallery is in the place of the house.[57]

The danger of the French Revolution, according to Burke, was that the gallery, the section of the auditorium identified with the lower orders (and with the ordinary soldier or sailor) was now dominating the political theatre of France. Order, hierarchy, and sexual propriety were threatened: the audience had thrown off passivity and was 'mixing' with the actors, usurping the latter's performance.

The fact that Burke should conceive the French Revolution in these terms is a measure of the potency of theatricality in British political discourse and behaviour at this period. In responding to *Reflections on the Revolution in France*, Thomas Paine also represented the events in France

---

[56] Cowper, *Letters*, iv. 344.
[57] Edmund Burke, *The Writings and Speeches of Edmund Burke*: viii, *The French Revolution*, ed. L. G. Mitchell (Oxford, 1989), 119.

as theatre but in a very different way from Burke. Instead of a disorderly gallery 'in place of the house', Paine postulated a 'manly' theatre of the people. In the second part of *Rights of Man*, he attempted to define the differences between the monarchical system and the new representative governments of America and France by comparing the former to

something kept behind a curtain, about which there is a great deal of bustle and fuss, and a wonderful air of seeming solemnity; but when, by any accident, the curtain happens to open, and the company see what it is, they burst into laughter. In the representative system of government nothing of this can happen. Like the nation itself, it possesses a perpetual stamina, as well of body as of mind, and presents itself on the open theatre of the world in a fair and manly manner. Whatever are its excellencies or defects, they are visible to all. It exists not by fraud or mystery; it deals not in cant and sophistry; but inspires a language that, passing from heart to heart, is felt and understood.[58]

Rights of Man posited a theatre where the audience would not be subordinated to the performers but would in fact become the performance; where there would be no symbolism of religion or rank, no 'fraud or mystery' to conceal the citizen from himself and from others; where everything would be 'understood' and nothing unknowable. This 'open theatre of the world' would have profound consequences for the status of theatricality in British political behaviour and discourse as well as for the role of the institutionalized theatre itself. Ever since the Restoration the patent theatres had functioned as images of the monarchical system of government, epitomizing the ideology of concealment or obfuscation in Paine's terms, or for Burke, the 'decent drapery' that made life tolerable. *Rights of Man* signalled the displacement of the theatre from this central, signifying role in British culture because it implicitly questioned whether the new political entity, 'the people', could be adequately represented there. The history of the theatre and of public culture as a whole after 1789 can be regarded as an attempt to come to terms with the implications of the new 'open theatre of the world'.

In so far as theatricality was crucial to the conduct of war at this period, military culture and practice were also affected by these changes. A key actor in Paine's 'open theatre of the world' was the citizen soldier fighting on behalf of Revolutionary principles. On a visit to Paris in 1796, Theobald Wolfe Tone witnessed an entertainment at the Opera which concluded with soldiers from the National Guard rushing on to the stage at the words '*Aux armes, citoyens!*' What most impressed Tone about the

[58] Paine, *Writings*, ii. 426.

performance was that the soldiers were not acting: 'I never knew what
enthusiasm was before, and what heightened it beyond all conception was,
that the men I saw before me were not hirelings, acting a part; they were
what they seemed, French citizens flying to arms, to rescue their country
from slavery'.[59] The Revolutionary fervour of the performance was reality: there was no sense that the soldier was playing a part; instead, he had
become the role. This book as a whole is concerned with exploring the
extent to which such ideology could be said to have penetrated British
culture. In defending itself against the French threat, the British government was compelled to raise its own people's army; to what extent did the
roles of 'citizen' and 'soldier' merge in Britain? What part was played by
the theatre in the mediation of the French wars and in the contestation
for the cultural meanings of the army and navy? Last, but not least, how
did the individual soldier and sailor perform as actors in the theatres of
war? These are some of the questions with which this book will be
concerned. Before I proceed, however, it is necessary to determine in
greater detail the kind of 'theatre of war' that was so profoundly changed
by the events of 1793–1815.

[59] Theobald Wolfe Tone, *The Autobiography of Theobald Wolfe Tone*, ed. R. B. O'Brien
(2 vols.; Dublin, 1893), i. 233.

2

Camp Culture: The War of Élites

THE idea of the soldier as a variety of *homo ludens* is one which still prevails in military organization and training—exercises are referred to as 'games' or 'plays', for example—but it was especially important in the eighteenth century. The limited European warfare of the period was often represented in terms which stressed its aristocratic, even festive *élan*. This, for example, is Goldoni's account of a truce during the siege of Pizzighetone in Italy in the 1730s:

A bridge thrown over the breach afforded a communication between the besiegers and the besieged: tables were spread in every quarter, and the officers entertained one another by turns: within and without, under tents and arbours, there was nothing but balls, entertainments, and concerts. All the people of the environs flocked there on foot, on horseback, and in carriages: provisions arrived from every quarter; abundance was seen in a moment, and there was no want of stage doctors and tumblers. It was a charming fair, a delightful rendezvous.[1]

In this martial interlude the boundaries between the besiegers and the besieged are temporarily broken down, as are those that separated the battle from fashionable life in general. War is not distanced from the rest of society but instead is assimilated and celebrated as an integral part of aristocratic sociability, as essential and as meaningful as the levee or the ball. This is not to imply that wars could be polite or civilized affairs—even the comparatively limited warfare of the eighteenth century was capable of inflicting horrific suffering on its participants and on the civilian population in general—nor does it suggest that eighteenth-century society was wilfully blind to these kinds of realities. Rather, it reflects the view of war as a necessary evil of polite society. As the social activities of governing élites—theatre-going, balls, assemblies—were infused with certain political meanings, so their wars had fundamental social and cultural significance.

---

[1] Carlo Goldoni, *Memoirs of Goldoni*, trans. John Black (2 vols.; London, 1814), i. 207.

Philadelphia and Valley Forge

There were no more energetic exponents of the idea of war as a gentle-man's game than the officers who were sent to quell the rebellious colonists of America. The Hessian officer van Ewald noted that whereas the Americans carried a few worn garments and textbooks of military science, the portmanteaus of the British officers were packed with 'bags of hair powder, boxes of sweet-smelling pomatum, cards (instead of maps), and then often, on top of all, novels or stage plays'.[2] Before his arrival in America as commander of the British forces General John Burgoyne was better known as a man of the theatre. In 1774 he was responsible for the spectacular *fête-champêtre* in honour of the marriage of the Lord Stanley, a fellow officer. With the help of David Garrick, the *fête* had been adapted for Drury Lane as *The Maid of the Oaks*.[3] On his arrival in Boston, Burgoyne deliberately outraged the anti-theatrical sentiments of the colonists by performing plays in Faneuil Hall—*The Busy Body* by Susannah Centilevre, Aaron Hill's *Zara*, and *Tamerlane* by Nicholas Rowe. A farce ridiculing the Yankees, *The Blockade of Boston*, was specially written and performed by Burgoyne and his fellow officers. Its opening night, 8 January 1776, was notorious for an incident which has entered the annals of the Revolution. During the performance the rebels attacked the British quarters nearby and when one of the actors interrupted the farce to give the news of what had happened, many of the audience assumed that he was part of the show and applauded him. According to the nineteenth-century theatre historian William Dunlap, 'real' and 'theatrical' worlds had become conflated: 'the prompter of the speaker was not behind the scenes, but behind the trenches.'[4]

British military theatricals did not stop with Boston. The campaigns of the American war were also theatrical campaigns. General Howe's 'strolling company', as one prologue styled them, established theatres in New York and later, Philadelphia. Officers solicited playbooks from local loyalists; scenery and costumes were made or procured; military

---

[2] Quoted J. F. C. Fuller, *British Light Infantry in the Eighteenth Century* (London, 1925), 153.

[3] Gerald Howson, *Burgoyne of Saratoga: A Biography* (New York, 1979), 63–4.

[4] William Dunlap, *A History of the American Theatre During the Revolution and After* (New York, 1832), 47. See also George O. Seilhamer, *History of the American Theatre* (3 vols.; Philadelphia, 1888–91), ii. 16–21; Kenneth Silverman, *A Cultural History of the American Revolution: Painting, Music, Literature, and the Theatre in the Colonies and the United States from the Treaty of Paris to the Inauguration of George Washington 1763–1789* (New York, 1976), 292–5; Sylvia Frey, *The British Soldier in America: a Social History of Military Life in the Revolutionary Period* (Austin, Tex., 1981), 66–8.

bands provided the music. By the end of the British occupation of New York, the military theatre was on a semi-professional footing; indeed its 'manager', General Clinton, has been described as one of the most successful in the history of the colonial theatre in America.[5] These dramatic performances took place in the context of other social activities such as balls, convivial dining and assemblies, and an expanding leisure economy. In the train of the occupying force in Philadelphia, for example, came hairdressers and perfumers: 'the new occupation newspaper, *The Royal Pennsylvania Gazette*, advertised a startling array of luxury goods—cards, cricket bats, "Velverett" (cotton cloth with a velvet surface), "fashionable crooked combs", "Lip salve", "Purified Italian shaving powder".'[6]

Military and political historians have questioned the wisdom of the British army's failure to prosecute the war during the winter season. General Howe, in particular, seemed content to confine himself to Philadelphia in 1777–8, fully aware that Washington's army, physically and mentally undermined by the conditions of a winter encampment, was only eighteen miles away at Valley Forge. It would seem that, to some extent, the military strategy of generals such as Howe was determined by the rules of the British social season. Winter was the period of greatest political and cultural activity in London. The actors of the patent theatres resumed their strolling careers in the summer when, like parliament and the law courts, Covent Garden and Drury Lane were in recess. For Howe's 'strolling company' to establish themselves in town for the winter was therefore unexceptional. In addition, the social activities of the British—the plays, the entertainments, the drinking, the mistresses—had an important political dimension. As stated previously, Washington's army was encamped in close proximity to the British lines—scouts and spies were in constant traffic between the armies and both sides were fully aware of what the other was doing. While General Howe established a royal box for himself in the military theatre at Southwark Street and Major John Andre was painting landscape scenery in the manner of Drury Lane's De Loutherbourg, Washington's army was encamped in huts made from turf and branches, suffering food shortages and rampant sickness. To adapt E. P. Thompson, both armies were watching each other, playing theatre

[5] Diane B. Malone, 'A Survey of Early Military Theatre in America', *Theatre Survey*, 16 (1975), 61. See also Jared A. Brown, '"Howe's Strolling Company": British Military Theatre in New York and Philadelphia, 1777 and 1778', *Theatre Survey*, 18 (1977), 30–43, and 'British Military Theatre in New York in 1780–81', *Theatre Survey*, 23 (1982), 151–62.

[6] Silverman, *Cultural History*, 333–4. See also Brown, '"Howe's Strolling Company"'.

and counter-theatre to the other's auditorium.[7] While the theatricality of British military behaviour in Philadelphia is obvious, that of Washington's army at Valley Forge was no less a performance. Washington had deliberately sequestered his men there, even though they were already hungry and exhausted, refusing to allow them to prey on the local civilian population.[8] The period at Valley Forge became a test of the virtue of the American army, but Washington needed Howe's 'strolling company' to highlight just how virtuous his men were. The proximity of Valley Forge to Philadelphia proved the ideological, cultural, and political differences between the two antagonists—Whig versus Tory, the country versus the city, the margin versus the centre, austerity versus luxury, manliness versus effeminacy, God versus Mammon.

Patterns of theatre and counter-theatre can also be detected in the conduct of battle itself. On 20 May 1778, as Howe was preparing to relinquish the supreme command of the army to General Clinton, a force of American soldiers under Lafayette mounted a break-out from Valley Forge. With 2,200 men, one-third of Washington's army, Lafayette established a position at Barren Hill, approximately half-way between Valley Forge and Philadelphia. The exact purpose of the expedition is unclear. It was ostensibly designed to interrupt communications with Philadelphia, but Washington may also have been allowing Lafayette, who had recently joined the American forces, to have an adventure. From the outset the British were aware of Lafayette's expedition and made preparations to welcome him as a captive to Philadelphia. Separate forces advanced to Barren Hill with the intention of trapping him, but Lafayette discovered their approach, as did Washington at Valley Forge by means of field glasses.[9] American scouts having discovered an escape route, Lafayette tricked the British into believing that he was attacking them by a series of feigned manœuvres. He used this as a cover to enable his force to escape across the river Schuylkill and back to Valley Forge before the British were aware of his absence.

Lafayette's escape was the final ignominy for Howe before his return to

---

[7] E. P. Thompson, 'Patrician Society, Plebeian Culture', *Journal of Social History*, 7 (1974), 402.

[8] Robert Middlekauff, *The Glorious Cause: The American Revolution 1763–1789* (New York, 1982), 411.

[9] Charles Stedman, *The History of the Origin, Progress, and Termination of the American War* (2 vols.; London, 1794), i. 377. See also Winthrop Sargent, *The Life and Career of Major John André, Adjutant-General of the British Army in America* (New York, 1902), 184–201; Christopher Ward, *The War of the Revolution*, ed. J. R. Alden (2 vols.; New York, 1952), ii. 562–7.

London. However, his departure had not gone unnoticed by his fellow officers. On 18 May 1778 Majors Andre and Delancy organized a grand pageant in his honour, the 'Mischianza', which has since become notorious as evidence of the 'degeneracy' of the British army in America. Charles Stedman, the loyalist historian of the war who had served under Howe and Clinton, compared it with the entertainments of that 'vainglorious monarch and conqueror, Louis XIV'.[10] The 'Mischianza', Italian for medley or mixture, began with a regatta on the river Delaware. Three divisions of galleys, decorated with streamers, brought General Howe and the company to the landing place at the Old Fort where the home of a local loyalist, Mr Wharton, had been specially prepared to receive them. The company proceeded to the Wharton house through an avenue formed by two files of grenadiers and a line of light horse. In front of the house was a square lawn lined with soldiers, on which a mock chivalric battle was to be staged. The square was decorated with two triumphal arches in honour of Howe, on each side of which were pavilions for the women of Philadelphia 'dressed in Turkish habits, and wearing in their turbans the favours with which they meant to reward the several Knights who were to contend in their honour'. At the sound of trumpets, a group of officers entered dressed as knights: they wore costumes of red and white silk, while their horses were 'richly caparisoned in trappings of the same colours'. After the mock battle, the company, with the ladies before them, moved in procession through the arches, one of which was decorated with 'a bombshell' and 'a flaming heart'.[11] They were received in the hall of the Wharton house: according to Winthrop Sargent, Major Andre's biographer, 'much of the decorations, as the Sienna marble, &c., was on canvas, in the manner of stage scenery'.[12] The 'knights' and ladies refreshed themselves in this hall and were then conducted to a ballroom. During the ball, 'the windows were thrown open, and a magnificent bouquet of rockets began the fire-works', organized by the chief engineer, Captain Montresor:

towards the conclusion, the interior part of the triumphal arch was illuminated amidst an uninterrupted flight of rockets and bursting of baloons [sic]. The military trophies on each side assumed a variety of transparent colours. The shell and flaming heart on the wings sent forth Chinese fountains, succeeded by fire-pots. Fame appeared at top, spangled with stars, and from her trumpet blowing the

[10] Stedman, *History*, i. 385.
[11] 'Particulars of the *Mischianza* in *America*', *Gentleman's Magazine*, 48 (1778), 354, 356.
[12] Sargent, *Life*, 184.

following device in letters of light, *Tes Lauriers sont immortels:*—A *fauteur* of Rockets, bursting from the pediment, concluded the *feu d'artifice*.[13]

The entertainment did not end here. At the stroke of twelve, 'large folding doors, hitherto artfully concealed', were opened to reveal an opulent supper. General Howe and the company were served by '24 black slaves, in oriental dresses, with silver collars and bracelets'. As the supper was concluding, one of the knights, to the sound of trumpets, led a toast to the royal family and the participants. Dancing and gaming continued until four o'clock in the morning.[14]

The 'Mischianza' has been dismissed by political and military historians, who have either regarded it as proof of the degeneracy of the British or ignored it altogether. Like the passion for amateur theatricals, the entertainment proclaimed the place of the officer class within the fashionable élite at home in Britain. With its emphasis on opulent display, spectacle, and the merging of indoor and outdoor space, the 'Mischianza' owed much to the fashion for the *fête-champêtre*, for which a military man, General Burgoyne, had been largely responsible. However, although the 'Mischianza' looked back to the fashionable world in London, it was not completely divorced from the real war that was going on around Philadelphia. Robert Middlekauff has described the battlefield of the American war as an 'intimate theater': 'the killing range of the musket, eighty to one hundred yards, enforced intimacy as did the reliance on the bayonet and the general ineffectiveness of artillery.'[15] Killing involved seeing or even touching the enemy: manœuvres in preparation for the bayonet assault constituted a code which every soldier on the battlefield fully understood. We have seen already how the American and British forces existed within close proximity of each other, how Washington had been aware of Lafayette being encircled by the British. Another significant element of the intimate theatre of war was topography. Lafayette's escape was due to the way that he had successfully integrated military performance—the feigned manœuvres which deceived the British into thinking that he was attacking them—with 'scenic space', that is, the landscape around Barren Hill against which the encounter was enacted. The configuration of the hill and the river Schuylkill had been crucial to his original strategy and had almost led to his downfall, but in that he used the hill to conceal his flight from the British it also enabled him to escape capture. The 'Mischianza' also made significant use of topography. Gen-

---

[13] 'Particulars of the *Mischianza*', 356.   [14] Ibid.
[15] Middlekauff, *Glorious Cause*, 500.

eral Howe and company moved from the strategically important river to
the site of the mock battle and thence to the Wharton house, thus demonstrating their control of Philadelphia. Every manœuvre and space was
regularized, from the aquatic procession to the dimensions of the battlefield, a perfect square. In theatrical terms, the move into the Wharton
house enacted a move behind the proscenium and into scenic space,
except the participants did not turn their backs, so to speak, on the world
beyond this interior theatre. Crucial points of the entertainment, such as
the throwing open of the windows to reveal the firework display and the
revelation of the doors 'hitherto artfully concealed', linked indoors with
outdoors, 'private' and 'public' worlds. As the term 'Mischianza' suggested, this was a medley of discoveries and surprises within the limits of
a perfected theatre of war. Its audience was not only the lower ranking
soldiers who formed the boundaries of the square in which the knights
performed, but also the soldiers of virtue camped at Valley Forge. The
'Mischianza' thus enacted the ideological differences between the British
and the American revolutionaries. George Washington had exhorted his
men to fight for the blessings of liberty: they were soldiers defending a
cause, not a king. It is significant that in the face of this, the British officers
at Philadelphia elaborated a neo-feudalism, a code of chivalric duty to king
and country that anticipated Edmund Burke's later response to the ideological charge of the French Revolution. As Linda Colley suggests, this
neo-feudalism can be regarded as a sign of a crisis of confidence in the
ruling élite as a result of the American Revolution.[16] The 'Mischianza' was
not only perfected war but also war fantasized. Rather than the conquering hero bearing his immortal laurels, General Howe was in fact a disappointed man, a leader whose failure to prosecute the war successfully had
brought Britain's arch-enemy France into the conflict and destabilized the
North ministry.

The contrast between the triumphalism of the 'Mischianza' and the
reality of Howe's achievements was such that it led even supporters of the
British to question the purpose of the entertainment—was it a joke after
all? What did war really mean to the British? As we have seen, the neo-
feudalism of the 'Mischianza' had a serious political import, but in performing war in such excessive terms the officers of Philadelphia were in
danger of parodying it. The theatricality of British military behaviour had
the potential to function as a kind of hermeneutic trigger. By drawing
attention to the fact that battle was a variety of performance, it inevitably

---

[16] Colley, *Britons*, 147.

led to a questioning of the meaning of war itself. In contrast, the American revolutionaries stressed immersion in the event, naturalizing battle as a sign of virtue by being, rather than acting, the soldier. This confrontation between a war of élites and a war of peoples—between Philadelphia and Valley Forge—prefigured what was to be enacted on an even larger scale later in the Revolutionary and Napoleonic Wars.

Camp Culture

While the 'Mischianza' was taking place in America, the British public was itself preoccupied with what the playwright Frederick Pilon described as 'military mania'. The entry of France into the American war led to the mobilization of both the regular army and the volunteers in case of an invasion. For the first time, the conflict with the American colonists was felt to be a threat to the security of Britain itself. A manifestation of this sense of national alarm was the establishment of military camps in the south of England along the routes of a possible invasion through Kent and Essex. The most significant of these camps was at Coxheath, near Maidstone; another important site was at Warley in the vicinity of Brentwood. In August 1778, when the *Gentleman's Magazine* was carrying news of the 'Mischianza', 17,000 soldiers were assembling at Coxheath, one of the largest military gatherings before the invasion scare of 1803.[17] The purpose of these camps was to enable the practice of large scale manœuvres in imitation of the conditions of a real war. Due to sensitivities over the issue of a standing army, it was impossible for the military to co-ordinate its activities on such a large scale except in conditions of emergency when war or invasion threatened, so the camps were essential in preparing an army for battle. The camps also had the important political function of accustoming the country as a whole to the prospect of war. The ostensible purpose of the 1792 camp at Bagshot, near Windsor, was to demonstrate new manœuvres in the presence of the King, but the widespread publicity given to the event also signalled that war with Revolutionary France was likely. In addition, the assembly of such a large body of soldiers, so close to London during a period of political tension, was an effective reminder

---

[17] J. R. Western, *The English Militia in the Eighteenth Century; The Story of a Political Issue 1660–1802* (London, 1965), 377–8, 385–8, 410–17; Brigadier Charles Herbert, 'Coxheath Camp, 1778–1779', *Journal of the Society for Army Historical Research*, 45–6 (1967), 129–48; J. A. Houlding, *Fit for Service: The Training of the British Army, 1715–1815* (Oxford, 1981), 322–46.

of the capacity of government to use soldiers against its domestic opponents.[18]

Late eighteenth-century military camps also had an important social and cultural, as well as political, valency. It is important to emphasize that for many people, military camps represented their only experience of warfare. England had not been invaded since the Jacobite rebellion of 1745: except for regulars who had seen service in Ireland, the West Indies, or the continent, the majority of the population, including the auxiliary forces, had never confronted war directly. What the people saw at the camps was war mediated as spectacle, extravaganzas of movement, sound, and colour which imitated the theatre of battle. During August 1793, for example, the British forces assembled at the camp near Brighton staged a mock invasion. The *Morning Chronicle* report was enthusiastic:

> To describe the effect of this business, is impossible. To SAY NOTHING of the sublime appearance of those military talents displayed by the different commanders; the different positions taken by the troops; the rapid movements of the cavalry, now in lines, crowning the brows of the hills; now in columns, descending in fast gallop down the steeps, or along the sides of these beautiful swells of ground; the firing of cannon and musquetry, and the immense crowds of spectators, were wonderfully pleasing; and displayed as gay and festive a sight, as can possibly be imagined.
>
> Everything had the appearance of festivity and pleasure . . . Carriages of the nobility and gentry, without number, and various groupes of people dining on the verdant lap of earth, furnished a scene as beautiful as it was uncommon.[19]

The camps were remarkable for their visibility. There was no attempt by the authorities to limit public access to these mock battles and parades, although occasional doubts were expressed in the press as to the wisdom of exposing Britain's military planning to continental spies. As the *Morning Chronicle* report made clear, large-scale manœuvres at the camps were occasions of 'festivity and pleasure': indeed, the report represents the spectators as an intrinsic element of the whole 'scene', 'dining on the verdant lap of earth' in a military version of pastoral. The camps attracted not only the nobility and gentry, who travelled from London or the resort towns of the south coast to witness them, but also the middling sort and artisans. The pot-bellied 'Cit' and his wife, *en route* for Coxheath, formed a frequent subject for caricature in the 1770s, while in a later ballad Charles Dibdin claimed that all London was 'gadding' to the camp at Bagshot Heath:

---

[18] Werkmeister, *Newspaper History*, 103–4.   [19] *Morning Chronicle*, 26 Aug. 1793.

> Talk not of London's busy joys,
> The camp's the only place for noise;
> Be buggies overthrown, and gigs,
> Be shopmen squeezed to death, and pigs.
> Though wedged in whiskies you've the cramp,
> Still great's the pleasure of the camp.[20]

A persistent trope in the 'camp literature' of the period is the military camp as a modern Babel, a site of confused multivocality. In *The Camp Guide*, a poem in dialogue, 'Ensign Tommy Toothpick' declares:

> With ladies, clowns, parsons, we have such intrusion,
> Our Camp is the picture of Babel's confusion!
> Here soldiers are drinking, there women are bawling,
> Here hautboys are squeaking, there children are squaling;
> In short, we're so merry, so joyous, and glad,
> From Drummer to Col'nel, you'd think we're all mad.[21]

This is echoed in *Coxheath-Camp: A Novel* (1779) when the heroine asserts that 'the similar confusion of Characters prevails in a Camp, as of tongues at the building of Babel'.[22]

The presence of large bodies of soldiers, and the crowds of civilians flocking to witness the manœuvres, offered considerable commercial opportunities. War was good for business at every level. The *Morning Chronicle* claimed that the Coxheath and Warley camps were 'of the greatest benefit to numbers of the industrious poor of the metropolis, as well as of the country, who occasionally carry provisions, hard-ware, &c. which they sell among the soldiery'.[23] In London entrepreneurs rushed to capitalize on the modishness of the camps. John Bell, enterprising publisher of *The British Theatre*, advertised a 'DRAMATIC, POETIC, and TRAVELLING CAMP LIBRARY', to be had 'compleatly bound, and packed in light cases for the convenience of Travellers, and Summer residence'.[24] Guided tours to the camps were advertised: the Coxheath outing included Chichester, Arundel, Brighthelmstone, Lewes, Tunbridge Wells, and Maidstone on its itinerary.[25] The camps also sold newspapers and

---

[20] Charles Dibdin the Elder, *The Professional Life of Mr Dibdin* (4 vols.; London, 1803), iii. 230.

[21] *The Camp Guide: In A Series of Letters from Ensign Tommy Toothpick, to Lady Sarah Toothpick, and from Miss Nelly Brisk, to Miss Gadabout* (London, 1778), 5.

[22] *Coxheath-Camp: A Novel in a Series of Letters by a Lady* (2 vols.; Dublin, 1779), ii. 168. See also George Huddesford, *Warley: A Satire* (London, 1778) and *The Second Part of Warley: A Satire* (London, 1778).

[23] *Morning Chronicle*, 1 July 1778.   [24] *Morning Post*, 16 July 1778.

[25] Ibid.

journals: detailed accounts of the goings-on there, both military and so-cial, occupied many column inches. On 9 July 1778 the *Morning Post* claimed that 'to extend the circulation of this Paper as wide as possible' it would be distributed on the same day of publication in the camps at Warley and Coxheath.

The *Morning Post* found it necessary to regard Coxheath as equivalent to London because its metropolitan readership, both military and civilian, was now to be found there. As mentioned previously in relation to British military behaviour in America, it was customary for the governing élite to leave the metropolis during the summer. August and September were also long established times of holiday for the lower orders, the period when the minor theatres were playing pantomimes and Bartholomew Fair was in operation. However, the spectacle of military manœuvres before an audi-ence of the fashionable élite *en militaire* was an attraction outrivalling any metropolitan entertainment in the summer of 1778. There were a number of complaints in the newspapers about poor attendance not only at the summer theatres of London but also at country establishments: 'we are apprehensive of a disagreeable visit from France', claimed the *Morning Chronicle*, 'and the publick seem more anxious to view the camps in the neighbourhood than any other diversion. When we are afraid of an enemy, the sight of men in arms who are to protect us, is of all spectacles the most agreeable.'[26]

The fact that the military camps became occasions of holiday for met-ropolitan society has significant implications, not only for that dominant theme in eighteenth-century culture—the relationship between the country and the city—but also for the politico-cultural status of war itself. The exile of soldiers and civilians to the heaths of Kent and Essex did not represent an abandonment of urbanity but its reinvention. Camps on the scale of Coxheath and Warley were in effect provincial towns, with all the facilities such centres would offer as well as all the usual distinctions of social geography. A newspaper tour of Warley described how the common soldiers were housed in the suburbs of the camp 'in Huts . . . built with Sticks, Straw, Turf and Boughs of Trees'.[27] These huts formed 'Streets, Courts, Lanes and Alleys' among which were to be found 'Butchers, Bakers, Taylors, Chandlers and Fish-stalls'.[28] Some of these streets were given names such as Westcote Street, Gloucester Street, and Pye-Corner, echoing well-known places in London. However, Warley was not a serious approximation of London but a London *en campagne*, a place

[26] *Morning Chronicle*, 7 Aug. 1778.
[27] *Morning Chronicle*, 3 Aug. 1778.   [28] Ibid.

1. The female invasion of the camps

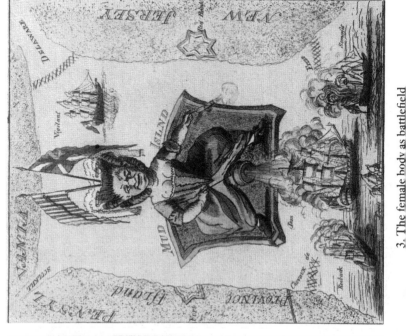

3. The female body as battlefield

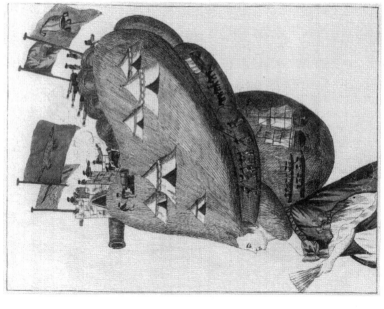

2. Fashion wars

4. The apotheosis of the camp, 1792

5. The French Revolution as theatre war

where the very material of urban society was transformed: 'One of the Drinking-Booths is called the *Green-House Tavern*, and very properly; for the whole of it is composed of boughs.'[29] The elaborate marquees of the officers at Warley, to which their occupants brought many home comforts, were bounded by miniature pleasure gardens in imitation of Ranelagh and Vauxhall, while on the borders of the camp were 'Coffee-Houses and Taverns of Mud-Erection, covered with Turf, at which the London Papers are taken in; so that the Traveller may suppose himself not only to enjoy *Rus in Urbe*, but *Urbis in Campania*'.[30] This latter phrase illustrates the extent to which the camps were places in which the normal boundaries distinguishing eighteenth-century society were merged or confused. For Michel Foucault, the military camp was one of the formative disciplinary apparatuses of the period, a 'short-lived, artificial city', the model of future sites of surveillance such as the hospital and the prison:

In the perfect camp, all power would be exercised solely through exact observation; each gaze would form a part of the overall functioning of power. The old, traditional square plan was considerably refined in innumerable new projects. The geometry of the paths, the number and disposition of the tents, the orientation of their entrances, the disposition of files and ranks were exactly defined; the network of gazes that supervised one another was laid down.[31]

In the British case, the emergence of this perfect camp did not take place until later in the eighteenth century, as a result of the impact of the war with Revolutionary France. In the 1770s and at least until 1792 the camp was very much identified with a culture in which power was manifested through display and theatricality rather than regulation. Coxheath and Warley were not only arenas which allowed the rehearsal of battle in the form of manœuvres and sham fights, they also dramatized the ideology of a war of élites in which what was at stake was the hegemony of the upper class. The camps' imitation of fashionable London was therefore of fundamental political significance as it demonstrated that war was a perpetual extension of the boundaries of the élite's theatre of action—London endlessly reproduced in the world at large.

One of the most controversial aspects of the camps of 1778–9 was the behaviour of some elements of the officer class as well as that of the women who associated with them. The American crisis was, to domestic eyes at least, a 'macaroni' war: it took place at the height of the fashion for

[29] Ibid.   [30] Ibid.
[31] Michel Foucault, *Discipline and Punish: The Birth of the Prison*, trans. Alan Sheridan (Harmondsworth, 1977), 171.

male foppery and female exhibitionism. The camps became Meccas for upper-class young men who, like their fellow officers on active service in America, treated war as another vehicle for the display of gentility, as socially significant as the race-track or the gambling club. Their marquees became home-from-homes, 'furnished with the most fanciful festoon-curtains, rich cabriolet chairs, chintz sophas, and other highly finished articles of the newest patterns'.[32] In the *Morning Post*, a letter from 'T. G. CENTURION' suggested that the indolence and extravagance of some officers was setting a bad example to the lower ranks, who in emulation of the macaronis had 'expanded over the field, in huts, &c. with their wives and families, like the wild Arab, instead of the British soldier'.[33] The *Morning Chronicle* printed a letter from one such 'soldier', complaining about the delicacy of the macaroni officers. The recent sun, he claimed, had 'not only tarnished the delicate texture of their fair faces, but likewise penetrated through their chicken gloves, and tanned their lilly hands to a frightful tawny'. The veterans and militia laughed 'heartily at their effeminacy' and wished 'they may be induced to throw up their commissions, in order to give place to more deserving men'.[34] There was no suggestion of widespread disquiet in the lower ranks—the authenticity of these letters of complaint is debatable—but it is clear that the camps, and the military in general, were subject to the broader cultural, political and gender issues of the 1770s. The theatricality of the macaroni officers was encoded with specific political significance; it was a means of projecting aristocratic influence and control, not only over domestic politcs but also over the conduct of war, appropriated in this way as the élite's theatre. Attacks on the frivolity and effeminacy of the macaronis could thus function as a form of critique of a system that rewarded aristocratic privilege rather than merit and 'manliness'.

The confusion of gender roles that characterized the behaviour of the macaroni officers also applied to the upper-class women who attended the camps. The most famous 'female volunteer' was Georgiana, Duchess of Devonshire who, with the wives of officers and other ladies, donned regimentals and formed 'battalions'. She spent the summer season of 1778 'entirely in camp' at Coxheath where the Duke had a tent large enough to contain a dining room, bed-chamber, and servants' quarters. The summer was absorbed in attending reviews and, on one occasion, dining on turtle.[35]

---

[32] *Morning Chronicle*, 16 July 1778.   [33] *Morning Post*, 17 July 1778.

[34] *Morning Chronicle*, 16 July 1778. On macaroni manners in general see Paul Langford, *A Polite and Commercial People: England 1727–1783* (Oxford, 1989), 565–613.

[35] The Earl of Bessborough (ed.), *Georgiana: Extracts from the Correspondence of Georgiana, Duchess of Devonshire* (London, 1955), 37–43.

The Duchess's presence at what were serious military preparations to resist the invasion of England was not exceptional. In the same way as the camps were open to civilians of all classes, so there was no segregation of male from female. It was common military practice in the eighteenth century for soldiers to be accompanied by their wives, while women in general made an important, if unacknowledged, contribution to the enterprise of war: 'as sutlers, trading in meat and drink, as wives, daughters, prostitutes, cooks, nurses, midwives, seamstresses and laundresses, women were an integral part of the military train and moved freely between these roles and others according to circumstance.'[36] What was remarkable about the camps of the 1770s was the way that the presence of aristocratic women, in particular, was represented as a sign of the eroticization of the military domain. The camps were identified in a number of different cultural texts as arenas of sexual licence. In *Coxheath-Camp*, the heroine claims that a camp 'like a masquerade, levels all distinction:—General Officers and Cadets, Duchesses and Demoiselles, are alike exposed to the snares of beauty, are alike susceptible to the tender passion'.[37] Sex, it seems, was everywhere. 'Half the girls in the country will get husbands by Coxheath-camp', declared the *Morning Chronicle*, while the same paper later claimed that when it was learned that the officers were 'conducting their ladies, *pro nocte*, secretly into their marquees', prostitutes in general were admitted behind the lines.[38] Women, rather than the French, were the force that 'conquered' Coxheath. In the significantly titled caricature 'A Trip to Cocks Heath', a group of genteel women are shown leading an 'invasion' of the camp. Fears of a rampant female sexuality (and possible emasculation of the male) are visually encoded by the centrality within the frame of a woman with an extravagant, quasi-phallic hairdress, mounted on a militia officer and evidently directing the female charge. In the background, her fellow female volunteers are fondling penis-shaped cannons.[39] This feminization of war is also apparent in a series of caricatures from the 1770s satirizing simultaneously the fashion for extravagant hairdress and the efforts of the British army in America. In 'Noddle-Island', the theatre of war is located on top of a woman's head. This absurd reduction of military topography has the effect of rendering ridiculous the achievements of Howe in America. Conversely, by magni-

---

[36] Myna Trustram, *Women of the Regiment: Marriage and the Victorian Army* (Cambridge, 1984), 11. See also Barton C. Hacker, 'Women and Military Institutions in Early Modern Europe: A Reconnaissance', *Signs*, 6 (1981), 643–71.

[37] *Coxheath-Camp*, i. 13.   [38] *Morning Chronicle*, 9 July 1778; 18 July 1778.

[39] For details of this caricature see M. Dorothy George, *Catalogue of the Political and Personal Satires Preserved in the Department of Prints and Drawings in the British Museum* (vols. 5–11; London, 1935–54), v. 313.

fying the hairdress as a battlefield, the exaggerated significance within national culture of the macaroni fashion wars is satirized.[40] Other caricatures equate the female body with the battlefield. In 'The Takeing of Miss Mud I'land', Mud Island in the River Delaware, contested by the British and the Americans in 1777, is represented as a grotesque female. Such an image could be said to be eroticizing war in terms of male sexual violence against women, except for the fact that the figure is firing a cannon from between her legs.[41] These representations suggest that far from being perceived in the exclusive terms of either male or female sexuality, war was regarded as destabilizing categories of gender. This destabilization is apparent in the following example of 'camp intelligence':

> We hear, that the Ladies connected with the different corps of militia, &c. are to be immediately *embodied* in *two* battalions, at *each* camp; the one consisting of the *wives*, the other of the *mistresses* of their respective officers . . . Accoutered in their different uniforms, they must necessarily produce a very pleasing effect, and their assistance will be very *sensibly* experienced by the officers, who *nightly* mount the several *quarter* guards; though it is apprehended the *General*, even with assistance of his Aids de Camps, will find some difficulty in settling the *Roster*.
>
> It is presumed the painful *chirugical* operation, to render them *complete Amazons*, will, at the solicitation of their brother officers, be dispensed with, as the injury the *breast-work* of the camp might sustain from such an operation, would not be sufficiently compensated by any little additional alertness in handling their arms.[42]

This passage exemplifies the sexualized representation of war in the 1770s. Military language—terms and phrases such as 'embody', 'mount the several *quarter* guards', '*breast-work* of the the camp'—is adapted for the purposes of innuendo in ways that destabilize meaning. As in the theatre, transvestism is used to explore the taboo subject of same-sex relations. Thus, the reference to the officers who 'nightly mount the several *quarter* guards' may be read as an ironic reference to the fact that these guards are actually women, or it can be interpreted in terms of a much more daring surface meaning, suggesting homosexuality between male soldiers. This ambiguity continues in the reference to the 'painful *chirugical* operation' which may imply the castration of the male officers, thereby rendering them '*complete Amazons*', or as it turns out, the masculinization of the female officers by the removal of the breasts. The word-play associated with '*breast-work*' of the camp, with its suggestions of female mutilation, makes an equivalence between the female body and

---

[40] For details of this caricature see George, *Satires*, v. 221.
[41] For details of this caricature see ibid. v. 252.   [42] *Morning Post*, 21 July 1778.

military fortifications, as in 'The Takeing of Miss Mud I'land'. The passage as a whole is characterized by a fluid ambivalence: while the references to mutilation suggest anxieties about the feminization of war and, at another level, its homoeroticism, such issues are very much in free play. The boundaries between male and female are crossed and recrossed; the demarcations of gender remain unclear.

The Camps in the Theatre: 'Coxheath by Candlelight'

As public entertainments on a grand scale, the camps of 1778–9 represented significant competition for the theatres. I have already referred to the numerous reports of empty benches in country theatres in contemporary newspapers and journals: the poor fortunes of provincial managers extended as far afield as Ireland, where the military camp at Cork was said to have 'impoverished' the local manager. Adapting a military metaphor so common in theatrical journalism of the period, the *Morning Chronicle* went on to state that 'the camps at Cox-Heath, Warley, Winchester, Plymouth, &c. &c. have been equally detrimental to the commanders of the various brigades detached from the head quarters'.[43] Faced with empty theatres, the commanders of these 'theatrical irregulars', as the *Morning Chronicle* styled them, gravitated to the military theatre of the camps, establishing their own tents in the vicinity of Coxheath and Warley. Like the coffee-house, the pleasure garden, or the masquerade, a distinctively urban form of public entertainment was relocated and reinvented. Strolling players found themselves deferring to military, rather than civilian, authority. In 1780, for example, a performance of *The Recruiting Officer* was bespoken by the Earl of Orford, encamped at Tenpenny Common in Essex with the Norfolk militia. According to the actor Charles Lee Lewes, 'his lordship, being afflicted with the gout, was led round the airy theatre on a poney, by a careful servant: the ridiculous distress of the actors was truly amusing; as his lordship, by his circular progression, obliged them, in good manners and profound respect to their patron, to wheel about occasionally, to show him a full front'.[44]

Strolling players, especially of the lower class, were used to such capriciousness. Their itinerant lives taught them adaptability and they did not always need the security of four walls in which to perform. For the patent theatres, however, the dominance of the camps in the cultural life

---

[43] *Morning Chronicle*, 29 Aug. 1778.
[44] Charles Lee Lewes, *Memoirs* (4 vols.; London, 1805), iii. 22.

of the 1770s was more problematic. Covent Garden and Drury Lane could not simply relocate to Coxheath, yet as the summer of 1778 passed into autumn, it became clear that the focus of cultural and political life had been effectively displaced from the metropolitan centre. The two patent houses were thus compelled to address the phenomenon of a militarized society. In representing Coxheath, however, playwrights and actors were not so much theatricalizing the camps as mediating events that already constituted theatre. The prologues to the two 'camp' plays of the 1778–9 season, *The Camp* at Drury Lane and *The Invasion* at Covent Garden, dealt with the 'military mania' of the times as a question of representation. In his prologue to *The Camp* Richard Tickell reasserted the traditional primacy of the stage as *theatrum mundi*—'The Stage is still the Mirror of the Day'—but the 'still' suggests that this authority was being challenged by the alternative *theatrum mundi* of the camps. The prologue went on to announce a virtual capitulation to the fashion for war, conceding that the only 'image' the theatre could 'yield' in the circumstances of war was 'the embattled Field' (*DW* 722). Similarly, Frederick Pilon, in his prologue for *The Invasion*, felt compelled to stake the claim of Covent Garden as a rival theatre of war to that of the camp. He represented the patent house as 'our encampment':

> Where walking Belles, and Irish chairmen ply;
> Where play-bills spread, seem like a centinel,
> To guard the entrance of the citadel.[45]

The contemporary crisis is redefined in Pilon's prologue in the terms of a 'theatre war' between Covent Garden and Drury Lane, as was indeed the case—the success of *The Camp* had compelled Covent Garden to reply in kind. Pilon describes the rival stages as 'the embattled plain' on which the muse in turn reveals 'a camp by candle light' and 'an Invasion, without wounds or blows'. Significantly, both prologues represent war in spatial terms—the 'embattled Field', of which the space of the stage and the territory of the theatre building itself (the 'citadel' of Pilon's prologue) become appropriations, not just in the sense of approximating the military theatre of Coxheath or Warley but also in the sense of ownership. In their versions of the camps the managements of Covent Garden and Drury Lane were declaring the pre-eminence of the theatre as *the* medium for the representation of war—the field of the stage was also the field of battle and vice versa.

45 Frederick Pilon, *The Invasion; or, a Trip to Brighthelmstone* (London, 1778), vii.

I would now like to consider these texts—*The Camp* and *The Invasion*—in some detail. Of the two, *The Camp* is the better known, largely because of its place in the canon of Richard Brinsley Sheridan's plays. However, the play could be described with more justification as a collaborative effort—the work of Sheridan, Thomas Linley (who produced the music), and in particular, Philippe Jacques De Loutherbourg who was responsible for the concluding scenic view of Coxheath before which mechanical soldiers undertook manœuvres. Produced on 15 October 1778, the piece was immediately successful and was performed a total of fifty-six times in the 1778–9 season.[46] 'In short, the Camp at Drury-lane is upon the whole very likely to rival the Camp at Coxheath', claimed the *London Evening Post* 'and the Managers (though they don't deal in brown bread) to exceed the profits of the Contractors' (*DW* 712). *The Camp* was later revived in the provinces in 1795, when a text of the piece was published for the first time, and it was produced again in 1803 in an adaptation to suit the circumstances of the invasion crisis.[47] The plot of the piece is slight, as many contemporaries noted. In a series of related incidents a number of characters meet on the plain of Coxheath: Gauge, an exciseman, is shown inveigling his fellow country people to cheat the soldiers at Coxheath. He is challenged by a spirited country girl, Nell, in a way which enables Sheridan to voice a criticism of corrupt contractors and sutlers. Nell has friends in high places, Lady Plume, Lady Sarah Sash, and Miss Gorget, female volunteers who were based on the Duchess of Devonshire and her sister 'Amazons'. According to contemporary reports, the ladies were costumed *en militaire* (*DW* 744 n. 2). *The Camp* also features an Irish painter called O'Daub who is producing drawings of the camp for 'Mr Leatherbag' (De Loutherbourg) of Drury Lane; in the course of his activities he is mistaken for a French spy. The other significant character in the piece is Nancy, a friend of Nell, who has followed her lover to the camp in the disguise of a soldier. Her introduction in *The Camp* seems to have been largely designed to allow the actress, Miss Walpole, to demonstrate the manual exercise 'in a style that would have done credit to any corps of regulars' (*DW* 713). (Part of the appeal of this performance to audiences was the way in which the movements of the

[46] Charles Beecher Hogan, *The London Stage 1660–1800: A Calendar of Plays, Entertainments and Afterpieces Together with Casts, Box-Receipts and Contemporary Comment Compiled from the Playbills, Newspapers and Theatrical Diaries of the Period, Part 5: 1776–1800* (3 vols.; Carbondale, Ill., 1968), i. 208.

[47] A 1795 production in Margate included a scenic representation of the local encampment at Birchington: see Malcolm Morley, *Margate and its Theatres 1730–1965* (London, 1966), 35–6. For the 1803 revival see *Gentleman's Magazine*, 73 (1803), 980.

exercise drew attention to the female body, particularly the breasts.)[48] The questions of O'Daub's identity and Nancy's gender are ultimately resolved and the play concludes with De Loutherbourg's spectacular representation of the manœuvres at Coxheath (*DW* 711).

The Camp follows a number of contemporary texts in emphasizing the reflexivity of war and fashion. In *The Camp Guide*, 'Miss Nelly Brisk' declares:

> Well, who can complain, at the tax that he pays,
> When war seems amusement, and battles seem plays.[49]

Likewise in *The Camp*, Sir Harry Bouquet, a 'Macarony Connoisseur', commends Coxheath as 'all the Parade, Pomp, and Circumstance of Glorious War—Mars in a Vis a Vis—and Bellona giving a Fete Champetre' (*DW* 713, 745). The figures of Lady Plume, Lady Sarah Sash, and Miss Gorget highlight the feminization of the military domain that I discussed previously; the weapons of war and those of beauty are linked in a comment by Lady Sarah Sash that echoes the mock epic of Pope's *Rape of the Lock*, another text identifying the interpenetration of war, fashion, and sexuality in eighteenth-century culture. According to Lady Sash, 'there is an Eternal Confusion between our Lords' Camp Equipage, and our dressing Apparatus—between Stores Military and Millinery . . . on the same Shelf Cartri[d]ges and Cosmetics, Pouches and Patches—here Stands of Arms, and there a file of Black Pins' (*DW* 744–5). Finally, *The Camp* also acknowledges the iconic relationship between a military encampment and urban space. In a comment that recalls the complaint of 'T. G. CENTURION' about British soldiers acting like 'the wild Arab' in emulation of their macaroni superiors, Sir Harry Bouquet notes an uncomfortable proximity between the officers and men at Coxheath: 'But now how will you excuse this, the Officers' Tents all close to the Common Soldiers—what an Arrangement is that? Now if I might have advised, there certainly should have been one part for the Cannaille and a *West End* of the Camp for the Noblesse and persons of a Certain Rank' (*DW* 746). This remark indicates the extent to which the camps, and military life in general, were perceived as violating the normal distinctions of social geography. Coxheath and Warley were 'artificial cities' in Foucault's terms, but they were also cities in holiday, 'airy theatres' of social and sexual interchange.

---

[48] See Dianne Dugaw, *Warrior Women and Popular Balladry, 1650–1850* (Cambridge, 1989), 180–2.

[49] *The Camp Guide*, 16.

In Frederick Pilon's *The Invasion*, the expanse of Coxheath, as represented in De Loutherbourg's *coup de théâtre*, is comically reduced to the dimensions of Sir John Evergreen's front parlour. Sir John, a boobyish squire immersed in the 'military mania' of the times, has transformed his home into an encampment and recruited two soldiers as servants to teach him the military exercise. Pilon identifies the preoccupation with war as a ludicrous fanaticism: significantly, the younger generation, in the form of Sir John Evergreen's son Charles and his friend Mr Beaufort have rejected soldiering, for which the squire has ostracized them. The two young men, with the help of a servant, Cameleon, trick the squire into believing that the French are invading with the intention of humiliating him and restoring their own position. Cameleon, played in 1778 by the virtuoso comic actor Charles Lee Lewes, stage-manages the deception of Sir John, recruiting the 'master of a puppet-show' and 'his merry-Andrew' to act the part of the French army. When he is informed that the 'French' are coming, the squire barricades his house with 'ploughs, barrows, wheelbarrows' and assembles a motley army of servants:

Enter a large party of servants armed with flails, pitchforks, &c.—The cook armed with a spit, the scullion with the poker, and all the others bearing something emblematical of their stations. In the middle two women stand with escutcheons tack'd to old curtains . . . they march across the stage and salute SIR JOHN with ludicrous solemnity.[50]

Pilon's burlesque was not only directed at the fanatical militarism of men like Sir John but also at the pretensions of De Loutherbourg and the Drury Lane management. Thus the *Morning Post* commented that 'the Baronet's review of his *household phalanx*' was 'a ludicrous contrast to the *Coxheath by candlelight* at the other house'.[51] The theatrical dimensions of the satire, not evident in the printed text, are suggested in the following comment on the costuming: 'Mrs Green wore upon her head a marquee in miniature, with a Lilliputian soldier standing centinel, the novelty and whimsical appearance of which created incessant laughter for the greater part of her first scene.'[52] Such an effect is comparable to caricatures such as 'Noddle-Island'; the camp site, and Drury Lane's representation of it, are comically reduced to the dimensions of fashionable headwear. In their meta- (and inter-) theatricality, both *The Camp* and *The Invasion* draw attention to the status of war as performance. As noted previously, the camps were rehearsals for battle which was itself an act, an attempt to

---

[50] Pilon, *Invasion*, 33. [51] *Morning Post*, 5 Nov. 1778.
[52] *Morning Chronicle*, 5 Nov. 1778.

implement the manœuvres and strategies practised on the camp field. The imitative relationship between sham and actual warfare is reflected in the practices of both Covent Garden and Drury Lane—Mrs Green's hat, the manual exercise performed by Miss Walpole, and the manœuvres of De Loutherbourg's mechanical soldiers, all highlighted the theatricality of military behaviour. Part of the metatheatricality of *The Camp* is the subplot involving O'Daub the Irish painter, who has come to 'take the Camp' for his master Mr Leatherbag of Drury Lane. Alone on stage, O'Daub sizes up the scene:

Well to be sure this Camp is a pretty Comical Place, with their Drums and their Fifes, and their Jigs and their Marches, and the Ladies in their Regimentals— upon my Conscience I believe they'd Form a Troop of Cavalry if there was any hope of an Invasion.— But now I am alone by myself, it's high time I should begin to be after taking my Place. . . . So—so—let me Study my orders a little, for I'm not used to this Stage Business. P. S. and O. P.—who the Devil now is to understand that?—O but here's the Explanation here, P. S.— the Prompter's Side and O. P.—opposite the Prompter—I'm to mark down the Side as it's to be on one Side or t'other. Very well—P. S. and O. P. Somewhere here about is certainly the best Point to take it from (*DW* 742).

What O'Daub is actually taking here are the dimensions of De Loutherbourg's scenic representations of Coxheath, as if it were 'reality'. His attempt to render the 'scene' in terms of stage space—the prompter's side and opposite the prompter—suggest that there are possibilities for an infinitely regressive series of stage Coxheaths—multiple theatres of war. The speech is followed by a comic incident in which some soldiers misinterpret O'Daub's references to O.P. and P.S. as suggesting that he is 'a Damn'd French Jacobite Spy' who is planning an attack on the camp. In representational terms, these soldiers have a point—the word play on 'take', as in to make a representation of something, or in the military sense of conquering the enemy's position, emphasizes that what both Drury Lane and Covent Garden were involved in was a struggle to define and appropriate the spectacle of war.

The Perfect Camp

It is clear then, that the camps were constructed in a variety of literary and other cultural texts as arenas of sexual licence, where the relationship between war and gender could be explored through the performance of the role of soldier by both men and women. They were also places where the boundaries between military and civilian life were fluid and uncertain and where the various classes of society could associate freely. In this sense the military camp could be said to resemble other forms of cultural activity in the eighteenth century—the masquerade and the fair—which have been defined by some critics in terms of the Bakhtinian carnivalesque. However, it is important to stress that Coxheath and Warley were never sites of subversion in the terms identified by Terry Castle in relation to the masquerade.[53] The cultural institution which the camp most resembled was in fact the theatre in the way that it encoded the political visibility and power of the élite. The macaronis and duchesses could be transgressive and exhibitionist, mainly because their status entitled them to be so. In making themselves a spectacle for 'metropolitan curiosity', they were proclaiming their importance to, as well as their control of, the gaze of others. Their behaviour was also saying something about the cultural politics of war. By successfully merging the worlds of war and the *bon ton*, the participants in the camp entertainment were able to socialize military activity as an integral part of fashionable life, for both men and women. The brutality of the wars of European absolutism was thus naturalized, made tolerable for those who had a political say in them. The cultural differentiation of the camps as fashionable spectacles also had the effect of reinforcing the élite's political control over the conduct of war, marking it as an affair of the great from which the rest of society was excluded.

However, the attack on the effeminacy of the macaronis and caricatures, such as 'A Trip to Cocks Heath', suggest that this construction of war as aristocratic theatre was being challenged and undermined. The camps took place during a period when upper-class behaviour, in particular that of aristocratic women, was coming under increasingly hostile scrutiny. The public and private adventures of the Duchess of Devonshire feature in a number of important discourses of the period concerning gender, class, and politics.[54] Her invasion of the supposedly masculine domains of Coxheath, and later, the Westminster election of 1784, and her flouting of dress codes by the wearing of breeches, placed her in the vanguard of an increasingly confident band of aristocratic women. The attacks on the Duchess in the press and polemical literature may have reflected a general unease in patriarchal society about the influence of such

---

[53] See Terry Castle, *Masquerade and Civilization: the Carnivalesque in Eighteenth-Century Culture and Fiction* (London, 1986); Peter Stallybrass and Allon White, *The Politics and Poetics of Transgression* (London, 1986).

[54] See Colley, *Britons*, esp. 242–8.

women, but they also had specific political implications. As Leonore Davidoff and Catherine Hall have indicated, gender played an important part in the making of the middle class, mainly as a means by which this class could define its status and values in opposition to those of the aristocracy and gentry.[55] Critiques of the excessive behaviour of upper-class women such as the Duchess of Devonshire and the stigmatization of the effeminacy of the macaronis were used to challenge aristocratic privilege and assert 'manly' middle-class probity. Even before the 1790s, therefore, the fluid ambivalence of the aristocratic theatre of war had been called into question.

The representation of war as the sexualized spectacle of the upper class persists after 1789. A print of 1792 depicting the camp at Bagshot Heath shows George III ogling a surrealistic display of military prowess— soldiers mounted on phallic cannons flying in the air, winged pavilions, and aerial manœuvres.[56] The Prince of Wales, in particular, relished the histrionic possibilities of military display. In 1795 a masquerade under his patronage took place in conjunction with the camp at Brighton; it was notable for the presence of 'a few lively Gentlemen in *Petticoats*, their Wives wearing the *Breeches*'.[57] There are indications, however, that as a result of the French Revolution the culture of war was changing. During the period 1793–1815 there was an increasing dissociation of the military from civilian society. Camps continued to be important militarily, but the army began to be associated in the public mind with the more restricted world of the barrack, as opposed to the 'airy theatre' of the heath or common. The barracks differed fundamentally from the camps in that they established actual boundaries between the military and the rest of society, indicating a withdrawal from the promiscuous domain of Coxheath or Warley. As such they can be related to the development at this period of other forms of social control such as the prison and the madhouse, and the increasing cultural differentiation of public space. Many of the convivial actitivities—drinking, gambling—that would have taken place in the 'taverns' or 'streets' of Coxheath and Warley were confined to the barrack buildings. Contact between officers and men, and between the military and the civilian community was comparatively restricted: 'the soldier, having risen and washed, if he had the stomach or the inclination, prepared his dress and weapons and spent his whole spare

---

[55] Leonore Davidoff and Catherine Hall, *Family Fortunes: Men and Women of the English Middle Class 1780–1850* (London, 1987).

[56] For details of this caricature see George, *Satires*, vi. 924.

[57] *The Times*, 5 Oct. 1795.

time in his barrack-room, unless he had a ticket for walking out.'[58] Barracks thus permitted an increasing masculinization of the military space: they were austere places with none of the chintz of Warley or Coxheath. Women were allowed to occupy them as 'wives', but only with the permission of the commanding officer; generally barracks were perceived, in McGuffie's terms, as 'bachelor establishments'. One of the arguments which John Thelwall used against them was that the separation of male from female would lead to the brutalization of the soldiery: 'when they are thus prevented from mixing with the innocent and estimable part of the softer sex, and when all the other circumstances attendant upon such confinement are taken into consideration, we cannot but dread the production of a degree of ferocity which they would never otherwise know'.[59]

The rise of the barrack system in England was symptomatic of more fundamental changes in the culture of war after 1793. The ideology of the 'nation-at-arms' as promulgated by the French *levée en masse* represented a challenge to the idea of war as a variety of aristocratic theatre, a 'delightful rendezvous', in Goldoni's terms, at which the people were insignificant spectators. Instead, the French Revolution assumed the right of these spectators to usurp and dominate the theatre of war on their own behalf. The effect of such ideology within Britain was to transform the perception of war as a vehicle for aristocratic display and licence into an altogether more serious affair. The government realized the potential dangers of a culture of war which stressed its significance as a game or performance. In order to counter the threat of an ideologically mobilized French army, it was necessary for the volunteer to believe in what he was fighting for; he had to be rather than act the soldier. While the camps continued to be strategically significant during the invasion scare of 1803, their politico-cultural value became more dubious, precisely because they accentuated the theatricality of war. The ludic element of practices, such as the mock battle, made much of the fact that both men and women could dress and play as soldiers, thus emphasizing the arbitrariness of not only gendered social roles but also the category of soldier itself.

As a consequence of this, the military camps of 1803 do not have the same cultural prominence as those of 1792 or the 1770s. The many satires and broadsides of the invasion scare are focused on the external threat of

---

[58] T. H. McGuffie, 'Early Barrack Life', *Army Quarterly*, 54 (1947), 66. See also Roy Palmer (ed.), *The Rambling Soldier: Life in the Lower Ranks, 1750–1900, Through Soldiers' Songs and Writings* (Gloucester, 1985), 77–8.

[59] John Thelwall, *Tribune*, 2 (1796), 101.

'Boney' and his minions rather than on the foibles of military fashion. 'A Peep into the Camp', a caricature which Dorothy George ascribes to 1803, reveals many of the conventions associated with earlier representations of camp life—effete officers, the elegance of the mess tent, the 'festivity' of the manœuvres—but as George notes, it seems 'out of touch' with the propagandistic impulse of other satires of the period.[60] The theatricality of military life as a whole was increasingly played down. The volunteers were warned that the sham fight or pageantry of the drill exercise were strictly rehearsals for a battle that would require acting of a different order. A broadside from 1803, for example, questioned military theatricality in the following way:

Who, Gentlemen, that witnessed (I speak of the last war) your tardy and ill-performed evolutions, and your commanders waiting, like actors not studied in their parts, the word of a prompter, who was generally some subordinate officer of the regulars—who, I say, Gentlemen, that witnessed these things, would anticipate ought but ruin and disgrace in the event of your being called out to act against a well-disciplined army? My friends, do not consider yourselves as idle pageants, strutting in regimentals, to gratify a paltry vanity. No; at a moment's notice you may be called to take an active part in the defence of your country. You have voluntarily promised to defend her; and if you neglect to render yourselves capable of performing that promise, you betray her.[61]

It is in this context that we find the emergence of the Foucauldian perfect camp in Britain. Writing in 1811, the military theorist (and MP) Henry Dillon, posited an idea of the camp as being transparent to warfare rather than a rehearsal or imitation of it: he wrote, 'let us not despair of seeing, in the plains of the south of England, an army arrayed as if for instant war, in a camp of toil and fatigue, no way differing from a scene of actual warfare, except in the loss of lives'.[62]

The problem for the generals and politicians directing the war was that the theatricality which had attracted many men of the middling and lower orders to the ranks of the Volunteers was a sign that their loyalty was not to be trusted. Performance and display were all very well for those who had a stake in the country on account of wealth and rank, but for the lower orders to 'play' at being soldiers in the same way was disquieting. Not only was it possible that the military energies of the Volunteers might be

---

[60] George, *Satires*, vii. 217.

[61] F. J. Klingberg and S. B. Hustvedt (eds.), *The Warning Drum, the British Home Front Faces Napoleon: Broadsides of 1803* (Berkeley, Calif., 1944), 41–2.

[62] Henry Augustus Dillon, *A Commentary on the Military Establishments and Defence of the British Empire* (2 vols.; London, 1811), i. 280.

directed against those in power in British society, but their full commitment as solders was also uncertain. Many suspected that lower-class men in particular were 'acting' the Volunteer in order to escape service in the regular army or militia, to make some money or simply in order to experience adventure. These suspicions were reinforced when some Volunteers refused to acknowledge the authority of their superior officers who were often men of civilian influence such as squires or magistrates, when they resisted the order to leave their local communities, and when they expressed a recalcitrant scepticism about the validity of the whole military exercise.[63] The failure of the Volunteers to become proper citizen soldiers, to renounce the theatricality of eighteenth-century militarism, was a factor in the rapid disbandment of the Volunteer Movement after 1804. This did not mean, however, that the British government and military had abandoned the lessons learnt from the ideology of the *levée en masse*. Instead they worked to divest the army as a whole of its amateurism by creating a professional fighting force attached not to a local community or to civilian rank, but to king and country and, above all, to one's fellow soldiers. This change did not happen overnight—the British army retained its amateur ethos well into the nineteenth century—but its beginnings can be traced in the response to the theatricality of both the Volunteers and the camps during the Revolutionary and Napoleonic Wars.

It is clear then, that theatricality was integral to the ideology and practice of war in late Georgian society. *The Camp* and *The Invasion* suggested ways in which the commercial theatre asserted its significance as the mirror of the broader 'theatre of war'. The following chapter will extend this analysis to consider how the theatre responded to the changing culture of war after 1789.

[63] See Cookson, 'Volunteer Movement' and 'Sutton Volunteers'. See also William Combe, *The Letters of Valerius* (London, 1804) and John Clare's account of his experiences as a volunteer in John Clare, *The Prose of John Clare*, ed. J. W. and Anne Tibble (London, 1951), 46–50.

3

War and Theatre

On 12 February 1798 the evening's entertainment at Covent Garden Theatre, which had consisted of Susannah Centilevre's comedy *The Busy Body* followed by the ballet *Joan of Arc*, concluded with a pageant. Before 'Britannia seated in Clouds, attended by Commerce, Plenty and Neptune' a series of scenes were enacted, representing significant moments in British history:

CARACTACUS' Magnanimity before the Throne of Claudius. ALFRED disguised in the Danish Camp as an Harper, and discovering himself to his desponding Countrymen. RICHARD COEUR DE LION imprisoned in Germany, & liberated by the Voluntary Contributions of his fair Countrywomen. KING JOHN uniting his Kingdom by singing [*sic*] Magna Charta. HENRY THE THIRD—The Effects of French Invasion—the Dauphine subdued, and the magnanimous conduct of England towards him. EDWARD and ELEANORA—The affectionate Wife sucks from her Husband's arm the Venom of a poisoned Arrow, by which Edward was wounded in Palestine. THE BLACK PRINCE—His taking the French King prisoner at the Battle of Poictiers, and his gallantly serving him at a Banquet. HENRY V—The Triumphs of Agincourt, and his Marriage with Catherine.[1]

This pageant was staged at one of the crisis points in the war between Britain and France: the mutinies at the Nore and Spithead had occurred the previous summer, a French invasion was in the offing, the government was facing acute problems in financing the war, and Ireland was in a state of virtual rebellion. Covent Garden's pageant reflects this perilous situation in that it begins with two beleaguered kings, Caractacus and Alfred, and stresses the need to unite the country, before reassuring its audience by portraying the 'triumphs of Agincourt'. Its message seems to have been mainly aimed at the female members of the audience: the symbol of the nation, Britannia, presides over the performance, while women are portrayed as helpmeets in the heroic male endeavour against the French; Richard is saved by the charity of his 'fair countrywomen' (an encouragement to the ladies to support the government's Voluntary Contributions scheme, an attempt to finance the war) while Eleanora aids her husband in

---

[1] Hogan, *London Stage*, Part 5, iii. 2043–4.

a time of crisis. Significantly, the last historical scene of the pageant represents the union of Henry V and Catherine, and not the battle of Agincourt, as the point of culmination. In an evening which had featured the work of a woman dramatist, Susannah Centilevre, it was appropriate that it should conclude by emphasizing that women too had a role to play in the war effort.

The significance of the pageant goes even further than this, however. Its political meaning lies in the way that it manages to suggest the dominant literary and cultural values associated with the patent theatres, effectively summarizing the way that mainpiece drama had constructed patriotism and British history for most of the eighteenth century. The majority of its scenes echo plays from the dramatic canon—William Mason's *Caractacus*, David Mallet's *Alfred*, Shakespeare's *King John* and *Henry V*, James Thomson's *Edward and Eleanora*, William Shirley's *Edward the Black Prince*—and as such, appeal to the collective consciousness of the theatre-going and play-reading public.[2] By reproducing these dramatic topoi of British history, Covent Garden was putting its own system of representation and its cultural prestige at the service of the national cause.

This pageant is indicative of one way in which the patent theatres responded to the war with Revolutionary and Napoleonic France. The managements of both Covent Garden and Drury Lane did more than represent the conflict; they implicated their own practices—the legitimacy of genres such as tragedy and comedy, the representation of politics by means of indirection, analogy—as part of the matrix of cultural values which were under threat from the French. Thus, in considering how Covent Garden and Drury Lane responded to the war, it is necessary to examine the whole politico-cultural enterprise of the patent theatres. To stage a genteel comedy such as *The Busy Body* in the context of February 1798 was a political act, making it a 'war' play. By carrying on as usual, the patent theatres were proclaiming as much about the war, as if they had staged a series of explicit representations of it.

A War like this

One of the practices implicated as part of the 'legitimate' values under threat from the French was that of politics by indirection, the tacitly

[2] The canonical status of these plays was reinforced by their appearance in multi-volume dramatic collections such as *Bell's British Theatre* (20 vols.; London, 1776–8) which was republished in 1797.

agreed contract between audiences and actors by which political meanings could be inferred from a play which was not supposed to be political at all. The framework in which this was accomplished was usually that of the history play, in which contemporary concerns could be effectively displaced to a distant time or place. An example from 1795 is George Watson's *England Preserved*, a propaganda play which sought to alarm audiences into patriotic loyalty by representing a French invasion in the guise of an episode from thirteenth-century English history. According to the *Oracle*, the play was designed to teach Englishmen 'to arise with vigour around the standard of a lawful KING, remain true to *themselves*, and confound both *treason* within, and *hostility* from without'.[3] The model for Watson's drama was the Shakespearian history play which was also much revived during this period. In 1789 John Philip Kemble anticipated the change in the public mood in relation to France by staging an adaptation of *Henry V*, giving it the subtitle of *The Conquest of France*. He also revived the now neglected *Henry VIII*, not only on account of Sarah Siddons's success in the role of Queen Katherine, but also because the play was an appropriate vehicle for the processions and ceremonies that were Kemble's directorial trademark, symbolic of his endorsement of the monarchy and the existing social order.[4]

But perhaps the most significant analogical drama of the period was Richard Brinsley Sheridan's *Pizarro*, first performed in May 1799. Although it has subsequently been neglected by both directors and literary critics, *Pizarro* was Sheridan's greatest commercial success and a cultural phenomenon of major significance.[5] Playgoers fought to see the initial London production, with stellar performers such as John Philip Kemble, Sarah Siddons, and Dorothy Jordan in the leading roles. The first edition of the printed text of the play, amounting to 29,000 copies, was quickly sold out, while the columns of newspapers and journals were full of commentary on the play (*DW* 641). *Pizarro* was also widely produced in the provinces throughout the rest of the French wars and survived in the repertory well into the nineteenth century. Its success was due to the way it represented the war, not through an explicit treatment of contemporary

---

[3] For *England Preserved* see Hogan, *London Stage*, Part 5, iii. 1731; *Oracle*, 17 Feb. 1795.

[4] See David Rostron, 'Contemporary Political Comment in Four of J. P. Kemble's Shakespearean Productions', *Theatre Research*, 12 (1972), 113–19; Bate, *Shakespearean Constitutions*, 61–4.

[5] For discussions of *Pizarro* see John Loftis, *Sheridan and the Drama of Georgian England* (Oxford, 1976), 124–41; J. W. Donohue Jnr., *Dramatic Character in the English Romantic Age* (Princeton, NJ, 1970), 125–56, and Sara Suleri, *The Rhetoric of English India* (Chicago, 1990), 68–74.

events or the figures of soldier and sailor, but through the strategies of indirection and analogy. I now want to consider the play in some detail as an example of how the patent theatres responded to the subject of the French wars.

Sheridan's career in the theatre was indebted to Britain's wars. We have seen already how in *The Camp* he sought to exploit and appropriate the theatricality of military culture. In *The Critic* (1779) he carried this a stage further by burlesquing pageantry and, in particular, the use of the history play as an analogy of contemporary events. The play-within-a-play in *The Critic*, Mr Puff's 'The Spanish Armada', ridicules a number of contemporary stage entertainments which had represented the prospect of a Spanish invasion in terms of the Elizabethan crisis of 1588. In 1799, when Sheridan produced his own 'Spanish Armada' in the form of *Pizarro*, some contemporaries, such as Thomas Moore, reacted with astonishment: 'When the author of the Critic made Puff say, "Now for my magnificence,—my noise and my procession!" he little anticipated the illustration which, in twenty years afterwards, his own example would afford to that ridicule' (*DW* 637). An adaptation of Kotzebue's *Die Spanier in Peru* (1796), *Pizarro* concerns the victimization of the Peruvian Indians by the colonizing Spanish, but audiences were encouraged to interpret the play in terms of a beleaguered British nation, threatened by a predatory France. In a speech from the play which became famous, the Peruvian general Rolla, played by John Philip Kemble, proclaimed the differences between the 'Peruvians' and the 'Spanish':

My brave associates—partners of my toil, my feelings and my fame!—can Rolla's words add vigour to the virtuous energies which inspire your hearts?—No—YOU have judged as I have, the foulness of the crafty plea by which these bold invaders would delude you—Your generous spirit has compared as mine has, the motives, which, in a war like this, can animate *their* minds, and OURS.—THEY, by a strange frenzy driven, fight for power, for plunder, and extended rule—WE, for our country, our altars, and our homes.—THEY follow an Adventurer whom they fear—and obey a power which they hate—WE serve a Monarch whom we love—a God whom we adore.—Whene'er they move in anger, desolation tracks their progress!—Where'er they pause in amity, affliction mourns their friendship!—They boast, they come but to improve our state, enlarge our thoughts, and free us from the yoke of error!—Yes—THEY will give enlightened freedom to *our* minds, who are themselves the slaves of passion, avarice, and pride.—They offer us their protection—Yes, such protection as vultures give to lambs—covering and devouring them!—They call on us to barter all of good we have inherited and proved, for the desperate chance of something better which they promise.—Be our plain answer this: The throne WE honour is the PEOPLE'S CHOICE—the laws we reverence are our brave Fathers' legacy—the faith we follow teaches us to live in bonds of charity with all mankind, and die with hope of bliss beyond the grave. Tell your invaders this, and tell them too, we seek no change; and, least of all, such change as they would bring us. (*DW* 669)

There was a distinct similarity between Rolla's words and the speeches which Sheridan had made in parliament on the prospect of a French invasion: parliamentary rhetoric and that of the theatre had been merged, like the roles of 'Sheridan' the orator and 'Rolla'/Kemble (*DW* 639). But why Peru and why Spain? In choosing to dramatize the conflict between Britain and France in terms of the Spanish conquest of America, Sheridan was able to accomplish a number of things at once. First, by adapting Kotzebue he could capitalize on the modishness of German drama and, in particular, its association with Revolutionary principles. Sheridan's identification of 'British' values with the heroic Peruvian Rolla was a way of reasserting the oppositional character of patriotism, its significance in the defence of rights rather than privileges. Thus another Sheridan which the play invoked was the Sheridan who had led the attack on Warren Hastings's abuses in India.[6] One of the number of public figures who went to see the play was William Wilberforce who made his first visit to the theatre in twenty years as an endorsement of the play's anti-imperialist message (*DW* 635).

In its appropriation of the Revolutionary energies of Kotzebue and its championing of the cause of an oppressed people, *Pizarro* would seem to be consistent with Sheridan's political identity as Foxite Whig and critic of Pitt's war policy. However, this does not seem to explain adequately the extent of the play's ideological appeal, the fact that it was the focus of loyalist, as well as radical patriotic expression. This was particularly the case in 1803–4, when *Pizarro* was staged in numerous theatres up and down the country and Rolla's speech was printed in handbill form as 'Sheridan's Address to the People' by the loyalist publisher Asperne. During a performance of the play in Chelmsford in 1803, the actor playing Rolla went so far as to interrupt Sheridan's text with his own personal tirade against Napoleon before resuming the role and going on to speak the famous denunciation of the Spanish/French. 'Both this preface and the speech were most warmly received,' claimed the *Monthly Mirror*, 'and Mr Seymour was called upon to repeat it on a subsequent evening.'[7] *Pizarro* was a text that seemed to offer itself to interpolation: not only had Sheridan interpolated his own parliamentary speeches, but actors and

---

[6] Suleri, *Rhetoric*, 71.   [7] *Monthly Mirror*, 16 (1803), 134.

audiences were able to insert themselves within it. As *Pizarro* was appropriated by Seymour and in turn by Asperne, so the celebrity of the play
was seized upon by Wilberforce, Pitt, Nelson, and George III who all
made well-publicized visits to see it. George III's presence at the Drury
Lane performance of 5 June 1799 was particularly significant, as it was his
first visit to Sheridan's theatre since 1795. Drury Lane had been perceived
by the King to be politically compromised when it allowed, and seemed to
endorse, republican sentiments expressed by the audience during a performance of Thomas Otway's *Venice Preserv'd* on 29 October 1795. According to *The Times*, the King was not disappointed by his reception at
Pizarro:

The bursts of patriotic enthusiasm and exulting Loyalty on the entrance and
departure of the ROYAL FAMILY, were reiterated, and appeared to catch an additional impulse from the prosperous state of public affairs both abroad and at
home.

His MAJESTY was peculiarly gratified with the noble and animated address of
Rolla to the Peruvians in support of their just rights as an independent and happy
people, against the lawless encroachments and savage ambition of foreign
invaders.[8]

George III had every reason to be happy with *Pizarro*, particularly with its
portrayal of kingship. The characterization of Ataliba, the Peruvian monarch, stresses his benevolent, paternalistic relationship to his people, a
style of kingship which George III had himself done much to promote.[9]
While Ataliba has an essentially minor role in the play, his people's love
for him and his centrality in the cause for which they are fighting are
firmly established and reiterated. Las-Casas, the Spanish priest who is
sympathetic to the Peruvians, questions his own people's moral right to
attack a king 'in whose mild bosom your atrocious injuries even yet have
not excited hate!' (*DW* 661). Ataliba's essentially 'Christian' qualities are
uppermost when he is forced to withdraw wounded from the battle declaring 'I will not repine; my own fate is the last anxiety of my heart. It is
for you, my people, that I feel and fear'. An old man, whose only role in
the play is to express the Peruvians' deep loyalty to their king, responds
chorically: 'The virtues of our Monarch alike secure to him the affection
of his people and the benign regard of Heaven' (*DW* 673). It is difficult to
imagine that a Drury Lane audience, conscious of the presence of its king,
would not have echoed such expressions of loyalty.

The significance of Sheridan's endorsement of George III's monarchy

[8] *The Times*, 6 June 1799.
[9] See Colley, 'Apotheosis', *Britons*, and Carretta, *George III*.

in *Pizarro* goes even further than this, however. As we have seen, *The Times* noted that the King was 'peculiarly gratified' with Rolla's address to the Peruvians, which ends by affirming that the ideological foundations of the Peruvian/British struggle are the monarchy, inherited laws, and religious faith: 'The throne we honour is the PEOPLE'S CHOICE.' This passage is crucial to the interpretation of the politics of *Pizarro* and its context requires elucidation. In 1797 the Foxite Whigs had seceded from parliament in protest against the corrupt electoral system and monarchical intransigence which, they felt, made it impossible to achieve reform through constitutional means. In January 1798 the Whig Duke of Norfolk toasted Charles James Fox at the latter's birthday celebrations by declaring 'Our Sovereign, the Majesty of the People', a deliberate challenge to the ultimate authority of George III. To the anger of Pitt, who regarded the toast as 'barely short of treason', Fox repeated it five months later at another Whig club function.[10] Typical of the sloganizing theatricality of late eighteenth-century politics, these toasts were calculated acts of defiance, designed to raise the temperature in the country and to provoke Pitt into making a political martyr out of Fox. They received a great deal of publicity at the time and were still very much in the public mind when *Pizarro* was first staged in May 1799. On 6 June, the day after George III had seen the play, *The Times* reported itself gratified that the health of the King had been toasted at the Whig Club 'with the warmest testimonies of affection to his person': 'There were no additions, which are always diminutions, and not the least allusion to the Whig-Pretender, his metaphysical *Majesty of the People*.' *Pizarro* is very much in line with what *The Times* described as 'the penitential wisdom' of the Whigs. Rolla's declaration that 'The throne we honour is the PEOPLE'S CHOICE' was a direct allusion to the controversy which, rather than proclaiming the sovereignty of the people with its revolutionary and even regicidal implications in the 1790s, instead stresses popular confidence in monarchical authority.

The event of *Pizarro* was therefore multi-layered in its significance. At one level it sought to reassert the libertarian dimensions of Whig patriotism by identifying British values with the heroic Rolla defending the oppressed and defenceless against a despotic enemy: at another level, however, it attempted a reconciliation with George III by endorsing the view of the monarch as the paternal figure-head of the nation. As such the play was amenable to both Whig and loyalist patriotisms, but I would argue that its bias was in favour of the latter. *Pizarro* was an important

---

[10] Wells, *Insurrection*, 156.

event in the process whereby patriotism was constructed as a set of values that transcended allegiancies of rank and faction, and because the play was about defining these values through war, this meant that the conflict with France was also removed from the realm of the political. As played by Kemble and later painted by Lawrence, Rolla became one of the most powerful totems of the British martial spirit, a fact recognized by Nelson, that other quintessentially British hero, when he made an appearance at the play after his victory at the Battle of the Nile.[11]

By depoliticizing patriotism and the war in this way, Sheridan was also effectively depoliticizing the practices of the patent theatres and, in particular, mainpiece drama. When he was criticized in parliament in 1795 for using Drury Lane for factional purposes, Sheridan had responded by arguing that the theatre was not a 'fit place' for politics. Significantly, he justified himself with reference to the status of the patent theatres as royal houses: 'With respect to the London stage, the fact however was, that the players were considered as the king's servants, and the theatre the king's theatre; and there was nothing so natural as that no pieces should be permitted that were not agreeable to his Majesty.'[12] The need to avoid offending the King is represented as a natural consideration, transcending factors of party or class allegiance—because the King was above factional politics, and Drury Lane was a royal theatre, it could not, by implication, be political. By extension, therefore, the tradition of mainpiece drama associated with the patent theatres and which other theatres such as Sadler's Wells were prohibited from performing, was also natural and outside politics. Sheridan's defence of British values in *Pizarro* was therefore synonymous with the defence of the cultural hegemony of Drama, in which war was intimated but not seen.

Spectacles and Re-enactments

Plays such as *Pizarro* should not be isolated from the broader context of the range of theatrical practices at Covent Garden and Drury Lane. Mainpiece drama was only one element of an evening's entertainment at the theatre consisting of music, song, interlude, occasional addresses,

---

[11] For Nelson's visit to the theatre see *Monthly Mirror*, 10 (1800), 396 and Charles Lamb, *The Letters of Charles and Mary Lamb*, ed. Edwin W. Marrs (3 vols.; Ithaca, NY, 1975–8), i. 254.

[12] Richard Brinsley Sheridan, *The Speeches of the Right Honourable Richard Brinsley Sheridan* (3 vols.; London, 1842), iii. 19–20.

afterpieces, pantomime, pageants, and spectacle.[13] It is to these forms that we must look in order to explore the explicit representation of the events of the French wars in the British theatre—indeed, considered together they reveal the extent to which the whole enterprise of the theatre at this time was dedicated to the commemoration of the war and the enhancement of patriotic values. In studies of the politics of the theatre, which have tended to focus on mainpiece drama, the other elements of the whole show have been neglected: I want to take some steps towards remedying this omission by examining the politics of spectacle in particular.

Spectacular effects—broadly speaking, the use of scenic devices, machinery, music, lighting, procession, and ceremony—were an integral element of all kinds of theatrical forms at this period, ranging from high tragedy to pantomime and ballet. At the patent theatres the evening's entertainment would often conclude with a spectacle, such as at Covent Garden in 1798, of which two main types can be distinguished—the pageant, derived ultimately from the Stuart masque, and the representation of military or naval engagements, related to the naumachia, another traditional form of court entertainment.[14] One of the most significant ways in which topical events were represented in the theatre was in the form of an afterpiece which would combine elements of dramatic action with a spectacular version of a military engagement, usually concluding with an effusion of patriotic pageantry. *The Camp* is a notable example of this, a success which Sheridan and Drury Lane tried to repeat in 1794 with *The Glorious First of June*, a commemoration of Howe's naval victory. As was the case with *The Camp*, *The Glorious First of June* featured a mechanical spectacle as its centre-piece. According to the *Salopian Journal*, the 'immense' stage of Drury Lane was 'turned into a Sea' and the manœuvres executed with more than usual verisimilitude:

Nothing can surpass the enchantment of this exhibition.—It is not the usual mockery of pasteboard Ships. The vessels are large, perfect models of the ships they represent, and made with such minute beauty, as to be worthy of a place in the most curious collection. All the manœuvres of the day are executed with nautical skill,—the lines are formed;—they bear down on each other; the firing is well managed, and kept up warmly for some time on both sides; at length, the French line is broken, several of their ships dismasted—boarded—taken,—and two sunk, as on the real occasion; and the expanse of sea affords a variety, which

---

[13] See George Winchester Stone Jnr. (ed.), *The Stage and the Page: London's 'Whole Show' in the Eighteenth-Century Theatre* (Berkeley, Calif., 1981).

[14] On naumachia see Richard D. Altick, *The Shows of London* (Cambridge, Mass., 1978), 97. For a discussion of spectacle see Michael R. Booth, *Victorian Spectacular Theatre 1850–1910* (London, 1981), 1–29.

it is not easy for the mind to conceive possible for mere scenic representation. (*DW* 757)

The drama surrounding the spectacular sea fight was not simply a pretext for it, but deals with the significant issue of the effect of the war on people at home. The dialogue of the afterpiece, the work of James Cobb, concerns a rural family, the Russets, whose sailor son Henry has died in battle. His role as the main bread-winner of the family has been taken by his messmate, William, who has deserted from the navy in order to fulfil his promise to Henry that he would take care of the Russets. A local lawyer, Endless, has designs on Susan, the daughter of the house, who has rejected his advances. Endless intends to force her hand by demanding unpaid rent from the impoverished family and when the landlord, an ex-naval man called Commodore Chace, will have nothing of it, he reveals William's presence, branding him a deserter. The Commodore is divided in his response but cannot extenuate William's 'crime'—'To encourage idleness and desertion from his Majesty's Service! But Russet's poor—yet such an example' (*DW* 768). Mrs Russet and Susan offer Commodore Chace the rent they owe with money given to them by William's friend Robin. They reveal to the Commodore that William has returned to sea of his own accord, at which news their landlord refuses to accept the rent, saying '—keep your money till I ask for it.—Don't think I want to be bribed by a fine speech to do an Act of Justice' (*DW* 770). At this point, the battle of the Glorious First of June takes place. When the dramatic action resumes, it is revealed that William has taken part in the battle alongside Robin—'stung' by his friend's act of generosity in supplying the Russets with money, he has decided to return to the navy. 'I went to my post', he declares, 'and I have shared your danger and your glory', to which Robin responds, 'I would share everything with a messmate I love as I do you William' (*DW* 773). This affirmation of naval fellowship is followed by Endless's come-uppance. Commodore Chace accuses him of committing 'the worst Act of Oppression—in grinding a poor Sailor's family' and authorizes the sailors to give him an appropriately naval form of punishment—'a good wholesome Ducking' (*DW* 774).

The Glorious First of June would thus seem to have been directed towards both a civilian audience and the sailors fighting the war, some of whom were present in the audience (an 'honest tar' in the gallery was said to have been so impressed with the verisimilitude of the naval engagement that he called out '*Dowse my lights, how I should like to be among them*' (*DW* 756)). The piece acknowledges that the sailors' concerns about the welfare of their families were to some extent justified. William is shown to have his reasons for protecting the Russet family, not only from poverty but also from the sexual attentions of men like Endless. In emphasizing the economic (and patriarchal) value of young men to the household, *The Glorious First of June* also participates indirectly in the controversy over impressment; indeed, when sailors are first referred to in the piece they are objects of fear rather than admiration. One of the Russet children tells her mother 'I am so frightened—there are some sailors talking together at the corner of the Orchard—I am afraid they want to rob us' (*DW* 765). The piece thus acknowledges civilian apprehensions of the navy, for the mention of lurking sailors would have evoked the press-gangs for many members of the audience, but it also attempts to allay such fears in two significant ways. First, it emphasizes the value of the navy as a transcendent national brotherhood, represented by the friendships between William and the dead Henry, and between William and Robin. Cobb suggests that humanitarian instincts—in the form of reified male bonding—will overcome the demands of predatory landlords and food shortages. There will always be a William or a Robin to lend a helping hand. (It could also be said that there is a democratizing tendency in *The Glorious First of June* in that 'true' charity is not identified with traditional figures of authority—the philanthropic squire or aristocrat—but with men of comparatively low social status. This is not necessarily inconsistent with the politics of the piece, however, as it suggests that the heroes are not only the admirals and generals but the people's own sons and brothers, thus identifying the civilian population even more strongly with its defenders.)

The second way in which Cobb attempts to reassure the audiences of *The Glorious First of June* is by suggesting that true justice will not be diverted from its path by men like Endless and that the families of sailors will be safe in the hands of civilian authority. It is significant that the figure who represents this authority in the piece is an ex-naval man, Commodore Chace, who effectively straddles both the civilian and naval worlds. In *The Glorious First of June* as a whole, national identity is effectively subsumed in that of the naval 'family', as represented by men like Robin, William, and Commodore Chace. This is indicated theatrically when Endless, the lawyer who has acted in an unpatriotic way by persecuting a sailor's family, is subjected to a form of naval rather than civilian punishment. This construction of the navy as emblematic of nationhood achieves its apotheosis at the end of the piece when the resources of spectacle come into their own. According to the *Salopian Journal*, *The Glorious First of June* concluded with

a beautiful transparency of Lord Howe . . . and a painting of Britannia holding the Cap of Liberty; while Neptune in a splendid and elegant habilment, surveys the stage, and the yards of the two men of war are manned by their hands. The conclusion was a brilliant display of Fire-works, one of which exhibited the words RULE BRITANNIA in capital characters, a shower of fire descending from each letter, while the Song was given by the performers in full chorus. (*DW* 757)

'Rule Britannia' rang out again in 1797 when *The Glorious First of June* was adapted to suit the circumstances of another victory by another admiral. The spectacle, song, and sentiment remained the same, but this time the piece was dedicated to the glory of Sir John Jervis who had achieved success in the battle of Cape St Vincent on 14 February 1797 (*DW* 831–2). The adaptation suggests the importance of topicality to this kind of theatre and its close association with how the war was commemorated in society as a whole. Managers and playwrights were adept at devising entertainments that could be staged within a few days of dispatches reaching London, thereby exploiting immediate public interest in the events of the war. The theatre thus enhanced its traditional significance as the mirror of the times, the place to which people went in order to comprehend their world. Its identification with society's experience of the war went even further than this, however, in that the theatre and the street shared a common repertoire of commemoration. A member of the audience at *The Glorious First of June* would have witnessed a display of fireworks, communal singing and dancing, and a transparency depicting the triumphant admiral; he or she could have left the theatre in London or any of the provincial towns and witnessed the same kind of events and devices on the streets. The transparency, a painted cloth through which light could be shone, is particularly significant in the link between urban ritual and the use of spectacle in the theatre. Its development as a feature of stage design, under the auspices of Philippe Jacques De Loutherbourg, seems to have occurred at the same time as it made an appearance on the London streets for political purposes.[15] By the period of the French wars the transparency had become a common feature of civic patriotism; in conjunction with illuminations, decorative arches, bell-ringing, and bon-

[15] Altick, *Shows*, 119; Sybil Rosenfeld, *Georgian Scene Painters and Scene Painting* (Cambridge, 1981), 55–9; John Brewer, *Party Ideology and Popular Politics at the Accession of George III* (Cambridge, 1976), 186.

fires it ushered in news of every major victory, transforming the townscape into a celebratory theatre. After the battle of Trafalgar, for example, the town of Titchfield was decorated with transparencies, one of which 'represented a Man of War, complete in all her rigging, as at the commencement of an action, with the portrait of the gallant Nelson as standing on the quarter-deck'. A house nearby 'displayed a ship with masts, yards, and rigging cut to pieces, representing the conclusion of an action'.[16] It was thus possible to read these transparencies as a narrative of Trafalgar, their superimposition upon the buildings and night sky of Titchfield signifying the way in which the naval victory had marked the community. Unlike monumental sculpture, transparencies and the theatrical entertainments with which they were linked, were ephemeral art forms. They were meaningful for so long as the events of the war were news: Howe had to give way to Jervis, while the Titchfield transparencies would only have lasted a few days. As such, they played an important part in registering the temporality of the war. For the majority of the civilian population of Britain, war was experienced as long periods of ignorance and anxiety about what was happening, punctuated by days or weeks of heightened significance as sketchy details of a major battle filtered through to the newspapers, followed ultimately by confirmation of victory or defeat. Communal celebrations such as illuminations, bonfires, and transparencies served the important purpose of expressing and enhancing patriotic fervour, but no less significant was their ritualistic function—the marking of these times of national catharsis. The fact that the theatre was an intrinsic part of these rituals bound it even more closely to the culture of war at this period.

The role of the theatre in mediating not only the events of the war but also how they were commemorated in society at large is illustrated by a topical afterpiece from 1797, Andrew Franklin's *A Trip to the Nore*, a musical entertainment in one act, first performed at Drury Lane on 9 November 1797.[17] The piece takes as its subject George III's departure from Greenwich to review the fleet at the Nore in commemoration of the victory at Camperdown.[18] This is represented in the form of a naumachia in scene two for which the scene direction is as follows: '*Greenwich Hos-*

---

[16] *Hampshire Telegraph, and Sussex Chronicle*, 18 Nov. 1805.

[17] Hogan, *London Stage*, Part 5, iii. 2019. For a discussion of the piece as 'nautical docudrama' see George D. Glen, '"Nautical Docudrama" in the Age of the Kembles' in *When They 'Weren't' Doing Shakespeare: Essays on Nineteenth-Century British and American Theatre*, ed. Judith L. Fisher and Stephen Watt (Athens, Ga., 1989), 141–4.

[18] For an account of the King's departure see *The Times*, 31 Oct. 1797. The review at the Nore failed to take place due to bad weather: see *The Times*, 1 Nov. 1797.

pital—Guns fire—Flags are hoisted on the vessels—The Royal Barge appears—The vessels sail—Martial music, which ceases when the vessels disappear.'[19] Around this spectacle, Franklin constructs a drama concerning the people who flocked to see the review. *A Trip to the Nore* is significant for the way that it attempts to theatricalize the energy and potency of the Georgian crowd—the piece begins with the scene direction '*Enter a Mob of People, shouting and running*'.[20] This representation of the people is closer to Paine's 'open theatre of the world' than to the disciplined, choric masses of pageantry. However, the energy of the mob in *A Trip to the Nore*, once theatrically realized, is directed towards the enhancement of patriotic values, rather than their deconstruction, as Paine was suggesting. Certain recognizable stereotypes are distinguished from the crowd—the Scotsman, the Irishman, the veteran tar, the sweetheart, the citizen and his wife, the tailor—some of these types representing elements whose loyalty was particularly in question in 1797. The heterogeneity of the British nation is thus acknowledged, but only to reinforce the idea that differences in the community can ultimately be subsumed in the great cause—the war against France. As in *The Glorious First of June*, civilian–military relations are identified as one of the most serious sources of dissension in the state. Bowsprit, the veteran tar, nearly comes to blows with the tailor Buckram over the question of the latter's loyalty. Buckram defends himself by claiming that he is one of the subscribers to the government's Voluntary Contributions scheme and that he nearly broke his neck forcing his way into the pit at Drury Lane for the sake of the widows and orphans of those who had fallen at Camperdown. The piece thereby suggests that the artisans and tradesmen who had not gone to war were equally capable of playing their part. Conversely, it is implied that the rumbustious disorderliness of a sailor such as Bowsprit has to be tolerated because ideologically he is at the centre of it all—he is the standard by which the loyalty of the community can be measured. This is represented in theatrical terms at the end of the piece when Bowsprit leads his fellow sailors, the civilian characters, and the mob beyond in the singing of a series of songs to the familiar tunes of 'God Save the King', 'Hearts of Oak', 'The Roast Beef of Old England', and 'Rule Britannia'.

It is probable that some elements of the audience would have joined in the singing that concluded the piece, thereby uniting actors and audience in a celebration of patriotic values. It is also highly likely that many of these spectators had themselves been part of the crowd that had rushed to

[19] Andrew Franklin, *A Trip to the Nore* (London, 1797), 10.   [20] Ibid. 5.

see the King at Greenwich or, like Buckram, been squeezed into the pit in order to demonstrate their gratitude to the heroes of Camperdown. The levels of signification are manifold: the performance of *A Trip to the Nore* at Drury Lane in 1797 represented an audience watching a topical afterpiece that in turn represented the audience's own participation in an event—a military review rendered as theatrical spectacle—which was itself an example of the theatricalized commemoration of war. (One might go further and claim that the battle of Camperdown, governed by the rules of naval engagements, was itself a kind of theatre.) The worlds of war, civic space, and the theatre are here synthesized, made inseparable, as are the actions of spectatorship and participation. *A Trip to the Nore* effectively represents war as a grand metatheatrical event, implying that the audience is as much on show as the spectacle of war itself, indeed that the audience *is* the spectacle. As Buckram's vindication of himself suggests, to endure the crush at Drury Lane is sufficient proof of one's loyalty—the identities of patriot and theatre-goer are one and the same.

Amphitheatrical Attacks

In representing the war as spectacle, Covent Garden and Drury Lane faced significant competition from the minor theatres—specifically Sadler's Wells and the amphitheatres of Astley and Hughes. The use of a fluid and dynamic spectacle of the crowd in *A Trip to the Nore* can be regarded as a response to what was happening south of the Thames and at Islington, where throughout the Revolutionary and Napoleonic Wars audiences could experience re-enactments of sieges, battles, and naval engagements. In this part of the chapter, I want to explore the representation of war at the minor theatres and the challenges posed by this to the cultural and political hegemony of the patent houses. But before I proceed, I want to establish the way in which these challenges are prefigured by the responses of the minor theatres to the fall of the Bastille in 1789, an event which was not only of totemic political significance but also profoundly influential in the later representation of war.

Censorship severely limited the capacity of the patent theatres to deal seriously with the subject of the French Revolution even during 1789–90 when events in France were generally welcomed in Britain. Frederick Reynolds's *The Bastille* was put into production at Covent Garden but was refused a licence by the Examiner for Plays, while at Drury Lane an opera entitled *The Island of St Marguerite* was trimmed of its allusions to the Revolution by the censor. L. W. Conolly claims that this was due to an official desire not to offend the French monarchy, but it is possible that the patent theatres were already girding themselves for the prospective reaction against the Revolution.[21] Kemble's revival of *Henry V* at this time clearly anticipated a swing in the public mood against England's traditional enemy and a resumption of the theatre's normal ideological role. There are other factors though, apart from censorship, which account for the failure of the patent theatres to mount conventional dramatic treatments of what had been happening in France. One is the nature of the public interest in the Revolution. While a significant number of people were radicalized by the fall of the Bastille and by subsequent events, the predominant response of the great majority of Britons was curiosity, a desire to read about and possibly see what was happening across the Channel. As an event, the fall of the Bastille thus belonged in the same category as any distant battle or siege. It was eminently suitable for representation as spectacle, the kind of theatre which the minors specialized in due to the limitations of the Licensing Act. Moreover, these theatres also had a significant commercial advantage as a result of the timing of the Revolution which occurred during the summer season when Covent Garden and Drury Lane were closed.

During late July and August 1789 a 'Bastille war' took place in London as managers of the minor theatres staged rival representations of the events of the Fourteenth of July. Hughes's Royal Circus offered *The Triumph of Liberty; or, the Destruction of the Bastille* on 5 August 1789 with John Palmer in the leading role of Henry Dubois. Palmer was the renegade actor who between 1785 and 1788 had mounted his own unsuccessful 'revolution' by building the Royalty Theatre and challenging the duopoly of the patents.[22] (During the seventy-nine night run of *The Triumph of Liberty*, Palmer, and the actor who replaced him, spent time in Bridewell prison for illegally speaking prose.)[23] Not to be outdone, Philip Astley, the ex-soldier and proprietor of the Royal Grove, obtained from Madame Tussaud waxwork models of the heads of notable victims of the Revolution and staged *Paris in an Uproar; or, the Destruction of the Bastile* on 17 August 1789. He advertised his amphitheatre as boasting 'one of the grandest and most extraordinary Entertainments that ever appeared,

[21] Conolly, *Censorship*, 87–93; see also Jeffrey N. Cox, 'The French Revolution in the English Theater' in *History & Myth: Essays on English Romantic Literature*, ed. Stephen C. Behrendt (Detroit, Mich., 1990), 33–52.

[22] W. Nicholson, *The Struggle for a Free Stage in London* (Boston, Mass., 1906), 98–123.

[23] J. Decastro, *The Memoirs of J. Decastro, Comedian*, ed. R. Humphreys (London, 1824), 125.

Grounded on authentic Facts', its chief attraction being a 'MODEL of PARIS . . . on a very large and extensive Scale, 50 feet by 84, covering the whole Theatre. The Streets, Squares, Public Gardens, Places of public Amusement, innumerable Houses, &c. . . . are strictly conformable to that City.'[24] Sadler's Wells was somewhat slower in its response than Astley's and the Royal Circus, but on 31 August 1789 it too announced its Bastille entertainment, *Gallic Freedom; or, Vive la Liberte*, in a double bill with *Britannia's Relief*, a spectacle representing the procession to St Paul's in commemoration of George III's recovery from illness.[25]

All three entertainments featured the attack on the Bastille as their centre-piece. According to the scene direction in the published version of *The Triumph of Liberty*, the Bastille was *'seen attacked, when Bombs are thrown into it for a considerable Time; a Breach then is made, and entered . . . After this the Scene changes to an inside View of the Bastille, when the attack is re-commenced.'*[26] In the advertisement for his entertainment, Astley claimed that the audience would be presented with an 'External Perspective View of the Bastile, the Draw-Bridge, the Fosse, &c. &c. shewing the Manner of storming and taking the Bastile, by the Military and Citizens'.[27] A synopsis for *Gallic Freedom* at Sadler's Wells referred to 'The Cannonade and general Attack . . . The Skirmish with the Garde Criminelle. . . . The actual Descent of the Soldiers and Citizens by Torch Light, into the SUBTERRANEAN DUNGEONS . . . And the plundering and final Demolition of the BASTILE by an exasperated Populace.'[28]

The fall of the Bastille was thus represented at the minor theatres in the same terms as a siege or battle, except that the politics of this particular war were very different from the norm. The army attacking the Bastille was an 'exasperated populace' and not a band of gallant Britons challenging a traditional enemy: the incident was still an act of rebellion by the people against authority, however much it was justified by the notorious reputation of the prison.[29] Moreover, the political implications of the fall of the Bastille were enhanced by its mode of representation at the minor theatres. In contrast to the static, two-dimensional quality of the patent theatres' tableau vivant, Sadler's Wells and the circuses peopled the theatrical space with a dynamic and destructive crowd—an 'exasperated populace' rising against the symbol of a despotic monarchy. The use of the

---

[24] *Public Advertiser*, 17 Aug. 1789.   [25] *The Times*, 31 Aug. 1789.
[26] John Dent, *The Bastille* (London, 1789), 12.   [27] *Public Advertiser*, 17 Aug. 1789.
[28] Quoted Denis Arundell, *The Story of Sadler's Wells 1683–1964* (London, 1965), 44–5.
[29] For the notoriety of the Bastille see David Bindman, *The Shadow of the Guillotine: Britain and the French Revolution* (London, 1989), 36–42.

circus ring as a stage enabled Astley and Hughes to choreograph their actors in ways that highlighted mass energy and movement.[30] In so far as these actors were representing 'the people', there were potential analogies to be made between the actions of the amphitheatrical crowd and the dynamics of mob behaviour on the streets, as familiar to the theatre-goers of Georgian London as they were to the people of Paris.

The Bastille entertainments thus had the potential to subvert the politics of spectacle at the patent theatres, recasting theatre war in terms of the contest between peoples and kings, and overturning the decorum of pageantry in their representation of the mobilized crowd. That this was recognized by the managements of the minor theatres is clear from the way that they themselves tried to reassert the values of patriotic pageantry within the framework of the Bastille entertainments. *The Triumph of Liberty* at Hughes's Royal Circus concluded with the descent of an actress representing Britannia along with two transparent portraits of George III and Queen Charlotte. Britannia then addressed the audience claiming that France had caught the 'Patriot flame' from Britain, at which '*The Statue of Liberty trampling on the Figure of Despotism is seen to ascend*'. The company then joined together in a Chorus celebrating Britannia:

> Hail! Britannia, 'tis to thee,
> We owe our liberty;
> Ev'ry clime, and ev'ry zone
> Ever must thy impulse own.
> May you ever hold controul,
> And bless us from pole to pole.[31]

Similarly, the Sadler's Wells management attempted to contain the potential subversiveness of *Gallic Freedom* by linking it with *Britannia's Relief*. A puff for the latter claimed that it formed 'a striking picture of national happiness, when contrasted with the present situation of our neighbours on the continent'.[32] *Britannia's Relief* was a representation of royal ceremonial, celebrating the centrality of the monarchy in the social order, while *Gallic Freedom* was an imitation of a revolution that would eventually threaten the authority of all kings. As the initial welcome given to the fall of the Bastille was followed by political reaction and, later, war,

---

[30] Martin Meisel, *Realizations: Narrative, Pictorial and Theatrical Arts in Nineteenth-Century England* (Princeton, NJ, 1983), 214. See also A. H. Saxon, *Enter Foot and Horse: a History of Hippodrama in England and France* (New Haven, Conn., 1968).

[31] Dent, *Bastille*, 23–4.

[32] Unidentified newspaper clipping, Collection Relating to Sadler's Wells, British Library, vol. 2, fo. 69.

so the spectacle of the crowd was quickly eclipsed by a revivified spectacle of patriotism—the kind exemplified by the spectacle that had concluded *The Triumph of Liberty*. However, *A Trip to the Nore* suggests that the lessons of the Bastille entertainments were not lost on the managements of the patent theatres—the spectacle of the crowd could be used to reinforce, rather than undermine, adherence to the crown and the constitution.

The 'Bastille war' of 1789 was also of crucial importance to the later representation of the French wars in the minor theatres. The success of *The Triumph of Liberty*, *Paris in an Uproar*, and *Gallic Freedom* showed that the circuses and Sadler's Wells were particularly suited to the staging of war. Unlike Covent Garden and Drury Lane, the minor theatres did not have to observe the hierarchy of dramatic forms implied by the relationship between mainpiece and afterpiece, and were able to place their enactments of sieges and battles at the centre of a night's entertainment. Because of the limitations of the Licensing Act, which compelled the minors to treat war as spectacle rather than drama, they could also align themselves more closely with the 'real' theatre of war—the culture of the military camps, of the Volunteers, of sham fights. This link was reinforced by the fact that the season for the minor theatres coincided with the height of military activity in the summer, enabling Astley and Hughes to mediate the idea of war as a time of festival or holiday. (The response of Sadler's Wells to the camp at Bagshot in 1792 was an entertainment entitled *Mars's Holiday*.)[33] Finally, the representation of war as spectacle at the minor theatres entailed a development of the symbolic relationship between stage space and the field of battle that I first raised in relation to *The Camp* and *The Invasion*. The use of the circus ring as a stage enabled Astley and Hughes to enact battles on a larger scale than at Covent Garden or Drury Lane, a scale that signified the scope of their ambition. Astley's boast that his model of Paris would cover 'the whole Theatre' suggests a desire to encompass the topography as well as the topicality of an event. 'The whole Theatre' was a Paris in the same way as it would later stand for Valenciennes, Seringapatam, or Salamanca.

Between 1793 and 1815 the minor theatres staked their claim as the most significant forum for the representation of war. In 1793, for example, Astley's staged 'a new military spectacle', *The Siege of Valenciennes*. Philip Astley had himself been present at the siege as a volunteer and, according to Charles Dibdin the Younger, had brought back for display in his

---

[33] Published as *Mars's Holiday; or, a Trip to the Camp* (London, 1792).

amphitheatre a cannon that had been captured from the French.[34] The scenery for the spectacle included a number of 'exact' views of the fortifications of Valenciennes. In 1794 Sadler's Wells competed with Drury Lane by offering its own tribute to the heroes of the First of June, an entertainment entitled *Naval Triumph; or, The Tars of Old England*, comprising a representation of the illuminations in London which had marked the news of the victory, a spectacular enactment of the battle, a pageant of famous British admirals dating from the Spanish Armada, and a procession of British seamen in historical costume.[35] In 1801 the Wells enacted the battles of Copenhagen and Alexandria. Referring to the latter, a puff for the theatre claimed that its representation of 'two armies engaging' had never been so well accomplished on the British stage.[36] Apart from naval and land battles, Sadler's Wells also marked notable events such as Sir Sidney Smith's daring escape from French custody in 1798 and ridiculed French invasion plans in entertainments such as *The British Raft* (also 1798). 'The Managers can never be sufficiently commended', proclaimed an advertisement, 'for their endeavours at this time, to convey through the medium of amusement, the solid lessons of loyalty and unanimity.'[37] The apotheosis of this form of drama came in 1804 with the installation of a water tank at Sadler's Wells, now renamed as the 'Aquatic Theatre'. The inaugural production, *The Siege of Gibraltar* (1804) was extensively described by Charles Dibdin in his *Memoirs*. He emphasized the pains taken by the theatre to represent the ships accurately. Shipwrights and riggers from the Royal Naval dockyard at Woolwich were recruited to construct them

upon a scale of one inch to a foot of those in the Navy ; in exact imitation of which they were made, even to the slightest minutiae; they had their regular tiers and number of brass Cannon, cast on purpose for them, which were regularly fired, recharged, etc. in action. The same precision was observed in regard to their rigging: The Sails were made to work; and when they were finished, they were the most [accurate] models ever exhibited to the public . . . and frequently have I been applied to by naval officers, to allow them a private inspection of our fleet, which

---

[34] Charles Dibdin the Younger, *Professional and Literary Memoirs of Charles Dibdin the Younger*, ed. George Speaight (London, 1956), 26.

[35] Unidentified newspaper clipping, Collection Relating to Sadler's Wells, British Library, vol. 2, fo. 159.

[36] Unidentified newspaper clipping, Collection Relating to Sadler's Wells, British Library, vol. 3, fo. 92.

[37] Unidentified newspaper clipping, Collection Relating to Sadler's Wells, British Library, vol. 3, fo. 43.

I always permitted, to the high gratification of my applicant. Our Ships' Crews were manufactured, not pressed, and not one of them ever flinched from his duty; these were made in the same scale of proportion to '*Real Men*', as the vessels were to *Real Ships*.[38]

The audience at the first night of the spectacle, 2 April 1804, was confronted with a drop scene covering the proscenium area and depicting the entire English fleet drawn up in battle lines against the French and the Spanish. When it was raised, the effect of the 'mimic ocean . . . acted like electricity', but this was exceeded by the response to the model ships: when they 'sailed down, in regular succession, . . . their sails shifting to the wind; their colours and pennants flying; and their ordnance, as they passed the front of the Stage, firing a grand salute to the Audience, the latter seemed in extacy'.[39] This was followed by an enactment of the incident in which Sir Roger Curtis had saved the lives of drowning Spanish sailors, involving the use of actual size rowing boats with children playing the parts of the sailors. At this, according to Dibdin, 'the enthusiasm of the Audience exceeded all bounds; and I think, that there are no persons who witnessed in 1804, *The Siege of Gibraltar*, at Sadler's Wells, will assert other than it was one of the most novel, imposing and nationally interesting Exhibitions they ever saw'.[40]

The representation of war thus involved the perpetual extension of the boundaries of what was theatrically possible. The livelihood of the minor theatres depended on them being able to outrival the patents, thereby attracting curious audiences; this meant ever more accurate representations of battle, superseding the conventions of Covent Garden and Drury Lane. The *coup* of *The Siege of Gibraltar* had been produced by the way in which the drop scene—a pictorial representation of battle—had been suddenly realized in the form of model ships and a 'mimic ocean', going beyond what any London theatre had done before. That the minor theatres were aware of the challenge they represented to Covent Garden and Drury Lane is suggested by the following puff for a spectacle at Astley's Amphitheatre entitled *The Brave Cossack*:

A battle on our principal stages [i.e. the patent theatres] has always produced a ludicrous effect.—According to Sir Philip Sydney—'*two armies* flie in, represented with *four swords and bucklers*, and then, what hard heart will not receive it for a pitched field.' But here the contrivance has nothing ridiculous in it—the horse and foot commingle, and an actual field of battle is realized to the sight.[41]

[38] Dibdin, *Memoirs*, 60.   [39] Ibid.   [40] Ibid. 62.
[41] *Monthly Mirror*, NS 3 (1808), 404.

Sir Philip Sidney's attack on the representation of war in the theatre, echoed by the Chorus in Shakespeare's *Henry V*, is here invoked in order to differentiate the practices of the minor theatres from those of the patents. War at Covent Garden and Drury Lane is stigmatized as being too theatrical; at Astley's, however, the actuality of conflict, significantly defined in the spatial terms of the 'field of battle', is 'realized to the sight' of the viewer. This emphasis on the verisimilitude of the theatre's representation of war is so persistent as to be worth consideration at this point. How realistic were entertainments such as *The Siege of Gibraltar* or *The Glorious First of June*? Why did Astley's management believe that an emphasis on the exactitude of the representation was a drawcard that could also be used to challenge the privileged status of Covent Garden and Drury Lane?

In his account of *The Siege of Gibraltar*, Charles Dibdin the Younger claimed that the audience was so taken by the 'gallant benevolence' of the British sailors in saving their enemies that 'they never for an instant saw the glaring abandonment of perspective, proportion and scenic propriety, exhibited by Man of War's boats, bigger than the largest ship of the line, and sailors compared with the 5 or 6 inch high mariners aboard the vessels, still more out of proportion'.[42] However, the empathy of the audience was also assisted by a deliberate effort during the rescue scene to obscure the model ships from the view by the use of smoke. The child sailors were made to leave the 'mimic ocean' as quickly as possible, the smoke then lifting to reveal the remnants of the Spanish navy. A later naval spectacle at Sadler's Wells in 1813, when the tank had ceased to be such a novelty, was not executed so successfully. The reviewer of a 'grand Melo-dramatic, Operatic and Aquatic Romance' commented that 'it would have been better' if the ships 'had not so often run aground; but this, indeed, was not surprising when a man was enabled to walk round one of them, with the water not higher than his knee; by which means it manifestly appeared . . . that even if a shipwreck had been the consequence, there was no imminent danger of drowning'.[43] This suggests that in spite of the boasts of actuality in the puffs, the representations of war in the minor theatres were as highly theatricalized as those in the patents. A print satirizing the 'Bastille war' of 1789 explodes the claims of Astley to verisimilitude by representing his entertainment in terms of a comically grotesque distortion of perspective and scale—the kind of 'glaring aban-

---

[42] Dibdin, *Memoirs*, 62.
[43] Unidentified newspaper clipping, Collection Relating to Sadler's Wells, British Library, vol. 4, fo. 27.

donment of perspective' that must have been apparent to audiences of *The Siege of Gibraltar*, in spite of the smoke.[44] In 'An Amphitheatrical Attack of the Bastile' a small cannon feebly puffs smoke at a scenic representation of the Bastille which is out of proportion to the actor who bulges from it, brandishing his dialogue in the form of a painted cloth. This is a theatre in which the forms of signification are excessively overdetermined—the drawbridge, which is also out of proportion to the rest of the Bastille, is labelled 'This is a Drawbridge'; the 'populace' are carrying the 'Standard of Liberty'. Astley's claim that *Paris in an Uproar* was based on personal experience of that city is also ridiculed in a fragment of a puff in the foreground of the image: 'Mr Centaur [i.e. Astley] can assure the publick since his return from Paris [above Dublin which has been struck through] that this here Bastile is the most exactest of any of the Bastiles existin.' In that the attack on the Bastille is represented in terms of a distortion of space and scale, this print can be compared with other images of war such as 'Noddle-Island' and the play on proportion and perspective that is apparent in both *The Camp* and *The Invasion*. This indicates how important visuality was to the conceptualization and representation of war in the late Georgian period. People attended Astley's and Sadler's Wells not because their entertainments were more or less theatrical but because the theatre, like the camp and the parade ground, catered to the desire to *see* war. The language of the puffs—as parodied in 'this here Bastile is the most exactest'—can be regarded as an appeal to this desire. The minor theatres attracted customers by constantly promising what they could never ultimately achieve—war completely penetrated by vision, 'an actual field of battle . . . realized to the sight'.

Panoramic War

The culture-critic Paul Virilio has emphasized how crucial the visualization of war is to its interpretation and perpetuation: '*the history of battle is primarily the history of radically changing fields of perception*. In other words, war consists not so much in scoring territorial, economic or other material victories as in appropriating the "immateriality" of perceptual fields.'[45] Virilio's *War and Cinema: The Logistics of Perception* is concerned with twentieth-century war and its relationship to cinematic and other

---

[44] For details of this caricature see George, *Satires*, vi. 628–9.

[45] Paul Virilio, *War and Cinema: the Logistics of Perception*, trans. Patrick Camiller (London, 1989), 7.

visual technologies, but his arguments can be applied to earlier periods of military history and other cultural practices such as theatre. Wellington's success at Waterloo, for example, was represented in terms of his visual command of the field of battle:

At the commencement of the action the Duke of Wellington on horseback, surrounded by his Staff, stood on the high ground to the right of the high road from Brussels to Genappe . . . To say where he afterwards was, is impossible—it would be more difficult to say where he was not; wherever his presence was most requisite, he was to be found; he seemed to be every where present. Exposed to the hottest fire, in the most conspicuous position, he stood reconnoitring with his glass, watching the Enemy's manoeuvres, and issuing orders with the most intrepid coolness, while balls and shells showered around him, and his Staff Officers fell wounded and dying by his side.[46]

Wellington's scrutiny of the battlefield becomes a sign of a quasi-divine military power; his soldiers' consciousness of his authority is rendered in terms of their sense that his vision, and his body, are everywhere. In the case of Waterloo, the metaphor of the battlefield as the warrior's theatre was more meaningful than ever. The conflict between the allies and France which had been conducted for years on a number of fronts was concentrated in a climactic encounter, acted out in a comparatively limited geographical space. The fate of Europe was decided on a plain outside Brussels, a plain, moreover, which Wellington had predetermined as the perfect site for battle. In 1814, on the way to Paris, he had taken 'a military view' of Waterloo; he then 'declared, that if ever it should be his fortune to defend Brussels, Waterloo would be the position he would occupy'.[47] Wellington's 'taking' of the site of Waterloo is comparable to the role of O'Daub in *The Camp* who, like the great commander, also takes a 'military view', in his case of the plain of Coxheath. As I indicated earlier, O'Daub's sizing up of the camp in terms of the dimensions of the stage is the key event of the afterpiece. Perspectival visualization, as represented here in a theatrical text and a work of military history, was part of the process whereby war was made meaningful: it was the way in which the enhanced significance of the battlefield/stage, both potential and realized, could be defined and understood.

The desire to see or 'take' the battlefield was instrumental in the development of another kind of spectacularization of war that I would like to consider briefly at this point—the panorama. The first permanent panorama in London was opened in 1793 by Robert Barker and in years

---

[46] *The Battle of Waterloo*, 4th edn. (London, 1815), xxii–xxiii.   [47] Ibid. xxiii.

following, the events of Britain's wars—the sieges of Seringapatam, Flushing, and Badajoz, the battles of Trafalgar, Vittoria, and Waterloo, for example—formed a succession of panoramic subjects. These consisted of pictorial representations, often on a massive scale ('The Storming of Seringapatam' at the Lyceum covered 2,550 square feet) which were displayed within a circular structure allowing a 360 degree view.[48] As in the theatre, the emphasis was on the verisimilitude of the representation. Promotional material constantly stressed that the paintings were based on sketches that had been taken at the actual battlefield. In the case of the panorama of the Battle of Waterloo Barker was at pains to emphasize that he had consulted with officers who had been there in order to verify the accuracy of the painting. The panoramists were also particular as to the time of the representation. Rather than a generalized treatment of battle, the paintings were supposed to show a specific time in its development. Viewers were encouraged to buy descriptions of the battle as a whole, thus enabling them to experience the panorama as a crucial stage in an unfolding temporal event. In his description of the Waterloo panorama Barker acknowledged that 'in the course of nine eventful hours, the field of Waterloo would furnish subjects for many Panoramas'. The period he had chosen to represent, however, was the triumphant conclusion of the contest 'about eight o'clock in the evening, when the British and their Allies, having finally repulsed all the attacks of the French, are attacking and routing them in their own position'.[49]

As a form of pictorial entertainment, the panorama represented another attempt to realize the field of battle to the sight. The advantage which it had over the theatres was its capacity to suggest the actual dimensions of the battlefield. The massive scale of the panorama painting—in comparison with the stages of the major and minor theatres—emphasized the spatial relationships between the armies and the enhanced significance of battlefield topography. Panoramas also implied a different sense of temporality—while entertainments such as *The Siege of Gibraltar* represented war as a series of actions in continuous time, in the case of the panoramas action was frozen. The sense of a battle having a dramatic continuum—as outlined in the printed narratives accompanying the panoramas—was thus subordinated to the apprehension of the moment, allowing the

---

[48] For account of the panorama see Altick, *Shows*, 128–97; Ralph Hyde, *Panoramania! the Art and Entertainment of the 'All-Embracing' View* (London, 1988), and William H. Galperin, *The Return of the Visible in British Romanticism* (Baltimore, Md., 1993), 34–61.

[49] *A Description of the Defeat of the French Army . . . Now Exhibiting in Barker's Panorama, Strand, Near Surry-Street* (London, 1816), 9, 3.

viewer to appreciate the ways in which battle altered the sense of time itself, giving it a peculiar intensity (as in Anton's 'it was a pause of death'). However, the most significant feature of the panorama entertainments, distinguishing them from the theatre, was the position of the viewer. According to Jonathan Crary, 'the circular or semicircular painting clearly broke with the localized point of view of perspective painting or the camera obscura, allowing the spectator an ambulatory ubiquity. One was compelled at the least to turn one's head (and eyes) to see the entire work.'[50] The 360 degree structure of the panorama had the effect of placing the viewer *within* the scene, rather than in front of it, as was the case in the theatre: the framing or mediating effect of the proscenium was thus eliminated. The position of the panorama viewer was in effect analogous to that of the military leader in the field; like Wellington at Waterloo, he or she had an 'ambulatory ubiquity', being able to command the view of the battlefield, free to examine whatever aspect of it he or she liked. In this respect, the civilian at home was in a much more privileged position than the ordinary soldier in the field. Accounts of warfare by those who have taken part in it often emphasize how difficult it is to gain an overview of what is happening. The individual soldier's knowledge of the pattern of the battle as a whole will often be a limited one. Thus it was the case that when the soldiers of the Royal Highland Regiment returned to Edinburgh after Waterloo, they were admitted free for two nights to the panoramic view of the battle. In order to comprehend what they had experienced the 'actors' had to become 'spectators'.[51] The fact that the Royal Highlanders who visited this panorama were effectively an audience indirectly highlights another difference between panorama entertainments and the representation of war in the theatre. The viewing of *The Glorious First of June* and *The Siege of Gibraltar* also entailed the experience of war as a communal event. In the theatre the individual perspective was subsumed in the larger 'view' of the audience—responses such as the collective 'extacy' which Sadler's Wells's ships had elicited. The panoramas, however, did not require an audience, only autonomous viewers who were free to come and go as they pleased. There was no time of performance, for example— the doors of the panorama were open from dawn to dusk.

The success of the panoramas was due to the ways in which they detheatricalized the representation of war, giving the impression that 'this' was what it was 'really' like—'an actual field of battle . . . realized to the

[50] Jonathan Crary, *Techniques of the Observer: On Vision and Modernity in the Nineteenth Century* (Cambridge, Mass., 1990), 113.

[51] Anton, *Retrospect*, 253.

sight'. This was war without the mediation of actors: there was no O'Daub to highlight the fact that it was a representation, no 'glaring abandonment of perspective', no framing device of the proscenium and, most importantly, no audience, only the autonomous viewer. The panorama was, in effect, a variety of Paine's 'open theatre of the world', a place in which the meaning of war was transparent to the viewer, without the obfuscations of the theatre. Ironically, the minor theatres, which had attempted to challenge the power of the patents by claiming that they alone could realize war, found themselves in competition with a form of entertainment that went even further in achieving this aim. Astley's *The Siege of Seringapatam* (1800) was produced after John Ker Porter's panorama of the same battle had been successfully exhibited at the Lyceum; increasingly military spectacles at the minor theatres used panoramas and large-scale paintings as primary referents, indirectly acknowledging the superiority of their competitors' realization of war.[52]

This diminution of the theatricality of war can be regarded as an early stage in the process whereby war, in Virilio's terms, has become the 'third dimension of cinema'.[53] Part of the politics of making war possible has involved the privileging of the vision of the civilian audience: the viewer at home must 'see' more than even the ordinary soldier in the field, assuming the position of a Wellington or a Napoleon. As long as the domestic audience can envision war, whether in the form of theatre, pictorial representation, or cinema, war can continue to be fought by the generals and strategists. The fear of mass conflict, especially when the domestic civilian population is not directly involved, is somehow assuaged. In this respect the people who crowded the panoramas of London and Edinburgh to see the battlefield of Waterloo shared the instincts of those who in 1991 crowded around the television screen to see the smart bombs penetrating the bunkers of Baghdad.

---

[52] For representations of the storming of Seringapatam at the Lyceum and Astley's see *Monthly Mirror*, 9 (1800), 240, 305. See also Dibdin, *Memoirs*, 107.

[53] Virilio, *War and Cinema*, 85.

4
'The Open Theatre of the World'

THE attempt to 'realize' the field of battle in the theatre was part of a complex pattern of cultural and political behaviour by which the French wars were being constantly mediated, re-enacted, and in some cases, transformed. One aspect of this was the significance of the theatre auditorium as a stage on which the tensions of a militarized society could be defined and played out. Any examination of what went on behind the proscenium also has to take into account the performances enacted before it. The significance of the theatre auditorium as a *de facto* military domain will form the subject of a later chapter: in the meantime, I want to explore the relationship between texts such as *Pizarro*, *The Glorious First of June*, and the Bastille entertainments and other cultural events of the period that were indebted to theatre—in particular Nelson's funeral of 1806 and the (premature) peace celebrations that took place in 1814. Both these events were occasions on which the meanings of war and patriotism were publicly articulated and contested: both events were also highly theatricalized in ways that confirmed as well as counteracted the practices of the institutionalized theatre.

Before I go on, however, it is necessary to define some of the methodological and interpretative issues that are raised by analysing events as texts. The recent work of historians such as Lynn Hunt and James Epstein, influenced by the cultural anthropology of Clifford Geertz and others, has led to an emphasis on the importance of 'symbolic practice'—the use of caps and flags, ribbons, songs and toasts—in the negotiation of political meaning.[1] This kind of approach, to which my own work is indebted, is redefining our perceptions of what constitutes the sphere of politics, extending it beyond written and verbal discourse to the 'languages' of costume, gesture, and the performative act. If there is a problem with this kind of cultural history, it lies in a tendency to overcompensate for previous neglect of these 'languages' by underesti-

[1] Lynn Hunt, *Politics, Culture, and Class in the French Revolution* (Stanford, Calif., 1984), and Lynn Hunt (ed.), *The New Cultural History* (Berkeley, Calif., 1989); James Epstein, 'Understanding the Cap of Liberty: Symbolic Practice and Social Conflict in Early Nineteenth-Century England', *Past and Present*, 122 (1989), 75–118.

mating the significance of the written discourses in which they are embedded.[2] We only have access to such symbolic practices through the mediation of a text, whether in the form of an official history, a newspaper account, or a work of imaginative literature. The analyses that follow in this chapter assume the impossibility of ever being able to retrieve what 'really' happened in a particular event. However, if an event only exists in the form of a text, then some texts are more privileged than others, making it necessary to look for which possible texts are being occluded or overlain. In the case of a theatrical or ritualized social occasion it is important to define the extent to which the 'performance' is being filtered or redefined by the influence of a discourse of theatricality within the printed text.

The representation of the funeral of Nelson, across a whole range of discursive and non-discursive practices, suggests the existence of a variety of 'theatricalities' in late Georgian culture with differing political nuances. The Nelson phenomenon is also interesting, not only on account of its immediate historical significance, but also because of his endurance as an icon of English patriotism. The key moments of the Nelson story, from 'I see no ships' to 'Kiss me Hardy' have entered historical folklore while biographies continue to be produced and Nelson societies flourish. In focusing on his funeral I want to go back to this legend in the moment of its cultural formation, in order to suggest that it is based on competing perceptions of heroism and the kind of theatre that should represent it.

Popular rejoicing at the news of the victory at Trafalgar on 21 October 1805 was tempered by grief over the loss of Nelson. Southey claimed that his death 'was felt in England as something more than a public calamity; men started at the intelligence, and turned pale, as if they had heard of the loss of a dear friend'.[3] Few public figures in Britain at this period would have been mourned in such a way. As a result of his naval victories and his reputation as a leader who was sensitive to the working conditions of his men, Nelson had achieved personal popularity of cult-like status, something which he had exploited in the manner of earlier popular heroes such as Wilkes by courting the urban crowd. His tours of England in 1802 were

---

[2] Epstein's comment in 'Understanding the Cap of Liberty'—'The cap of liberty allowed certain things to be said without actually saying them'—would seem to suggest the possibility of retrieving the 'pure' meaning of this particular symbolic practice (Epstein, 116). It neglects the way in which this meaning is filtered through the 'saying' of the historical document. For a discussion of how the behaviour of crowds at this period was mediated by 'a language of crowd description' see Mark Harrison, *Crowds and History: Mass Phenomena in English Towns, 1790–1835* (Cambridge, 1988), 168–91.

[3] Robert Southey, *The Life of Nelson* (London, 1909), 260.

reputed to have been more popularly acclaimed than those of George III and like the monarch, he enjoyed making well-publicized visits to the theatre where he would be the focus of attention.[4] In defining a public role for himself, Nelson was following in the footsteps of earlier eighteenth-century naval commanders. Victorious admirals such as Edward Vernon had exerted considerable political power because they were regarded as men of disinterested virtue, who put their country before the competing claims of place or party.[5] In this capacity, Nelson was able to exert an appeal across the political spectrum and was the toast of radicals and loyalists alike.[6] As far as Pitt's government was concerned, the Admiral's significance as a patriotic hero could only be advantageous to the war effort, but it is not clear to what extent it was either willing or able to exploit the Nelson phenomenon. George III and his placemen had every reason to be uneasy about the political implications of Nelson's popularity, especially its suggestion that men of vision and aptitude were more entitled to respect than those who possessed titles and property.

However, the political establishment could not afford to neglect the opportunities of a funeral. In his will, Nelson had expressed a wish to be buried at his birthplace, the Norfolk village of Burnham Thorpe, but instead he was given a state funeral at St Paul's Cathedral. The last commoner to receive such an honour had been the Elder Pitt in 1778.[7] The ritual of the funeral began with a period of lying in state at Greenwich, after which the body was transported in a flotilla of barges to the Admiralty. On 9 January 1806 it was borne in procession to St Paul's Cathedral, the burying place of military and naval heroes (Westminster Abbey being reserved for royalty). The very route of the funeral was meaningful in that it traversed an urban space—bounded by the Thames, Whitehall, and Westminster—which was traditionally associated with the monarchy and government. Additional efforts were made to enhance the

[4] See Jordan, 'Admiral Nelson as Popular Hero', 114–15.

[5] See Jordan and Rogers, 'Admirals as Heroes' and Wilson, 'Empire, Trade and Popular Politics'.

[6] Nelson's appearance in court as a character witness for Colonel Despard, the United Irishman who had plotted to assassinate the King, enhanced his reputation with radicals. In 1805 John Thelwall commemorated his death with an 'Epic Effusion' in poetry entitled *The Trident of Albion* (Liverpool, 1805).

[7] For the history of the state funeral in Britain at this period see two articles by Paul S. Fritz: 'From "Public" to "Private": the Royal Funerals in England, 1500–1830' in *Mirrors of Mortality: Studies in the Social History of Death*, ed. Joachim Whaley (London, 1981), 61–79, and 'The Trade in Death: The Royal Funerals in England, 1685–1830', *Eighteenth-Century Studies*, 15 (1982), 291–316.

iconic significance of the event: the sarcophagus in which the coffin was laid was the one which had been designed by an Italian artist for Cardinal Wolsey and at the end of the interment, the members of the College of Arms who were officiating broke the ceremonial staves, an event which in royal funerals was the occasion for the cry 'The King is dead: long live the King'.

The ritual of Nelson's funeral was thus encoded with a crypto-royalist mystique, a symbolic enactment of Burke's claim in *Reflections on the Revolution in France* that the significance of institutions resided in persons. Of particular importance was the way that the ceremony had exploited the concept of the king's two bodies. Nelson had been accustomed to playing the role of the surrogate monarch in his public appearances; aspects of the ritual, such as the breaking of the staves, amplified this by suggesting that while the physical body of the admiral was dead, the patriotic myth was immortal. At the same time the pageant of the funeral was circumscribed in ways which defined the limits between real and metaphoric monarchy. While the Prince of Wales and his brothers attended, George III did not, on the grounds that 'such national marks of gratitude . . . should be exclusively paid to royalty'.[8]

Like any significant public occasion of this period, Nelson's funeral was commodified and marketed by entrepreneurs of all persuasions. Charles Lamb claimed that the vergers of St Paul's were making £100 a day from people eager to see where the hero was to be buried.[9] Commemorative ceramics, special editions of journals, newspapers, and prints depicting every aspect of the proceedings could be bought to mark the occasion, while those who wished to relive it could visit a number of exhibition venues showing 'exact representations' of the event. Nearly a year after the funeral, copies of the coffin, the flags, and the decorations were still to be seen at 'No. 11 Beckett Street, west of Temple Bar'.[10] Public interest, moreover, was not confined to the metropolis. An 'exact copy' of the coffin was exhibited at the Assembly Room in Lincoln, in order to 'gratify' country families.[11]

The theatres also tried to capitalize on this interest in Nelson. After the news of Trafalgar had reached London in early November, both Drury Lane and Covent Garden mounted commemorative afterpieces. On 7

[8] Jordan, 'Admiral Nelson as Popular Hero', 118, and Colley, 'Whose Nation?', 107.

[9] Lamb, *Letters*, ii. 197.

[10] A Collection of Cuttings from Newspapers containing Memoirs of Lord Nelson, British Library.

[11] A Collection of Cuttings from Newspapers Containing Memoirs of Lord Nelson, British Library.

November Covent Garden presented a 'LOYAL MUSICAL IMPROMPTU', entitled *Nelson's Glory*, which concluded with a representation of the naval engagement at Trafalgar.[12] A few days later 'A New Melo Dramatic Piece' appeared at Drury Lane featuring leading actors in the company such as Elliston and Mrs Powell.[13] The piece was the second item in the bill between a comic opera, *The Cabinet*, and a farce, *The Irishman in London*. In representing Nelson's death in this way, the theatres were following the usual practice when it came to important topical events. A precedent for the Nelson entertainments was the response to the death of Captain Cook in Hawaii in 1778. Between 1789 and 1792, for example, an afterpiece entitled *The Death of Captain Cook* had met with considerable success in both London and the provinces. An adaptation of a French original, the piece was described as 'A Grand Serious-Pantomimic Ballet'. It depicts Cook as a hero of Enlightenment rationality, first intervening to save a young Hawaiian woman from the attentions of an unwelcome suitor and then preventing his execution, between interludes of music, dance, and song.[14]

In 1805, however, audiences were much more resistant to the representation of Nelson's death in such a way. The *Monthly Mirror* acknowledged that 'the late victory, clouded as it was with the death of the conqueror' presented some difficulties for dramatic treatment, and it commended the management of Drury Lane for being 'very judicious' in restricting its commemoration to solemn music and dialogue. The words of Richard Cumberland or an air from Handel were felt to be more suitable than the conventions of theatrical representation: 'A few pasteboard ships, a squib or two, let off by carpenters, and some sorry daub, bearing the name of the victorious hero, which are generally resorted to, throw a sort of ridicule upon events that, out of the theatre, we contemplate with mingled gratitude, delight and admiration.'[15] Audiences seem to have agreed with this view. They objected to a ballet at the King's Theatre entitled *The Naval Triumph* on the grounds that the 'circumstances were too recent and too sorrowful for theatrical representation; they must be of far older date before they will bear "sporting with"; for such we must call every endeavour, in ballet, to describe the mournful day'.[16]

By early January, and Nelson's funeral, this kind of response had

---

[12] Playbill, Theatre Museum, London.   [13] Playbill, Theatre Museum, London.
[14] *The Death of Captain Cook, A Grand Serious-Pantomimic Ballet, in Three Parts* (Hull, 1789). For this and other representations of the death of Cook see Bernard Smith, *European Vision and the South Pacific*, 2nd edn. (Sydney, 1985), 118–21, and Greg Dening, *Mr Bligh's Bad Language: Passion, Power and Theatre on the Bounty* (Cambridge, 1992), 272–8.
[15] *Monthly Mirror*, 20 (1805), 339.   [16] Ibid. 407.

become even more intense. Drury Lane decided not to use drama at all in marking the funeral but performed music by Handel instead.[17] At Covent Garden a two-act piece was in preparation for the evening of 10 January but it was prohibited by the Lord Chamberlain, presumably on the grounds of the insensitivity of dramatic representation. Much offended, the playwright Richard Cumberland claimed that 'the objections, which so palpably bore against the exhibition of that affecting scene at the opera house, were in no respect whatever applicable to my composition, and I am to this hour uninformed of the reasons which actuated the Lord Chamberlain for the suppression of it'.[18] The Lord Chamberlain would presumably have been even more alarmed had he witnessed an attempt by the Manchester Theatre to commemorate Nelson's funeral. This particular production took the form of a panorama before which a series of puppet figures re-enacted the procession from the Admiralty to St Paul's Cathedral. The *Thespian Review* reported that the figures

looked as well as could be imagined, considering what they were;—but owing to some imperfection in the mechanism, horse, foot and carriages, lords and commons, sailors, soldiers, and even kings at arms, tumbled down by dozens . . . Decorous solemnity, on the part of the audience, was out of the question, and the funeral procession was the occasion of more laughing than generally takes place at the representation of a highly finished farce.

The *Thespian Review* went on to claim that 'the nature of the shew was improper' and argued that the 'proper tenants' of the stage on such occasions were Shakespeare and Otway who could 'influence the patriotic feelings, and melt the soul to the luxury of sympathy'.[19]

The response to these theatrical representations of Nelson's death and funeral would seem to suggest a change in public attitudes. If the staging of Captain Cook's death as a pantomimic ballet had been relatively successful in 1790, why then were these conventions felt to be inadequate in 1805–6? This question has significant implications because the failure of *Nelson's Glory* and the other entertainments represented a major challenge to the propriety of these forms of commemoration. As I noted in the previous chapter, the conventions of the topical afterpiece were closely linked with the theatricality of contemporary political behaviour, especially patriotic celebration. A devaluing of this mode of theatrical

[17] A Collection of Cuttings from Newspapers Containing Memoirs of Lord Nelson, British Library.

[18] Richard Cumberland, *Memoirs of Richard Cumberland 1806*, ed. Henry Flanders (orig. edn. London, 1856, New York, 1969), 361.

[19] *Thespian Review*, 7 (1806), 55.

representation would seem to have implications not only for the status of theatricality within political culture but also for the configuration of patriotism.

One possible reason for the reaction against the theatre at this time was the fact that Nelson's death and funeral took place at the height of a period of renewed anti-theatricalism associated with the evangelical movement.[20] This would have made the public more sensitive to the propriety of such events being represented in the theatre. The sources of anxiety for the *Monthly Mirror* critic—action and visual simulacra as opposed to words and music—were the traditional targets of anti-theatrical prejudice. The exhibitions of Nelson's coffin escaped criticism, not only because they were deemed as culturally inferior to the theatre but also because they did not attempt a dangerous dramatic mimesis of the funeral. However, this reaction against the theatre's treatment of Nelson can also be linked to specific changes in cultural politics at this period, in particular the status of theatricality within discourses of the French Revolution. As I indicated in the first chapter, political debate in Britain after 1789 was focused around the competing claims of two forms of theatre—Burke's theatre of order and tradition which clothed the state in the 'decent drapery' of respect, veneration, and awe, and Paine's 'open theatre of the world' in which the mechanisms of power were completely open to the scrutiny of the people. The response to the dramatic treatments of Nelson's funeral interestingly suggests the influence of a Paineite discourse of theatricality, manifested by a desire to efface the complications of theatre, the framing devices, the curtains, and disguises, that might obscure the integrity of the event. Thus, in the view of the *Monthly Mirror*, the problem of *Nelson's Glory* was that it could 'throw a sort of ridicule upon events that, out of the theatre, we contemplate with mingled gratitude, delight and admiration'. This was the same kind of argument that had been used by the organizers of the Revolutionary festivals in France. There, too, there was a sense that the theatre was an unreliable medium for political expression with the capacity to throw 'a sort of ridicule' upon the Revolution.[21] It would seem that, in widely differing contexts, the politically dominant cultures of both Britain and France were in the process of rejecting the

---

[20] e.g., Ingram Cobbin, *Stage Playing Immoral Vain and Dangerous in its Tendency* (London, 1802); Rowland Hill, *A Warning to Professors: Containing Aphoristic Observations on the Nature and Tendency of Public Amusements*, 2nd edn. (London, 1805); John Styles, *An Essay on the Character, Immoral and Antichristian Tendency of the Stage* (Newport, Isle of Wight, 1806).

[21] See Mona Ozouf, *Festivals and the French Revolution*, trans. Alan Sheridan (Cambridge, Mass., 1988), 207.

traditional role of the institutionalized theatre as a political signifier, in favour of the more numinous 'open theatre of the world'.

Evidence of this 'open theatre of the world' is apparent in Charles Lamb's account of Nelson's funeral. This is how he wrote to William Hazlitt on 7 January, two days before the funeral took place:

You know Lord Nelson is dead. He is also to be buried. And the whole town is in a fever. Seats erecting, seats to be let, sold, lent &c . . . the whole town as unsettled as a young lady the day before being married. St Paul's virgers making their hundred pounds a day in sixpences for letting people see the scaffolding inside, & the hole where he is to be let down; which money they under the Rose share with the Dean and Praecentors at night.—Great Aquatic bustle tomorrow. Body to come up from Greenwich with Lord Mayor & City Barges. Fillets of Veal predestined to be demolished at The Temple in the afternoon. All Cheswick, Pimlico & Pancras emptying out in the morning into the Temple . . . If you with your refinements were here you could neither eat, sit, read nor paint, till the corpse were fairly laid.[22]

Lamb had resisted the cult of Nelson, describing his attendance at a performance of *Pizarro* in 1799 as little more than a 'Clap trap', but he was fascinated, as always, by the vibrancy of London.[23] He represents the funeral in terms of a release of urban energies: the clerics of St Paul's distributing the proceeds of the day under the rose-window of the Cathedral, the veal 'predestined to be demolished', the 'emptying out' of the denizens of Chiswick, Pimlico, and St Pancras. The solemnity of the water procession is comically undermined in the phrase 'Great Aquatic bustle' which equates the event with the activities of that other aquatic theatre in the metropolis—Sadler's Wells. Lamb also caricatures the sentimental response to the funeral in the form of the 'eldest Miss Squeeze', a fictional spokeswoman for the spectators who cannot predict how she will react to the procession 'for she is afraid it will be too affecting. She is sure she shall turn her head away from the window as it goes by. O the immortal Man!'[24] Lamb's account of Nelson's funeral neglects the sublime theatre within St Paul's to focus on the urban comedy going on around it. This is a theatre of the margins—literally so in terms of the geographical relationship between Chiswick, Pimlico, and St Pancras and the urban space which the funeral procession symbolically defined. Although this text is in no way explicitly politicized, it suggests the existence within contemporary discourse of an alternative, and also feminized, theatricality, an Elian version of Paine's 'open theatre of the world'.

[22] Lamb, *Letters*, ii. 197–8.   [23] Ibid. i. 254.   [24] Ibid. ii. 198.

Evidence of this unofficial theatre can also be found within the boundaries of the ceremony itself. One of the aristocratic spectators at the funeral, Lady Bessborough, expressed her surprise at the spontaneous expression of the crowd:

The moment the car appeared which bore the body, you might have heard a pin fall, and *without any order to do so, they all took off their hats.* I cannot tell you the effect this simple action produc'd; it seem'd one general impulse of respect beyond anything that could have been said or contriv'd.[25]

This is an indication of the way in which the focus of the political theatre had altered, the gallery, in Burke's terms, having taken the place of the house. The crypto-royalism of the funeral ritual had been a deliberate attempt on the part of the organizers to revive the pomp and circumstance of monarchical spectacle with all this implied in political terms. To an extent this was unsuccessful, primarily because the élite was aware that nationalism was a two-edged sword which could be used to undermine its right to rule and was thus unprepared to make a king out of Nelson. But it was also unsuccessful because the audience had been unwilling to play a passive, subordinate role in the spectacle and had imposed one of its own instead. The most notable example of this occurred when Nelson's flag was about to be lowered into the grave. In a premeditated act, of which the organizers of the funeral had been unaware, 'the sailors who assisted at the ceremony with one accord rent [the flag] in pieces, that each might preserve a fragment while he lived'.[26] The decorum of the funeral ritual was violated as these sailors imposed their own rite, one which expressed the significance of Nelson as a popular hero rather than as a pseudo-monarch. The future dean of St Paul's (and dramatist) Henry Milman, witnessed the event as a young boy: 'I heard, or fancied that I heard, the low wail of the sailors who bore and encircled the remains of their admiral.'[27] Like Lady Bessborough's amazement, Milman's uncertainty as to what he heard symbolizes the sense of marginalization felt by those who had been accustomed to dominating 'the show'. It is possibly the most intriguing aspect of an affair which, rather than denoting a kind of hegemonic theatricality, the all embracing spectacle of state, instead suggests its susceptibility to the challenge of alternative rites and performances.

[25] Bessborough to Lord Granville, 9 Jan. 1806, *Lord Granville Leveson Gower (First Earl Granville): Private Correspondence, 1781–1821*, ed. Castalia, Countess Granville (2 vols.; London, 1916), i. 154 (quoted in Gerald Jordan, 'Admiral Nelson as Popular Hero', 118, my emphasis).

[26] Southey, *Nelson*, 260.

[27] Henry Hart Milman, *Annals of S. Paul's Cathedral*, 2nd edn. (London, 1869), 485.

The Regent's Holiday

The funeral of Nelson suggests that the authorities were fully aware of the propaganda value of a public spectacle that would reinforce the identification of the monarchy with patriotic values. However, both the royal family and Pitt's government were careful not to endorse a form of spectacle that might invoke the Revolutionary nationalism of the festivals in France. As Linda Colley has indicated, in late 1797 there had been a debate about this in the pages of the *Anti-Jacobin*, prompted by the Naval Thanksgiving in November of the same year.[28] Ostensibly to commemorate the victory at the Battle of Camperdown on 11 October, the thanksgiving at St Paul's Cathedral was generally regarded as a sign of the authorities' relief at the suppression of the mutinies at the Nore and Spithead. Significantly, the organizers had broken with precedent by including 250 ordinary seamen and marines in the procession from the Admiralty to the Cathedral. This smacked too much of Revolutionary egalitarianism, even for an opposition paper such as the *Morning Chronicle* which described the thanksgiving as a 'Frenchified farce'.[29] As the war wore on, the royal family and Pitt's government put considerable financial resources into the kind of event which would not draw this criticism; if the Revolutionary festivals stressed the importance of 'reason' or 'the People' they would reply with spectacles that represented British nationhood in terms of George III's special relationship with his people. Thus there were no explicit 'festivals of Britain' during this period but a series of events celebrating royal birthdays and anniversaries such as the King's Jubilee in 1809.[30]

However, the defeat of Napoleon in 1814 could not afford to go unnoticed. It signalled the triumph of those forces which had mobilized against the French Revolution. Across Europe monarchs were reassuming their thrones in the name of legitimacy, a fact which caused William Hazlitt, for one, to walk the illuminated London streets in a state of profound gloom.[31] The successful conclusions of war had been celebrated before in British history: in 1749, Horace Walpole had witnessed a firework display in the royal parks of London to commemorate the Peace of Aix-la-Chapelle, followed by one of the most lavish masquerades of the eighteenth century.[32] The Prince Regent turned to this precedent in 1814

[28] Colley, 'Apotheosis', 109–10.   [29] 19 Dec. 1797, quoted ibid. 110.

[30] See Colley, 'Apotheosis'.

[31] Stanley Jones, *Hazlitt: A Life; from Winterslow to Frith Street* (Oxford, 1989), 139.

[32] Horace Walpole, *Correspondence*, ed. W. S. Lewis (48 vols.; New Haven, Conn., 1937–83), xx. 46–50.

by again using the royal parks as a venue for public celebration. However, he sought to play down any suggestion of national triumphalism by choosing 1 August as the date for the festival, conveniently coinciding with 100 years of Hanoverian rule in Britain, as well as the anniversary of the Battle of the Nile in 1798. Such was the royal family's desire to be seen to be above party politics that soldiers and MPs were excluded from the Royal Booth at the celebrations. The *Gentleman's Magazine* saw fit to observe that 'some disappointment' was felt at this measure.[33]

The 'Jubilee Fête', as it was described in the London newspapers, was the culmination of a series of events commemorating the peace. On 20 June the Officers of the City of Westminster had travelled in procession from St James's Palace to read the King's Proclamation of Peace to the Lord Mayor, Aldermen, and Sheriffs of the City of London. This ritual derived from a period when the monarch and the City had not been united in their interests. By 1814 its function was largely symbolic. It represents an aspect of the theatricality of urban life which was declining in importance at this period, according to the urban historian Peter Borsay, who has suggested that the 'socially cohesive' role of this kind of civic ritual was being replaced by that of patriotic celebration.[34] Borsay has also noticed an increasing stratification in urban ritual and ceremony; in particular, the withdrawal of the élite into their own socially exclusive forms of entertainment. This exclusivity is apparent in the second phase of the commemorations: the lavish private fête which the Prince Regent staged on 21 July at Carlton House in honour of the Duke of Wellington and the visiting dignitaries from Europe. The Prince's favourite architect, John Nash, was called in to augment the resources at Carlton House with a specially constructed polygonal hall, decorated with allegorical transparencies and rare plants from Kew Gardens.[35] The Jubilee at the royal parks on 1 August represented the extension of the Prince's bounty to the people as a whole, a paternalistic reward for their services during the war, though as criticisms in the radical journals and prints made clear, they would pay for it with their taxes later.

The date of the Jubilee coincided with the traditional holiday period in London. Bartholomew Fair was about to commence, Edmund Kean had been startling audiences at Drury Lane with his performance as Richard

---

[33] *Gentleman's Magazine*, 84 (1814), 182.

[34] Peter Borsay, '"All the town's a stage": Urban Ritual and Ceremony 1660–1800' in *The Transformation of English Provincial Towns 1600–1800*, ed. Peter Clark (London, 1984), 228–58. See also his *The English Urban Renaissance: Culture and Society in the Provincial Town, 1660–1770* (Oxford, 1989).

[35] John Summerson, *The Life and Work of John Nash Architect* (London, 1980), 98.

III, and Sadler's Wells was staging entertainments such as *The Wild Man* with Joseph Grimaldi.[36] The form which the Jubilee took—fireworks, illuminations, trickwork, and mock sea battles—represented an extension of this summer theatre, a sort of Sadler's Wells writ large. It took place across three locations—Hyde Park, Green Park, and St James's Park. In 1749 Horace Walpole had noted no obvious social demarcation at the fireworks display to celebrate the Peace of Aix-la-Chapelle, except for specially built galleries for members of the Houses of Parliament and 'chief citizens'. In 1814, however, the crowd was excluded from St James's Park by means of a ticketing system. Joseph Farington, who purchased his ticket far in advance of the event, found the company in St James's Park 'numerous, but not the least crouded' which is not surprising as admission cost 10s. 6d., higher than the price of the most expensive box at the patent theatres.[37] While the Jubilee was ostensibly open to all, such measures ensured that social privilege and status were not compromised.

The proceedings began with a mock naval engagement by two minia-ture fleets on the Serpentine in Hyde Park, while at the same time a hot air balloon was let off from Green Park carrying a Mr Sadler. At ten o'clock the fireworks display began, the centrepiece of which was the 'Grand Metamorphosis' of the Castle of Discord, representing the war, into the Temple of Concord. This edifice, which was similar to devices in stage pantomime and had been built by the scene designers of Drury Lane, moved on an axis and was decorated with allegorical paintings. The topical significance of the latter is clear from this description in the *Gentleman's Magazine*: '. . . the Genius of France is [seen] restoring the sceptre to the dynasty of the Bourbons, personified by a female seated on a throne, in a regal mantle, ornamented with the fleur-de-lis, and on the other, Russia, Prussia, Austria, and Sweden, are witnessing the event with delight.'[38] In St James's Park the evening concluded with another fireworks display at a Chinese pagoda designed by Nash.

Joseph Farington remarked that the Jubilee 'by no means justified the sour, cavilling remarks profusely made in the opposition papers', but whether it amounted to much of a success is doubtful.[39] Even a govern-ment newspaper such as *The Times* was unenthusiastic about it. The event assumed the dimensions of tragedy when the Chinese pagoda in St James's Park caught fire, causing crowds to abandon events in the other

---

[36] *The Times*, 4 July 1814.
[37] Joseph Farington, *Diary*, ed. Kenneth Garlick, Angus Macintyre, and Kathryn Cave (16 vols.; New Haven, Conn., 1984), xiii. 4569.
[38] *Gentleman's Magazine*, 84 (1814), 182.   [39] Farington, *Diary*, xiii. 4569.

parks in order to see it. Two men died as a result of their injuries. There were other, less serious technical problems which diminished the success of the event. Sadler and his balloon came down ignominiously in Mucking Marshes in Essex while *The Times* felt that some of the devices compared unfavourably with their equivalents in the theatre. The metamorphosis of the Castle of Discord into the Temple of Concord 'took place with some-what less than the celerity generally witnessed in our theatrical panto-mimes; it resembled the cautious removal of a screen rather than the sudden leap into a new shape'.[40] *The Times* was also disturbed by the presence at the festival of 'all the deliciae' of Bartholomew Fair which had been given permission by the authorities to move from its usual location in Smithfield to the proximity of the royal parks. After the Jubilee was over, the fair remained

with its usual accompaniments of swings, roundabouts, wild-beast shows, fat women, and dramatic entertainments, to which were added the attractions of *E. O. tables—Black and White Cocks—Dice Tables*—and a game with dice, called *Under and over Seven*. This gambling the police did not even make a show of stopping. There were donkey racing, jumping in sacks, running for smocks, &c.—and there were printing presses, where, on payment, people had the privilege of themselves pulling off a typographical souvenir of the fair. Nay, it was even contemplated to print a *Jubilee Fair Journal*.[41]

The Times deplored the effect all this might have on the susceptible lower orders 'who can be secure against temptation only by its being remote . . . Idleness thus held out and sanctioned to the servant and the mechanic, produces not merely a waste of his time, but a diminution of his means of life,—not merely an expensive indulgence, but a disgust to future industry.'[42] Responding to such objections, the Home Secretary, Lord Sidmouth, ordered the fair to be closed on 6 August, but he was defied, and wild beasts and fat ladies did not eventually leave the royal parks until 11 August. The presence of Bartholomew Fair at the Jubilee should not be regarded as a deliberate attempt to subvert its meaning in the form of a carnivalesque 'anti-Jubilee'. The fair was in fact a logical extension of the showmanship of the official festival with its extravaganzas of sight and sound. Any subversive impact which it had lay in the way that it ignored the paternalistic ethos of the Jubilee to make its own distinctive entertainment, carrying on beyond the temporal and geographical limits

---

[40] *The Times*, 2 Aug. 1814.
[41] John Ashton, *Social England under the Regency* (London, 1899), 206–7.
[42] *The Times*, 1 Aug. 1814.

which the Prince Regent had imposed. It also had an implicit cultural significance in the way that it realized one of the nightmares of the Augustans—the fear of a dangerous misalliance between 'low' culture and the monarchy. The locus of Pope's anxiety in *The Dunciad*—Smithfield—had moved lock, stock, and barrel to the territory of the royal parks and, as sponsor of the festival, the Prince Regent was responsible for this in the view of newspapers such as *The Times*. A contemporary print depicts him as a fairground manager picking the pocket of John Bull while the latter ogles 'The Regency Puppet Show': the tastes of royalty are shown to be thoroughly immersed in those of Smithfield.[43] 'Peter Pindar' also satirized the fête as an unwarranted extravagance on the part of the Prince Regent pandering to the lowest instincts of the populace. Royalty and the mob, according to Pindar, were united in their taste for 'low' theatre:

> Why ought the *vulgar* low to sate,
> On what's denied the *vulgar great*?
> Why not great men, just like the many,
> Have privilege to play the zany?[44]

The Jubilee Fête also had a military significance. Hyde Park was the traditional site of military reviews such as that which took place in October 1803 at the height of the invasion scare when an estimated two hundred thousand people had watched George III inspect his troops.[45] The military role of the royal parks also included their use during periods of domestic political crisis as places of assembly for the army. In 1780 troops had been stationed in Hyde Park and St James's Park as part of the effort to quell the Gordon rioters.[46] The military character of the Jubilee was noted by a number of commentators. In Peter Pindar's 'The R—l Showman, or the R—t's Gala', the Prince Regent, exasperated by the incursions of Bartholomew Fair, declares:

> I'll have no more sea-fights and sieges,
> No more pagodas, booths, and bridges;
> Nor turn my Park into a camp;
> No, suttlers, players, all shall tramp.[47]

A poem published in the radical newspaper *The Statesman*, entitled 'The Soliloquy of a Sailor', also refers to the event in terms of 'a camp',

[43] George, *Satires*, ix. 430.
[44] Peter Pindar, *The R—t's Fair, or Grand Galante-Show!!* (London, 1814), 11.
[45] *Gentleman's Magazine*, 73 (1803), 977.
[46] J. Paul De Castro, *The Gordon Riots* (London, 1926), 118, 177, 198.
[47] Peter Pindar, *The R—l Showman or the R—t's Gala* (London, 1814), 27.

a grotesque travesty of the war which mocks the sailor's injuries and sacrifice:

> Blind as I am, methinks a camp I view—
> Many the Tents, but faith, the Contents few . . .
> For this, *I* lost an eye, an arm, a leg,
> For this poor NAN, too, is compelled to beg.
> Illumination!—O the shame and scandal,
> *God's light they grudge, and tax my farthing candle.*[48]

In a letter to William Wordsworth, Charles Lamb complained that the Prince's festival of peace had laid waste the natural beauty of the parks: 'the very colour of green is vanishd, the whole surface of Hyde Park is dry crumbling sand . . . not a vestige or hint of grass ever having grown there, booths & drinking places go all round it for a mile & half I am confident . . . the stench of liquors, bad tobacco, dirty people & provisions, conquers the air.'[49] The transformation that the Jubilee had effected was such that for Lamb 'the unusual scene in H. Park, by Candle-light in open air, good tobacco, bottled stout, made it look like an interval in a campaign, a repose after battle, I almost fancied scars smart-ing & was ready to club a story with my comrades of some of my lying deeds'.[50] Like the camps of 1778, the Jubilee Fête represented a cultural and political space—'Mars's Holiday'—mediating between the con-ditions of war and peace. The Prince Regent's festival was thus the apotheosis of the practice and ideology of a war of élites, an appropriate celebration of the restoration of monarchs to thrones across Europe. It was a merging of the theatres of war in late Georgian society, a coming together of the practices of the institutionalized stage—the naumachia, the mechanical spectacle, the transparency, fireworks—with the festive culture of the camps, in which the sutler was naturally allied with the player.

However, the response to the Jubilee suggests a challenge to this cul-ture of war from two directions—the plebeian counter-theatre of Bartholomew Fair, and the concerns among some elements of the upper and middling orders that the theatricality of the military was no longer sufficient to resist Britain's enemies. The latter increasingly wanted war to signify more than pasteboard ships or paper fortresses. A comment in *The Times* associated the Jubilee with previous misgivings over the represen-tation of Nelson in the theatre. It questioned whether the miniature fleet on the Serpentine could not

---

[48] *Statesman*, 26 July 1814. [49] Lamb, *Letters*, iii. 96. [50] Ibid. 97.

be sunk or blown up without mimicking the manœuvres of the immortal Nelson in the greatest of his victories? We recollect to have seen him introduced dancing in a ballet, at the Opera House, shortly after his last triumph. The absurdity was too offensive, and the piece was driven off the stage . . . But this is for the 'happiness' of the people. Possibly so; but if things like this are to make Englishmen happy, the world has strangely misconceived their character.[51]

The 1814 Jubilee was the apotheosis of theatricalized patriotism in that the expression of an 'official' national identity was increasingly channelled into forms, such as civic sculpture, which could be trusted not to throw 'a sort of ridicule' upon the people and events they were commemorating.[52] This change was only incipient, but is none the less discernible, the result of the complex pressures of war and revolution that exposed the inherent instability of theatricality as a medium for political expression. Its major problem was that it permitted the unpredictable—the transformation of the decorum of a hero's funeral into farce, the rending of the flag at Nelson's burial in a way that appropriated his memory for the people, the incursion of Bartholomew Fair on the territory of the Jubilee. The magnitude of the task facing Britain was such that dancing admirals and pantomimic public festivals were felt to be inadequate forms of representation, by radicals and loyalists alike. The Revolutionary and Napoleonic Wars thus ultimately led to a profound shift in British culture whereby a certain kind of political behaviour, identified with the institutionalized theatre, was increasingly regarded with suspicion by polite opinion. Such a change inevitably influenced the perception of war itself, which was wrested, in both a cultural and a political sense, from the control of those gentlemen amateurs who treated it as another forum of pleasure, as 'Mars's Holiday'. These gentlemen did not relinquish their authority without a struggle: significantly, one of the forums in which they defended their hegemony was the theatre itself. Having analysed in Chapter 3 how the field of battle was approximated by the field of the stage, I now wish to explore how the space of the auditorium also constituted a kind of battlefield, as the officer class sought to assert its presence in the political theatre of Britain.

---

[51] *The Times*, 26 July 1814.

[52] For the development of civic sculpture at this period see Alison Yarrington, *The Commemoration of the Hero 1800–1864: Monuments to the British Victors of the Napoleonic Wars* (New York, 1988).

5

Riotous Assemblies:
the Army and Navy in the Theatre

AFTER the fire which destroyed Covent Garden Theatre in September 1808, the manager-proprietor, John Philip Kemble, quickly made plans to rebuild it. Part of these plans involved the staging of an elaborate public ceremonial, the laying of the corner-stone of the new building. On 30 December 1808 Life Guards were assembled around the site of the new theatre while detachments of infantry were deployed to control curious spectators. Deputations of masons gathered at the Freemason's Tavern in Queen Street and marched in procession to Covent Garden where they were met by the Prince of Wales, who was to lay the stone: 'The Grenadier companies of the Foot Guards, were stationed at the grand entrance door, flags were hoisted at the four corners of the building, and about forty Life Guards, who were Masons, lined the space along which the procession was to pass.'[1] The specially constructed platform on which the ceremony took place was reserved for the bands of the Coldstream and Life Guards. While they played 'martial music', Sarah Siddons and other members of the company looked on as the Prince laid the corner-stone, a twenty-one gun salute booming out the new theatrical era.

What is remarkable about this event is its symbolic enactment of the significance of the theatre as a masonic-military domain. The actors of Covent Garden were supernumeraries in a spectacle dominated by two closely associated masculine élites—Freemasonry and the officer class. Synthesizing parade ground ceremony with the theatre's own penchant for military spectacle, the elements of the occasion—the procession, the regulation of the crowd, the lines of the Life Guards, the firing of the salute—enacted a marshalling of the physical and cultural space that was to be occupied by the theatre. It had been ritually marked as the military's own. This event was also significant in that it was the prelude to another kind of 'war', the sixty-seven nights of the Old Price disturbances in which elements of the audience—some of whom were likely to have been spectators of the stone-laying ceremony—struggled with Kemble for con-

---

[1] *Monthly Mirror*, NS 5 (1809), 123.

trol of Covent Garden.[2] The Old Price riots, moreover, took place at a time when the fortunes of the Napoleonic Wars were going against Britain. The Walcheren expedition had been a failure, causing 16,000 casualties, while the Mary Anne Clarke affair, which had highlighted corruption in the military, was reaching a crisis point.

This was not the first occasion on which one of Britain's wars had been paralleled by a celebrated war in the theatre. David Garrick's use of French dancers during the tensions leading up to the Seven Years War had caused a sustained period of rioting at Drury Lane, Noverre and his troop becoming the target for anti-Gallic chauvinism. In 1809 the *Monthly Mirror* expressed disbelief that the metropolis could be 'agitated by a kind of miserable civil war . . . while fire and sword are at the gate', but the rioters carried on regardless, contesting the territory of the theatre as if it were as important as any field of battle.[3] In the same way as the theatre's representation of war—the scenic oceans, the pasteboard ships, the mechanical sentinels—mimicked the scale of battle, so did the behaviour of audiences. In this chapter I want to examine the reflexivity of wars both within and without the theatre.

The Army and Navy as Audiences

The prominent part played by the military in the stone-laying ceremony at Covent Garden was a sign of how deeply implicated the armed forces were in the representational practices, the ideology, and the commercial survival of the Georgian theatre. Managers such as Kemble were aware that soldiers and sailors of all ranks formed a substantial element of theatre audiences, in many cases determining their character. Officers bespoke plays and sometimes even took to the stage themselves, paying handsomely for the services of theatre professionals. Lower-ranking soldiers and sailors dominated the will of the gallery, while playgoing was an integral part of the sociability that sustained the Volunteer Movement. An evening at the theatre was often the culmination of a day's mustering and parading for the Volunteers, an occasion on which these amateur soldiers could celebrate their place in the community.

---

[2] For the O.P. riots see Baer, *Theatre and Disorder*; Gillian Russell, 'Playing at Revolution: the Politics of the O.P. Riots of 1809', *Theatre Notebook*, 44 (1990), 16–26, and Elaine Hadley, 'The Old Price Wars: Melodramatizing the Public Sphere in Early-Nineteenth-Century England', *PMLA*, 107 (1992), 524–37.

[3] *Monthly Mirror*, NS 6 (1809), 386.

The significance of the theatre as a source of ideological enrichment for the military and as a venue for recreation and display was a long-established one. During the Revolutionary and Napoleonic Wars, however, the association between the theatre and the military was accentuated as a result of a relaxation of the Licensing Act in 1788, which allowed the construction of permanent theatres in the provinces. New playhouses took their place beside the expanding naval dockyards and barracks in the south and east of England as a response to the leisure economy of war. Sarah Baker, for example, who was one of the most resourceful entrepreneurs of the period, mounted a campaign of theatre building across Kent after 1788. In 1790 she opened theatres in Canterbury and Faversham, followed by establishments at Rochester (1791), near the naval dockyard at Chatham, and at Maidstone (1798), not far from Coxheath. According to her will, made in 1815, she was the proprietor of two small theatres on the coast at Folkestone and at Ore near Hastings.[4] While theatres in manufacturing towns suffered as a result of the war, those associated with military or naval establishments were flourishing. Exeter, for example, 'stirred to the colour and ceremony of military occasions . . . The officers of smart cavalry regiments entertained Exeter society, supported benefit nights at the theatre and applauded fashionable stars of the London stage.'[5] The demand for entertainment from the sailors and dockyard workers of Plymouth was such that it was able to maintain two theatres during the French wars. One, located in the town, was patronized by civilians and neighbouring county gentry while the other, situated in the dock area of East Stonehouse, was designed for the use of the navy, dockyard workers, and their female companions. James Winston claimed that the latter was remarkable for its 'nightly scene of riot and debauchery, notwithstanding the constant presence of the Magistrates'.[6] The reliance of towns such as Plymouth on the military establishment was such that when peace finally came in 1815, their economies, and their theatres, suffered temporary eclipse. For playhouses in the smaller coastal towns, the end of the war signalled catastrophe. Places such as Southend and Sheerness, where the father of the Victorian dramatist Douglas Jerrold maintained two theatres in the latter stages of the Napoleonic Wars, became virtual ghost towns. Faced with the loss of an audience of officers

⁴ Norma Hodgson, 'Sarah Baker (1736/7–1816) "Governess-General of the Kentish Drama"' in *Studies in English Theatre History in Memory of Gabrielle Enthoven* (London, 1952), 65–83.
⁵ Robert Newton, *Eighteenth Century Exeter* (Exeter, 1984), 104.
⁶ James Winston, *The Theatric Tourist* (London, 1805), 69.

and men who had provided a lucrative income in the war years, Samuel Jerrold quickly went bankrupt. His grandson Blanchard, writing in 1859, noted a fundamental change in the culture of Sheerness: 'the sailors repair to sad beershops, while the serious attend those sleepy, soulless lectures, of which the soiled syllabus may be seen in the bakers' windows. There is no theatre in Sheerness; and more, I could not find a single inhabitant who wished to see a theatre there.'[7]

It was different in the unreformed days of the French wars. Apart from the alehouse, the theatre offered the most accessible and affordable form of entertainment for the soldier and sailor—a place where he could enjoy conviviality with his mates or make contact with prostitutes. It functioned as a place of celebration after victory, a venue for strut and swagger, or alternatively, a site where the tensions and frustrations of military life could be vented in the form of minor skirmishes with other members of the audience, or even the ritual of a full-scale theatre disturbance. For sailors in particular, the theatres of the coastal towns were important as places of mediation between shipboard life and that of the civilian hinterland. Small provincial theatres such as Jerrold's at Sheerness were enclosed, hierarchical institutions, very like the naval vessel with its strictly enforced divisions of quarter, middle, and lower deck. Commentators often noted how sailors in the theatre behaved as if they had never left ship, descending from the gallery to the pit below as if they were on rigging and using naval terminology to describe the theatrical space: 'the pit they called the hold; the gallery, up aloft, or the maintop landing; the boxes, the cabin; and the stage, the quarterdeck.'[8] Playgoing was especially important for those soldiers and sailors who had returned to Britain after a long period of service overseas. A foray into the theatre at Plymouth Dock or Portsmouth was a ritual of reintegration, a reminder to civilian society of the individual sailor's place within it.

The playhouses of London and the provinces thus offered the army and the navy more than mere recreation (though recreation is always a serious business). They were places of self-definition, especially for the sailor. One of the most important stereotypes of the late eighteenth and early nineteenth centuries was that of the 'Jolly Jack Tar', whose qualities usually consisted of a fondness for grog, women, and salty lingo, honest goodheartedness, a tinderbox temperament, and above all, loyalty to his ship, his country, and his king. The emergence of the stereotype can be

---

[7] Blanchard Jerrold, *The Life and Remains of Douglas Jerrold* (Boston, Mass., 1859), 10.

[8] John Bernard, *Retrospections of the Stage* (2 vols.; London, 1830), ii. 129.

regarded as a response to the sub-cultural status of the navy within Georgian society that I discussed in Chapter 1. The strangeness of the sailor—a deracination represented by a different way of speaking, a distinctive costume, and in many cases, a loyalty to a ship and mates that superseded previous ties to family and community—contained a potential threat to civilian society that was most powerfully realized in the naval mutinies of 1797. The events at the Nore and Spithead demonstrated that some sailors were not unthinkingly loyal, a point that was driven home by the experiences of civilians in towns such as Plymouth and Sheerness, where sailors were often identified with disorderly criminality. As in the case of many stereotypes, such as the stage Irishman of the period, the 'Jolly Jack Tar' image functioned as both a social control, an image of how the sailor should be, and as a way for civilian society to relieve its fears of the navy's alterity.[9]

The 'Jolly Jack Tar' was largely a creation of the theatre. His antecedents are to be found in the character of Ben in Congreve's *Love for Love* and Garrick's imitation of a drunken sailor in the prologue to David Mallet's masque *Britannia*, produced during the Seven Years War with France. Garrick's sailor was a figure of disruptive excess, manifested in his drunkenness and by the fact of his being located in the prologue, a form that traditionally exploited the boundaries between stage fiction and the theatricality of the audience. At one point Garrick nearly left the stage altogether, a stage direction within the prologue suggesting the actor's physical movements: 'he staggers forward, then stops.'[10] This action symbolizes the construction of the sailor within the prologue as a whole. The potentially disruptive energies of the navy are realized on stage, if only to be reined in, controlled. Garrick's tar is a figure of comic ridicule who confuses the distinctions between 'high' and 'low'—he misinterprets the title of the mainpiece tragedy of the evening, Aaron Hill's *Zara*, as Sarah, declaring *'I'm glad 'tis Sarah—Then our Sall may see | Her namesake's Tragedy'*—but at the end he stands as a figure of authority, capable of indicting civilian society for not being sufficiently loyal or united:

[9] For discussions of the sailor in fiction and drama see Jim Davis, 'British Bravery, or Tars Triumphant: Images of the British Navy in Nautical Melodrama', *New Theatre Quarterly*, 4 (1988), 122–43; Michael R. Booth, *English Melodrama* (London, 1965), 93–117; C. N. Parkinson, *Portsmouth Point: The British Navy in Fiction 1793–1815* (Cambridge, Mass., 1949); C. N. Robinson, *The British Tar in Fact and Fiction* (London, 1909). See also J. S. Bratton, 'British Heroism and the Structure of Melodrama' in *Acts of Supremacy: The British Empire and the Stage, 1790–1830*, ed. J. S. Bratton, Richard Allen Cave, Breandan Gregory, Heidi J. Holder, and Michael Pickering (Manchester, 1991), 18–61.

[10] David Mallet, *The Plays of David Mallet*, ed. Felicity A. Nussbaum (New York, 1980), 185.

I wish you landsmen tho, would leave your tricks,
Your factions, parties, and damn'd politics:
And like us, honest tars, drink, fight, and sing!
True to yourselves, your Country, and your King![11]

The conclusion of the prologue highlights the potential value of the sailor as a symbol of a patriotic ideal existing outside factionalism and politics. However, it is important to stress that this idealization of the honesty and loyalty of the tar is bound up with an awareness of his disruptive potential, constantly threatening to topple over, to violate boundaries and distinctions. In this respect, the metatheatricality of the prologue and Garrick's highly self-conscious playing were of crucial importance. At the same time as the sailor was being represented as an image of patriotic integrity he was also caricatured as a role, a part to be performed. This was 'Mr. GARRICK, in the character of a sailor', in the terms of the prologue, and this 'character' was being defined as predominantly histrionic.[12] Theatricality, it must be emphasized, not only allowed for the transgression or transformation of rules, hierarchies, or identities, it also functioned as a kind of discipline or restraint. To act successfully involved staying within the boundaries of a role and not going beyond them: the actor could threaten to fall on top of the audience in the pit but he must pull back at the end. In representing the 'Jolly Jack Tar' in this way, Garrick was communicating a powerful message about the proper role of the sailor in Georgian society as someone to be respected but who also needed to exercise self-restraint, constantly monitoring his own public role.

The part played by the theatre in the political and cultural identity of the sailor was particularly important after 1793, as both loyalist and radical patriotisms struggled over the meanings of the armed forces. The expansion of theatrical entertainment after 1788 also enhanced the significance of the playhouse as a school or mirror in which the navy could define itself. One of the most effective ways in which this was achieved was through the nautical song. An integral part of the whole show of an evening's entertainment, the song was an important link between the theatre, the culture of the street, and ultimately, that of the ship. As many nautical memoirs confirm, singing was one of the ways in which life on board a man-of-war could be made tolerable, enlivening the sailor's recreational moments as well as assisting him in his daily tasks. Theatre songs, reproduced in broadside or chap-book form and sung outside the

---

[11] Mallet, *Plays*, 186–7.   [12] Ibid. 185.

theatre were capable of reaching a wider audience than the usual range of playgoers, including the illiterate. Many of the most popular patriotic anthems of the period, such as 'Rule Britannia', 'Britons Strike Home', and 'Hearts of Oak', had their origins in the theatre, highlighting the fact that eighteenth-century patriotism was at base a performance, an assumption of a role (that implicitly could be counteracted).

The propaganda value of the theatre song was recognized by loyalists. One provincial manager, Henry Lee, claimed that 'humble' though his station was in the theatrical hierarchy he had 'several times received (free of any expence) packets and parcels, containing popular songs, &c. with polite requests from persons of consequence, that such songs might be sung at my different Theatres'.[13] The most notable exponent of the patriotic nautical song, Charles Dibdin the Elder, received a government annuity of £200 as recognition of his achievements. After his death in 1814 he was commemorated by a statue at the Royal Naval Hospital at Greenwich, paid for by a subscription dinner at which the Duke of Clarence was the principal guest.[14] A collection of nautical ballads, published in 1798, suggests the image of the sailor which the sponsors of Dibdin and Lee wished to convey. The preface to the collection describes the sailor's thoughts as not reaching 'much above the topmasthead . . . He has seen in his days more than enough to have made any thinking creature wise and honest; but this brave fellow views all things as sheep do the stars, or a dray-horse what passes in Cheapside, without any afterthought, or reflection.'[15] The representation of the navy in such a way was a sign of an anxiety, especially powerful around 1797–8, that the 'brave tars' were not as bovinely passive as the authorities would have liked. Dibdin's version of the tar was on the whole a more subtle one, while at the same time reinforcing the basic features of the type. Henry Lee was convinced that his nautical ballads had done much to define the characteristics of the sailor whom, he claimed, had been 'taught to think and to be (what he often is) "All as one as a piece of his ship!"—"A Lion in battle, and afterwards a lamb!" and "when on board"—he "braves all! dreads nought!" for he knows that "There is a little cherub that sits up aloft to keep watch for the life of poor Jack!" '.[16] Dibdin's tar was simple, loyal,

[13] Henry Lee, *Memoirs of a Manager; or, Life's Stage with New Scenery* (2 vols.; Taunton, 1830), ii. 12.

[14] *Songs, Naval and National of the Late Charles Dibdin* (London, 1841), xii, xiv–xv; Robert Fahrner, *The Theatre Career of Charles Dibdin the Elder (1745–1814)* (New York, 1989), 155.

[15] *The Naval Songster, or Jack Tar's Chest of Conviviality, for 1798* (London, 1798), 6.

[16] Lee, *Memoirs*, 12.

and true to his king, his sweetheart, and his mates but he was also capable of expressing some resentment of those in positions of privilege. 'The Heart of a Tar', for example, questions whether 'Your lords, with such fine baby faces, | That strut in a garter and star, | Have they, under their tambour and laces, | The kind honest heart of a tar?'.[17] In 'The Forecastle Man' Dibdin suggested that the ratings were much more deserving of respect than the officers strutting on the quarter-deck:

> Your finiking sirs may in finery appear,
> Disdaining such tars as can hand, reef, and steer,
> On the decks, spruce as tailors may cautiously tread,
> And live at the stern, without minding the head.
> Old tough experienced sailors know,
> Where'er they take their trip,
> Whether rising on mountains, or sinking below,
> The forecastle man's the ship.[18]

The construction of the ordinary sailor as a locus of patriotic identity and a more authentic 'man of feeling' than the effete officer or aristocrat is comparable to the heroicization of Robin and William in *The Glorious First of June* and of Bowsprit in *A Trip to the Nore*. The importance to the war effort of the lower orders was thus acknowledged but in a way which gave this contribution a distinctive character or role—that of the kind, honest, and steadfast tar who was morally superior to his betters but always malleable and unquestioning. The tar, as conceived by Dibdin and played by numerous male (and female) actors during the French wars, anticipates his later status in Victorian melodrama as a model of working-class identity, based around loyalty to king and country. In this respect the role of gender in the construction of the tar image is significant. For the stage sailor was not uncomplicatedly masculine, as might be expected. His martial vigour is combined with a 'feminine' capacity for tenderness and feeling: a 'lion' one moment, he could suddenly become a 'lamb'. In many of Dibdin's songs he reveals a 'feminine' capacity for monogamy, in contrast to the sailor's reputation for promiscuity, a girl in every port, and the more taboo view of the ship as concealing rampant homosexuality. The tar is often represented either as a boy or as a promising adolescent. Dibdin's 'Tom Bowling', which later became a Victorian parlour-room standard, is a lament for a lost sailor boy which, like many masculine elegies, has a sub-text of homoerotic desire.[19] Indeed, it is possible to regard the stage-sailor as evidence of a continuing homoeroticism in

---

[17] *Songs*, 16–17.   [18] Ibid. 17.

[19] 'Here, a sheer hulk, lies poor Tom Bowling, | The darling of our crew; | No more he'll hear the tempest howling, | For death has broached him to. | His form was of the manliest

Georgian theatre practice, related to the significant part played by
the army and the navy within homosexuality in the community as a
whole.[20] In 1791 the actress Dorothy Jordan was depicted as the sailor
Little Pickle in Isaac Bickerstaffe's farce *The Spoil'd Child* in a way that
suggests that on this occasion martial cross-dressing was not being used
to draw attention to the female body but instead to create an image
of androgyny—the adolescent sailor as 'masculine–feminine'. The fact
that the stage-sailor could represent a congruence of so many strands
of erotic desire—both heterosexual and homosexual—is an indication of
the powerful fascination exerted by the navy upon Georgian society.
To some extent, the feminization of the sailor is linked to the persistent emphasis on him as passive and unthinking. If the heroicization
of the tar represented a legitimation of plebeian patriotism, to charac-
terize the sailor as a creature of feeling rather than intellect, like a woman,
was one way of ensuring that the legitimation would not go too far.
The femaleness of the tar was also a reflection of a more general sense of
the navy as being different from civilian society in which masculinity
defined the norm. The tantalizing androgyny of Dorothy Jordan was
one way of embodying the alterity of the navy, at the same time
allowing civilian society to express its desire to know or appropriate that
alterity.

However, the audiences for Dibdin's songs and Dorothy Jordan's
boy-sailor did not consist of civilians only. The 'Jolly Jack Tar' was more
often than not performed for the benefit of a predominantly naval audience. How did actual sailors respond to this image of themselves? The
behaviour of sailors in audiences was often commented on in theatrical
literature, usually in relation to their tendency to interpret the fiction of
stage representation as reality. The playwright John O'Keeffe described
one such incident during a performance of Tobias Smollett's nautical
drama *The Reprisal* at Portsmouth in the 1770s. The prompter of the
theatre had recruited some sailors to act as supernumeraries in a battle
scene. They joined in the performance enthusiastically but then began to
act in earnest:

they totally forgot the *tame* instructions they had received from their present
captain, the prompter of a play-house, and began to hack, and cut about furiously.

beauty, | His heart was kind and soft, | Faithful, below, he did his duty, | But now he's
gone aloft.': ibid. 41.

[20] See Kristina Straub, *Sexual Suspects: Eighteenth-Century Players and Sexual Ideology*
(Princeton, NJ, 1992); Arthur N. Gilbert, 'Buggery and the British Navy, 1700–1861',
Journal of Social History, 10 (1976), 72–98, and 'Sexual Deviance and Disaster During the
Napoleonic Wars', *Albion*, 9 (1977), 98–113.

The audience themselves (amongst whom were many maritime people, and their families), not aware of the prompter's ingenious device, considered them as acting, and were in the highest rapture, applauding their performance, and when it came to tearing down the French white *rag*, and hoisting the English entire *flag*, the shouts of joy and victory were quite glorious.[21]

The Portsmouth theatre was also the venue for a similar incident, recorded by the actor Edward Cape Everard. In the course of the third act of Sheridan's *School for Scandal*, when Charles Surface was shown drinking, a group of sailors had clambered down from the gallery. Filling the stage, they had approached 'Charles' 'exclaiming "My eyes, you're a hearty fellow! Come, my tight one, hand us a glass"'.[22] During a nautical drama at the Plymouth theatre one sailor responded to the cry of 'Man overboard!' by 'scrambling over heads, shoulders, seats and slips' to get to the scene of distress. 'When the acting-manager remonstrated, the interrupter directed a stream of tobacco juice in his face, and protestingly remarked "Why there was a man overboard, and no one shall be in distress so long as I can lend a hand!".'[23]

These anecdotes, which have the status of a trope in accounts of behaviour of sailors in the theatre, confirm the perception of the tar as naïve and unsophisticated, unable to make the distinction between fiction and reality. What they also reveal, however, is the sailor's sense of himself as an actor who finds the theatre as familiar an environment as his other home, the ship. Encouraged by the stereotype of the 'Jolly Jack Tar' to think of himself as a role to be performed, it is not surprising that the sailor should have disregarded the rules of theatrical mimesis and the distinctions between stage and auditorium. This refusal to maintain his place, spectacularly negating the physical and social barriers distinguishing the gallery from the pit and invading the territory of the stage, countered the model of self-discipline represented by the stage-tar of actors such as Garrick. The fact that the theatricality of the sailor in the audience often exceeded that of his stage image was noted by Charles Lamb in his account of the acting of Bannister as the sailor Ben in Congreve's *Love for Love*. Lamb claimed that Bannister's success was in making the audience feel that this was a real sailor, a combination of

[21] John O'Keeffe, *Recollections of the Life of John O'Keeffe* (2 vols.; London, 1826), i. 370–1.

[22] Edward Cape Everard, *Memoirs of an Unfortunate Son of Thespis* (Edinburgh, 1818), 105.

[23] Henry Francis Whitfeld, *Plymouth and Devonport in Times of War and Peace* (Plymouth, 1900), 308.

naïvety, warm good-heartedness, and blithe indifference. He contrasted Bannister to the generality of stage-tars who were played as

a downright concretion of a Wapping sailor—a jolly warm-hearted Jack Tar—and nothing else—when instead of investing it with a delicious confusedness of the head, and a veering undirected goodness of purpose—[the actor] gives it a down-right daylight understanding, and a full consciousness of its actions . . . we feel the discord of the thing; the scene is disturbed; a real man has got in among the dramatis personae, and puts them out. We want the sailor turned out. We feel that his true place is not behind the curtain but in the first or second gallery.[24]

Lamb's account of Bannister reveals how deeply the stereotype of the tar had penetrated British consciousness and how powerful the need was to conceive the sailor as simple, good-hearted, and unthreatening. For Lamb, Bannister was successful because he satisfied this need. His Ben has a 'delicious confusedness' and a 'veering undirected goodness'. The 'Jolly Jack Tars' of other actors are disturbing because they are too close to the image of themselves in the gallery. There is no 'delicious confusedness' about the latter, only the challenge of a 'full consciousness' as unmistakeable as a jet of tobacco juice in the face. The failure of the stage-sailors, in Lamb's view, is due to the fact that they are too theatrical; the irony of his comments is that in being too theatrical, they become like the 'real' sailors in the gallery. The genuine sailor was even more of a stereotype than the 'Jolly Jack Tar' on stage. This suggests the complex dimensions of the representation of the sailor in the theatre, one kind of theatricality—that of Garrick, Jordan, or Bannister—interacting with that of naval culture as a whole. As Henry Lee suggested, the stage-sailor of Dibdin's ballads may have been important in determining the character of the British tar, but the naval community was far from being a group of eager students, ready to be moulded. As much as the stage was a vehicle for propaganda, conveying an image of what the authorities and civilian society would have liked the navy to be, the auditorium was the place in which these pressures could be challenged and resisted. In going to the theatre, one was confronted not only with the idealized sailor on stage but also with the sailor as he really was in the audience—rum-drinking, lascivious, and brutalized. The theatre was profoundly important to the French wars because it became the place in which the civilian community's ambivalence in relation to its armed forces could be acted out. Civilian society needed their heroicized images of Robin, William, and

[24] Charles Lamb, *The Works of Charles and Mary Lamb*, ed. E. V. Lucas (7 vols.; London, 1903–5), ii. 141.

Bowsprit not only as a means of shaping the character of the navy but also because they themselves needed to establish a belief in the forces that were defending them, in spite of the fact that these men were often 'the scum of the earth' whose loyalty was always in question. In the theatre these two faces of the army and navy were constantly in evidence, testing each other out in performances both on stage and in the auditorium—in other words, the theatre had become a battlefield.

Such Little Tyranny

Sometime between 1793 and 1795 the American sailor Jacob Nagle made a visit to a London theatre. As is typical with many accounts of theatre-going in this period, Nagle seems to have been more interested in the communal aspects of the evening than in what was happening on stage. He describes the tremendous crush of bodies on the way into the theatre and his apprehensions that his pocket would be picked:

Arriving at the playhouse, the croud [sic] was numerous. Mr. Goodall gave us warning to secure our pockets. We entered the stair case, which was very broad, but so throng [sic] that it was difficult to squese [sic] along, but Mr. Goodall and Mr. Hunter led the van along side each other, the pusser [sic] and his wife next to them, the capt. and myself bringing up the rear, keeping close together. There hapened [sic] to be a great big bussen gutted gentleman got a long side of me, and being so much scrouged, he would come bump up against me. I claped [sic] my hands to my side and my elbo [sic] sticking out would lunge against his ribs, made him cry out, 'You hurt me verry [sic] much, Sir, with your elbo.' 'I cannot avoid it, Sir'.[25]

Discovering that he was not properly dressed for the boxes, although his companion Mr Goodall had already bought a ticket on his behalf, Nagle found himself in the one shilling gallery. There Mr Goodall caused a minor disturbance when he knocked off the hat of a woman who was obstructing his view. The removal of the hat took the woman's wig with it, exposing her as bald before the company: 'There was such a cruel laugh and uproar in the gallery, made them stare from all quarters of the playhouse. The lady being elegantly dressed ketched [sic] up hur [sic] bonnet and cap and got out of the playhouse as fast as posseble [sic].'[26]

[25] John C. Dann (ed.), *The Nagle Journal: A Diary of the Life of Jacob Nagle, Sailor, from the Year 1775 to 1841* (New York, 1988), 152–3.
[26] Ibid. 153.

Nagle's account of his evening illustrates the casual violence of theatre-going in the late eighteenth century: the violence of an agglomeration of bodies, pushing, fighting for space; the threat to personal space and property posed by pickpockets and the constant undertone of male aggression against women, related to the status of the theatre as a sexual market-place. It is not surprising that in such an atmosphere of disorder there should be flare-ups, disturbances, and even full-scale riots. In 1789, for example, *The Times* expressed a doubt 'whether COVENT GARDEN Theatre, gains most by its theatrical exhibitions or pugilistic sports, for it may be fairly computed that there is at least one battle at that theatre to every play and entertainment'.[27] Soldiers and sailors played a significant part in these 'battles' which assumed greater importance than ever before in the highly charged political contexts of the Revolutionary and Napoleonic Wars. After 1793 the already fraught relationship between the military and civilian society was exacerbated by the magnitude of the war effort and by the tensions of domestic politics. Billeting, domestic recruitment, and army manœuvres imposed severe burdens on many communities, while the political temperature of towns with a strong radical identity was raised considerably by the constant presence of soldiers on the streets and by the newly raised barracks. *The Times* of 21 February 1793 claimed that Nottingham 'has more the semblance of a camp than of a manufacturing town' due to the 'number of recruiting parties and the presence of the militia'. In the Norwich of 1794 'officers could hardly appear in the streets without insult from the populace', a situation which had not changed six years later when R. B. Sheridan reported that the town 'had been for some time a scene of incessant tumult and affray between the military and . . . the people'.[28] According to John Bohstedt, issues involving the military account for 21.6 per cent of the riots that occurred in England and Wales between 1790 and 1810: these included the crimp riots of 1794 in London and the opposition to recruitment for the supplementary militia in rural areas between 1796 and 1797.[29] These were major events which were reported nationally: at another level, however, but no less important politically, were what Bohstedt classifies as 'miscellaneous' riots, which included theatre disturbances. This latter class of riot reflects the sus-

---

[27] *The Times*, 3 Nov. 1795.

[28] James McGrigor, *The Autobiography and Services of Sir James McGrigor, Bart.* (London, 1861), 41; Richard Brinsley Sheridan, *The Letters of Richard Brinsley Sheridan*, ed. Cecil Price (3 vols.; Oxford, 1966), ii. 126.

[29] John Bohstedt, *Riots and Community Politics in England and Wales 1790–1810* (Cambridge, Mass., 1983), 14.

tained level of political and social tension throughout the period of the French wars. In the view of Roger Wells, 'the duration of the crises, the fierce polarisation of conflicting interests, ensured that social tensions remained high for very long periods. Nobody was immune, for the theatre for conflict was universal.'[30] This 'theatre for conflict' could encompass chance encounters between the military and civilians at a street corner, the tavern ante-room, or even the church.[31] It also included the theatre proper: between 1793 and 1815 there were a number of publicized disputes involving the military in the theatres of Portsmouth, Plymouth, Norwich, Sheffield, Manchester, Lewes, Brighton, Belfast, Edinburgh, Nottingham, Wolverhampton, Sheffield, Maidstone, King's Lynn, Canterbury, and Waterford.[32] With the notable exception of E. P. Thompson, these disturbances have received very little attention from social and cultural historians.[33] In the context of major public disturbances such as the food riots of 1795–6 and 1799–1801 and the complexity of political activity in general, altercations in the theatre may seem of minor importance but I would argue that a consideration of them is necessary to an overall picture of British society during the French wars and, in particular, the role of public culture within it. These disturbances had long term implications for the political atmosphere of the provincial theatres; they also reflected significantly on the distinctive theatricality of military behaviour itself.

A typical incident was that which occurred in the Edinburgh theatre in April 1794. The *Thespian Magazine* reported that the manager, Stephen Kemble, had announced the performance of a tragedy, *Charles the First; or, the Royal Martyr*:

previous to the play beginning, some persons ordered the music to play, '*God Save the King*;' but the clamour against the tune was so loud and unanimous, that the band was obliged to obey almost the universal call of the house, by striking up 'Moggie Lauder.'

The democratic parts of Cromwell's speech were heard with thundering plaudits, while the dignified and pathetic speeches of Charles were received with hisses, groans, and laughter. About the fourth act, '*God save the King*,' was again called for by a number of officers of the Fencibles, and others who had made their appearance in the pit after the first contest.

---

[30] Roger Wells, *Wretched Faces: Famine in Wartime England 1793–1801* (Gloucester, 1988), 94.

[31] *The Times* of 26 Dec. 1795 reported a disturbance between a 'carpenter of respectability' and a former militia officer in the parish church of Chatham, Kent, over who was entitled to enter a particular pew.   [32] This list is not intended to be comprehensive.

[33] For Thompson on theatre riots see *The Making of the English Working Class*, 2nd edn. (Harmondsworth, 1968), 808–9.

A part of the audience in the pit took off their hats; and the Highland officers, to prove their loyalty to their King, and their affection to the people, drew their *Maiden Swords*, and attacked all those who were covered. A stout battle took place, which was only decided by the interposition of a party of soldiers, who rushed in with drawn bayonets to assist their officers, and who even, with swords in their hands, were like to be overcome.[34]

Throughout the eighteenth century theatre disturbances involving the military had followed a similar pattern to this one. In 1749 the Edinburgh playhouse had been the site of a battle between supporters of Jacobitism and 'certain military gentlemen' who had 'called out to the band of music to play *Culloden*'. A contest had ensued during which the officers were 'assailed from the galleries with apples, snuff-boxes, broken forms'.[35] Recurrent patterns of behaviour—the contest over 'tunes', particularly 'God Save the King', the symbolism of hats, the physical struggle over meaningful territory within the theatre—suggest that these riots were highly ritualized affairs. Many of these elements, particularly the singing of 'God Save the King', were shared by other forms of sociability and political expression outside the playhouse, such as celebratory dinners, civic gatherings, public demonstrations, and effigy burnings, another in- dication of the theatre's importance within the overall matrix of urban political behaviour.[36] There was therefore nothing innovative in the form taken by the disturbances of the 1790s. What was different were the political circumstances: 'God Save the King' was being contested by new anthems such as 'God Save Tom Paine' and 'Ca Ira', while the refusal to doff a hat signalled disrespect not only to the Hanoverians but to the institution of monarchy itself.

Many of the theatre disturbances of this period took place in manufac- turing towns identified with Jacobinism—centres such as Norwich, Nottingham, and Sheffield where barracks had been constructed in the 1790s. Others occurred in towns with a long history of political engage-

---

[34] *Thespian Magazine*, 3 (1794), 178. Among those present at the disturbances was Walter Scott: see James C. Dibdin, *The Annals of the Edinburgh Stage: With an Account of the Rise and Progress of Dramatic Writing in Scotland* (Edinburgh, 1888), 224–5.

[35] John Jackson, *The History of the Scottish Stage* (Edinburgh, 1793), 374–5. For an account of a theatre riot involving Jacobites and officers in Norwich in 1716 see Sybil Rosenfeld, *Strolling Players & Drama in the Provinces 1660–1765* (Cambridge, 1939), 50–1. See also Paul Monod, 'Pierre's White Hat: Theatre, Jacobitism and Popular Protest in London, 1689–1760' in *By Force or By Default? The Revolution of 1688–1689*, ed. Eveline Cruickshanks (Edinburgh, 1989), 159–89.

[36] For 'God Save the King' see V. C. Clinton-Baddeley, *All Right on the Night* (London, 1954), 87–102. For a discussion of the custom of 'calling for tunes' see W. J. Lawrence, *Old Theatre Days and Ways* (London, 1935), 113–23.

ment such as Maidstone and Manchester. In Maidstone the theatre had been the traditional arena for the expression of conflict and the settling of scores. In 1778 'party divisions' in the town were such that 'very serious consequences have arisen from the existence of a playhouse; and the corporation have wisely determined to prevent such in future'.[37] Assembly rooms and other forms of public entertainment were also felt to be dangerous, much to the consternation of the pleasure hungry officers of nearby Coxheath. Very little had changed by 1797 when Thomas Dibdin performed for the Volunteers of Maidstone as a member of Sarah Baker's touring company: 'Political party at that time ran very high . . . and a fierce dispute, amounting almost to a tumult, occurred, in the course of the evening, respecting an encore of "God save the King!".'[38] Manchester also had a long tradition of factional politics being expressed at public entertainments, again involving the military. After the Jacobite rebellion of 1745 the local Whigs seceded to form their own dancing assembly as a result of 'some quarrels that arose . . . between the people of the town and the officers quartered there'.[39] During the 1790s Manchester was again a town divided. Democrats and Church and King supporters became engaged in a public struggle: effigies of Tom Paine were paraded and burnt in the streets, tavern keepers put up signs declaring 'No Jacobins admitted here' and the theatre resounded to the contest over 'God Save the King'.[40] The *Monthly Mirror*'s Manchester correspondent reported in 1796 that 'some imagined irreverence on the part of two or three persons' when the anthem was requested had led to a 'violent dispute', causing one gentleman to be 'dangerously hurt'. 'An action at law it is said will be the consequence.'[41]

Disturbances in the theatre involving the military were therefore more likely in towns which had an established tradition of such behaviour. But it is clear that many more officers, in many more towns, were using the theatre as a forum for political expression, a place where they could 'have a go' at their opponents. In *The Wandering Patentee* Tate Wilkinson noted

[37]   *Morning Chronicle*, 8 July 1778.

[38]   Thomas Dibdin, *The Reminiscences of Thomas Dibdin* (2 vols.; London, 1827), i. 209.

[39]   J. Aikin, *A Description of the Country from Thirty to Forty Miles Round Manchester* (London, 1795), 190.

[40]   S. W. Ryley, *The Itinerant: or Memoirs of an Actor* (9 vols.; London, 1808–27), iii. 306; Archibald Prentice, *Historical Sketches and Personal Recollections of Manchester* (London, 1851), 7; J. L. Hodgkinson and Rex Pogson, *The Early Manchester Theatre* (London, 1960), 144–5.

[41]   *Monthly Mirror*, 1 (1796), 310. The evidence of Maidstone and Manchester would tend to challenge the view of Peter Borsay that the theatre promoted social cohesion among the élite. See Borsay, 'All the Town's a Stage' and *English Urban Renaissance*.

the activities of 'those in cockades', who in Hull, Portsmouth, Sheffield, and Edinburgh were 'degrading' the theatre in the name of loyalty:

> Were our sovereign to witness the behaviour of such *gentlemen*, as when sick from a load of wine discharging it in a stage-box—jumping on the stage, because a bet had been laid over a bottle that it should be done, and singing 'God save the King,' during the *time* of a *principal scene* of a play, thereby interrupting the performance, and insulting the sober part of the audience, as well as the actors and actresses, alarming the ladies, and by such means rendering themselves lower than the *meanest* person at that time in the theatre, I am fully persuaded that his majesty, would not thank such heroes for their *compliment* (*WP* iv. 211).

The privileged position of the theatre in urban culture meant that even a minor victory over the democrats could have significant ramifications, receiving publicity in the local and even national press. A theatre disturbance could be thus more meaningful than a street corner altercation or even a full-scale riot in which the military were likely to play a more anonymous role. Such behaviour enabled officers in particular to assert themselves politically as well gratifying their own sense of theatricality.

Many disturbances were undoubtedly premeditated. A performance at the Norwich theatre in March 1800 was disrupted when a party of officers from Ireland demanded the playing of 'God Save the King'. In the context of local tensions prevailing at the time, such action was likely to have been deliberately provocative.[42] A number of theatre disturbances were significantly associated with the performance of plays by Elizabeth Inchbald and Thomas Holcroft. The first performance of Inchbald's *Every One Has His Fault* at the Brighton theatre was the occasion of an incident involving officers from the Brighton camp and the Revd Vicesimus Knox, a well known opponent of the war with France. The Revd Knox

> had, it seems, preached an obnoxious sermon on Sunday last, and was discovered in one of the boxes; and the officers belonging to the Camp, who happened to be in the house to the number of 30 or 40, loudly called for his exclusion, declaring that no person should sit in that house who was a promoter of sedition and anarchy. The gentleman charged with the crime stood up to vindicate himself from that imputation, but he was not allowed to speak, and was consequently obliged to retire with his family, who accompanied him, after being very ill-treated.[43]

---

[42] C. B. Jewson, *The Jacobin City: A Portrait of Norwich in its Reaction to the French Revolution 1788–1802* (Glasgow and London, 1975), 100.

[43] *The Times*, 26 Aug. 1793.

Every One Has His Fault was also the occasion of a riot in the Portsmouth theatre in February 1795, caused by a group of young officers who rushed into the playhouse with a 'hideous yell' and 'terminated the performance'.[44] In 1805 the Portsmouth theatre was again the scene of a disturbance, coinciding with the performance of Thomas Holcroft's *Hear Both Sides*.[45]

It is impossible to determine whether any political motivation on the part of the theatre management is revealed by the staging of plays by Inchbald or Holcroft in the potentially volatile atmosphere of naval towns such as Portsmouth. Elsewhere, however, managers were certainly implicated in the disturbances by publicly identifying with certain political factions. Stephen Kemble had contributed to the riots at the Edinburgh theatre in April 1794 by reviving *Charles the First*. In case the democrats missed the point, the accompanying playbill stressed the analogies between Charles I and Louis XVI 'and insinuated that the reformers of the present day were a set of hypocrites, like Cromwell and his followers'.[46] The manager of the Belfast theatre, Michael Atkins, demonstrated his political loyalties by staging a play which was sympathetic to the Revolution—*The Guillotine; or, The Death of Louis XVI*: 'as soon as the performance began on Monday, 27 May [1793], cries of "Off, off!" came from the pit and the boxes, while the gallery shouted "Go on".' A full-scale riot was averted but Atkins was forced to curtail the theatrical season because of the controversy.[47] His actions, like those of Kemble, suggest that in certain circumstances managements could be less politically circumspect than some theatre historians have maintained.

The effect of these disturbances was to intensify the political role of the provincial theatres in the 1790s. While other places of entertainment—the assembly room, the pleasure garden, the race-ground, or the circulation library—were being clearly demarcated as the public spaces of the polite and the genteel, to the exclusion of the lower orders, the theatre remained socially heterogeneous in its audience composition. Its accessibility to all social ranks but the most impoverished became especially significant after 1795 when government restrictions on public demonstrations caused radicals to retreat to the alehouse and to clandestine open air assemblies. The theatre was one of the few places of public entertainment where democrats and loyalists of all ranks could legitimately confront each other.

---

[44] *Hampshire Chronicle*, 16 Feb. 1795.

[45] H. Sargeant, 'A History of Portsmouth Theatres', *Portsmouth Papers*, 13 (1971), 9.

[46] *Thespian Magazine*, 178.

[47] W. S. Clark, *The Irish Stage in the County Towns 1720 to 1800* (Oxford, 1965), 275.

In this context the socially encoded hierarchy of pit, box, and gallery became more highly charged than ever, especially in rapidly industrializing centres such as Sheffield and Leeds where the will of the gallery dominated. It is not accidental that many of the conflicts involving the military were fought in the playhouses of these manufacturing towns, many of which were centres of radical disaffection. Disturbances at the Wolverhampton and Sheffield theatres in 1800 and 1812 respectively involved a struggle for territory between the gallery and those officers stationed in the boxes and the pit: as usual, the disputes had been initiated by calls for 'God Save the King'.[48] Such behaviour can be regarded as a response by previously dominant social groups to the changing class composition of theatre audiences in these towns—an attempt to curb the cultural, and by implication, political assertiveness of the lower orders by reminding them of their duties of deference and place within the audience hierarchy.

The fact that galleries in provincial theatres contained a fair proportion of lower-ranking soldiers and sailors suggests another dimension to these disturbances—their significance as expressions of class hostility or tension within the ranks of the military itself, or between the services. As will have become clear, the causes of the riots were often ascribed to the actions of a few officers. Their assumption of the right to disrupt the evening's entertainment, and their often violent incursions into the territory of other social groups within the theatre, represented assertions of class privilege as well as interventions in local politics. One of the ways in which the upper-class men had traditionally demonstrated their authority was through disruptive behaviour in the theatre—being sick in the boxes, parading themselves on stage, attacking, or even murdering, actors and actresses.[49] It is significant that this kind of 'performance' became more widespread, exactly at a time when the prerogatives encoded by it were being contested by radical politics.

The 'enemy' within the theatre could assume a number of forms. In December 1803 artificers then building the barracks at Lewes in Sussex bespoke a performance of *Richard the Third* at the local theatre, taking their seats in the boxes in order 'to render their patronage more profitable to the Managers'. This usurpation of the privileges of the military was regarded as an affront by local officers who challenged the interlopers: according to *The Times* 'the whole house was . . . thrown into an uproar

---

[48] Wells, *Insurrection*, 193; Thomas Asline Ward, *Peeps into the Past* (London, 1909), 196.
[49] For an example of violence against a theatre worker see Everard, *Memoirs*, 105–7. See also Straub, *Sexual Suspects*, 151–73.

that threatened a catastrophe more serious than that which awaited the crook-backed Tyrant'.[50] There were similar problems between the navy and civilian dockyard workers who were amongst the most unionized and politically radical groups in the country.[51] After 1795 the navy itself underwent a change in its social composition as a result of Pitt's Quota Acts. Many failed artisans, shopkeepers, and clerks took the opportunity of increased bounties to exchange the debtor's prison for the man-of-war, bringing with them higher standards of literacy and the seeds of political disaffection. These conditions were exacerbated by the presence within the fleet of many Irishmen who had been sent there by the government on suspicion of insurrectionary activity. The regular army and its auxiliaries were therefore likely to have been wary of the loyalties of those lower ranking sailors who were hurling bottles and benches at them from the galleries of the provincial theatres. Indeed, mutual suspicion between the services stood the government in good stead when it came to suppressing the naval mutinies at the Nore and Spithead in 1797. The Portsmouth theatre became the venue for a contest between the mutinous sailors and the military, described by James McGrigor in the following way:

At first a military officer dared not go to the theatre in uniform. 'God save the King' was not allowed to be sung . . . At length the soldiers in strong parties dared to go to the theatre and officers ventured to appear there in uniform. At this time, the corps of officers of the 88th—about thirty in number—took places and went to the theatre together. A great body of the soldiers, all Irishmen, got tickets for the gallery, where there were many disorderly sailors, with their dissolute female companions. We called for, 'God save the King.' This was the commencement of a trial between the parties; the sailors and several of the inhabitants resisting the loyal song being sung. However, we carried it, and the soldiers turned out all the malcontents. After this, the song was sung, I believe, half a dozen times in the course of the evening, every individual standing up and joining in the chorus. After this struggle it was never omitted in the Patent Theatre.[52]

McGrigor's account suggests that the military's conquest of the theatre was a significant event in the suppression of the mutiny. The loss of this cultural bastion must have dealt a severe blow to the morale of the mutineers and their supporters in Portsmouth: without the theatre there was no public institution in which they could so effectively insult the prerogatives of the élite and parade their dominance of the town. This

[50] *The Times*, 14 Dec. 1803.
[51] See Roger Morriss, *The Royal Dockyards During the Revolutionary and Napoleonic Wars* (Leicester, 1983).
[52] McGrigor, *Autobiography*, 91.

incident serves to emphasize the extent to which theatre disturbances were not isolated, one-off events but part of the continuing negotiation of relations between the military and civilian society. Like other forms of theatre riot, disputes over the singing of 'God Save the King' may have functioned as a ritualized release of tension, a safety-valve for confrontation that might otherwise have been expressed in more politically explosive forms. But as Tate Wilkinson's remarks and other accounts of disturbances make clear, they were not spontaneous eruptions of the carnivalesque in which both sides of the contest were equal, ludic participants, but events which were deliberately initiated by officers for politically motivated reasons. The presence of the armed forces in the theatre was a reminder to the rest of society of its reliance on them. The fact that this presence constantly threatened to become a violent one also reminded playgoers that no aspect of their lives was free of the pressure of an increasingly militarized society. The theatre was thus unable to offer a relief from the daily tensions of living with the army or navy—the constant apprehension of the soldiery that was part of even the most casual encounter—and it is clear that many officers exploited this special intimidatory power. In 1800, for example, the patrons of the Belfast theatre were confronted with a disturbance that followed a similar pattern to those elsewhere. While 'God Save the King' was being played two officers leapt from their box and attacked a man in the pit, whom, they claimed, had not shown the proper sign of respect by taking off his hat.[53] As we have seen from the evidence beforehand there was nothing exceptional in this behaviour—this disturbance does have a special significance, however, because it took place in a town which was still suffering the effects of martial law, twenty months after the rebellion of the United Irishmen. There had been house-to-house searches and public executions and floggings of the rebels; indeed, the inhabitants were so cowed that when the military ordered the streets to be cleaned 'never was [sic] brooms used with more activity than the following day'.[54] In this context, the actions of the officers in the theatre have an accentuated political significance, demonstrating that even in this domain they were able to exert the authority of violence. The disturbance was doubly significant in that the Belfast theatre had been associated with the growth in civic and national

[53] Martha McTier to William Drennan, 25 Feb. 1800, letter no. 837, Drennan Letters, Public Record Office Northern Ireland. This letter has been substantially edited in D. A. Chart (ed.), *The Drennan Letters* (Belfast, 1931).

[54] Martha McTier to William Drennan, undated letter no. 725, Drennan Letters, Public Record Office Northern Ireland.

consciousness that had led, ultimately, to the rebellion. The prologue on the opening of the new theatre building in 1793 had contemplated the rise of 'a second Athens' while a number of its shareholders were local men who were closely associated with the United Irish movement.[55] The behaviour of the officers on 24 February 1800 was therefore of powerful symbolic significance, signalling, as much as any public execution, the defeat of a community's aspirations.

The intimidatory behaviour of officers in the provincial theatres can thus be seen as an unauthorized aspect of their role as policemen in late Georgian society. What was the response of playhouse managers to this marshalling of the theatrical space? As we have seen earlier, Tate Wilkinson deplored the actions of these 'upstart dictators of a theatre' but claimed that to intervene against them 'would only make bad worse, and heat and fire animosity and party, which wants quenching, not stirring the flames' (*WP* iv. 215–16). Managers such as Wilkinson were placed in a difficult position when it came to dealing with the disruptive behaviour of the military because of their occasional need to resort to soldiers in order to discipline unruly audiences. Throughout the eighteenth century it had been the practice to station two grenadiers on either side of the stage. Although the origins of the custom are obscure, it is likely that the sentinels were intended to prevent members of the audience, in particular upper-class males, from invading the space of the performance. Later in the century the use of the sentinels became mainly symbolic—they were noticed only when they fell asleep or collapsed with exhaustion during performances—but the very fact of this symbolism indicates the need for some kind of disciplinary authority in the theatre.[56] It is clear that managers occasionally used soldiers in order to 'police' the behaviour of certain elements of the audience, in particular the gallery. On 25 April 1791, for example, there was a disturbance at Drury Lane following a change in the published playbill. According to the *Morning Post*, 'the confusion was augmented by the unadvised introduction of some soldiers into the galleries'. This action had the effect of intensifying the significance of the dispute as a struggle between the perceived rights of playgoers and the authority of the management. The audience negotiated for the 'removal' of the soldiers 'which being complied with, the tumult sub-

---

[55] W. J. Lawrence, 'The Annals of "The Old Belfast Stage"', typescript dated 1897, Linenhall Library Belfast, 167–8.

[56] Hogan, *London Stage*, Part 5, iii. 1824; Allardyce Nicoll, *The Garrick Stage: Theatres and Audience in the Eighteenth Century* (Manchester, 1980), 97–8, 101 n. 30.

sided'.[57] During rising tensions in Ireland in 1797 Philip Astley went so far as to install a sentry box in the gallery of his amphitheatre in Dublin, in addition to deploying 'a military Guard at each of his doors, and the usual number of police officers'. The effect of this was to provoke the gallery even more. Charles Dibdin the Younger, who witnessed the incident, reported that 'the discordant yell with which he [Astley] was received . . . must have completely convinced him how much the audience felt themselves insulted; he was pelted from the Gallery; and among other missiles I saw a large and sharp clasp knife, opened; which just missed his head'.[58] Astley's actions can be seen as part of the general attempt to discipline a politicized and assertive gallery. In this context the actions of officers in the theatre could be politically useful to the local magistracy. In Sheffield and Wolverhampton, for example, magistrates used the pretext of riots instigated by the military to install special constables in the galleries of the theatres.

It is clear though, that in many cases the military were acting without official sanction and often to the considerable embarrassment of local authorities. Their behaviour had the effect of intensifying the political role of the theatre, thereby making it a potential focus for disaffection within the community as a whole. During the 1790s magistrates closed the Portsmouth theatre on at least two occasions, while in 1798 Sarah Baker was refused a renewal of her licence to perform in the theatre at Rochester due to the frequency of riots involving soldiers and sailors from Chatham. The disturbances also raised the politically sensitive issue of the relationship between military and civilian law. To which authority were rioters legally responsible—the civil courts or the military tribunal? In most parts of the country the military was subject to civil jurisdiction but in some towns, such as Portsmouth, which were to all intents and purposes military domains, martial law was the *de facto* authority. The theatres of such towns functioned as places where the relationship between martial and civilian law could be ritually tested. It is clear that many soldiers and sailors regarded playgoing as a holiday activity and the theatre as a space where they were temporarily free of the drill sergeant or the boatswain. When a midshipman at the Plymouth dock theatre was ordered to desist from rioting by his captain, he asserted the liberties of playgoing by declaring 'No martial law here!'. This challenge to naval authority was met by force from his captain who, after a pitched battle in the theatre with the midshipman's supporters, escorted the rebel to his ship where he

---

[57] Ibid. ii. 1343.   [58] Dibdin, *Memoirs*, 24.

was publicly stripped of his uniform and sentenced to two years solitary confinement.[59]

In the face of this kind of incursion on civil authority, the closure of theatres by local magistrates can be seen as a challenge to local military hegemony, a reminder to an overweening captain or colonel of who was actually in charge. Local communities found the disorderliness of soldiers and sailors in the theatre increasingly wearisome. After an incident in Portsmouth in 1795 the *Hampshire Chronicle* commented with irritation: 'we have witnessed so many instances of unqalified violence on the part of subaltern officers towards poor country actors that it is worth some enquiry to ask where such little tyranny originates.'[60] Instead of closing theatres some magistrates took the decision to punish officers directly. The disturbance over Holcroft's *Hear Both Sides* at Portsmouth in 1805 was followed by the arrest of those who had instigated it. At Lewes in 1803 the officers who had challenged the right of the barrack artificers to occupy the boxes sent for a peace officer and charged their opponents with assault. However, one of the barrack artificers later brought a civil suit against the officers for false imprisonment and was successful. Two of his military assailants were fined substantial sums. In this case civil law had triumphed against an attempt by the military to manipulate it in its interests.[61]

While managers such as Stephen Kemble and Michael Atkins encouraged political factionalism in their theatres, others regarded the behaviour of the military as a threat, not only to their income, but also to the status of playgoing as a genteel or polite activity. The masculinization of the theatre associated with the French wars undoubtedly contributed to its declining popularity amongst upper-class women and those who wished to emulate them. The threat of a disturbance at the playhouse often led to the immediate exit of the ladies in the audience, though at Belfast in 1800 it was a woman, Mrs Mattear, who confronted the officers, telling them that they belonged in the gallery rather than in the boxes. Managers such as Sandford at Plymouth attempted to restrain the disorderliness of the sailors and their female companions. The *Monthly Mirror* of March 1804 commended his efforts, claiming that 'instead of the inebriety and confusion which used to prevail, order and regularity are introduced'.[62] Sandford later used the standard recourse of the period—pricing—in order to make the theatre less affordable to these undesirable elements and

---

[59] Whitfeld, *Plymouth and Devonport*, 307.　　[60] 16 Feb. 1795.
[61] *Hampshire Chronicle*, 26 Mar. 1804.　　[62] *Monthly Mirror*, 17 (1804), 207.

more attractive to those who were increasingly regarding it with disdain. In 1810 he curtailed the system of half-price, leading to riots at Plymouth Dock theatre that took their inspiration from the O.P. conflict at Covent Garden in the previous year. Like John Philip Kemble, Sandford was forced to capitulate as the tars reasserted the disorder which had for so long been one of the customary privileges, and the attraction, of playgoing.[63]

The dominant presence of the military in the provincial playhouses thus had the effect of intensifying the political role of the theatre in the 1790s, making it a potential flash-point for local tensions and a source of anxiety for the magistracy. The provincial theatre became a contested site where the military and their opponents in the gallery struggled for political control of public space, the officers in many cases winning the battle. The *'internally disciplined'* theatre audience of the mid-nineteenth century, which Peter Stallybrass and Allon White have described as a sign of 'an almost geological shift in the cultural threshold of shame and embarrassment which regulates the body in public' can thus be seen to be the product of an overt disciplining of audiences by the military during the period of the French wars.[64]

The military's politicization of the theatre, associated with its general tendency towards riotousness and other forms of licentious behaviour was a significant factor in the declining cultural status of the theatre. The appropriation of the theatrical space by soldiers and sailors increasingly made it a suspect domain, to both the élite and middle-class polite opinion. This appropriation also had significant implications for the relations between the military and civilian society in general. Both officers and lower ranks regarded the theatre as an adjunct to the parade-ground, the camp, the ship, or the barrack; it was as much a place of performance and display as any specifically military venue. Playgoing, whether or not it involved violence, thus had the important function of endorsing the military's sense of its own theatricality; it confirmed what the armed forces believed themselves to be—actors in a domestic theatre of war. This ran counter to the emerging philosophy and practice of total war which sought to divest military behaviour of its theatricality by fusing the categories of 'soldier' and 'citizen'. For the officer class, the changes induced by the Revolutionary wars led ultimately to its professionalization in the nineteenth century: the excessive, flamboyant younger brothers of the aristo-

---

[63] Whitfeld, *Plymouth and Devonport*, 207–8.
[64] Stallybrass and White, *Transgression*, 85.

cracy who treated war as another forum for pleasure were to become the servants of the state, increasingly seen and not heard. The 'little tyranny' which officers exhibited in the theatre was a considerable embarrassment to the authorities; their assertion of political independence in such a public fashion threatened to undermine the edifice of patriotism, based as it was on the concept of passive military loyalty and steadfastness. As we saw earlier in relation to Nelson and Sheridan's *Pizarro*, the factional neutrality of the soldier and sailor was crucial to the construction of a patriotism, centred around loyalty to the king, that transcended party and class allegiances. The behaviour of officers in the theatre negated the idea of a neutral armed force. Every occasion on which someone was forced to sing 'God Save the King', or was physically attacked for failing to doff his hat, was a reminder that patriotism was not a matter of naturalized morality but one of personal political choice.

The behaviour of the army and navy as theatre audiences thus highlighted, in a culturally significant way, the paradox of the military's role within society as a whole: that is, those who were the guardians of the state, its defenders against the Revolution and Bonaparte, were also sources of instability and danger. The paradox was realized on 15 May 1800 when James Hadfield, an ex-soldier who had fought and been severely wounded in the Flanders campaign, stood up in the audience at Drury Lane and fired a shot at the royal box where George III was sitting.[65] Earlier on the same day the King had also survived a probable assassination attempt during a military review at Hyde Park; while a celebratory *feu de joie* was taking place, a shot had been fired from a billet window injuring an official only 20 feet away from him. The conjunction of these two incidents was not accidental; rather, it demonstrates the status of the theatre as a *de facto* military space, an extension of the political theatre of the parade ground. In both cases the decorum of events which were designed to reinforce the prestige of monarchy was disrupted by individuals who, like the sailors at Nelson's funeral, had gone beyond the prepared script. As in the case of Nelson's funeral, what incidents such as this demonstrate is not the intimidatory power of public ritual, but in fact the opposite—its very susceptibility to other kinds of performance. There is an appropriateness to Hadfield's choice of Drury Lane as a forum in which to shoot the King because military culture and society in general would have taught him that he was, in a basic sense, an actor. Like the

[65] See Wells, *Wretched Faces*, 147–9; McCalman, *Radical Underworld*, 61; Harry William Pedicord, *'By Their Majesties' Command': The House of Hanover at the London Theatres, 1714–1800* (London, 1991), 60–8.

loyalist officers in Portsmouth or Belfast, Hadfield was in effect exploring the political logic of this, showing that while theatricality could enhance the power of the military in British society, it also had its own inherent dangers of destabilization.

6

'Mars and the Muses':
the Army and Navy as Actors

THE effective colonization of the theatre by the military was not confined
to the auditorium: many soldiers and sailors took the stage as performers
in their own amateur productions, not only in Britain but also overseas in
the theatre of the Peninsular War, for example, or in imperial outposts
such as the Cape of Good Hope or Australia.[1] My aim in this chapter is to
describe and analyse some of these productions with a view to defining the
significance of such ritualized performance within military culture of the
late Georgian period.

The army and navy's penchant for theatricals was part of an histrionic
mania which swept British society in the late eighteenth and early nineteenth centuries. Its historian, Sybil Rosenfeld, dates the beginning of 'the
craze' to Garrick's retirement in 1776: it 'reached its climax in the 1780's,
declined somewhat in the 1790's, increased again slightly in the first
decade of the 19th century and, after that, petered out'.[2] The amateur
theatricals of the élite, in conjunction with the activities of the macaronis
and fashionable aristocrats such as the Duchess of Devonshire, denoted an
increasingly confident and exhibitionist upper class, prepared to defy the
criticisms of the middling sort as well as any kind of plebeian 'counter-
theatre'. The practice also indicated a cultural shift which would have
profound implications for the patent theatres, confirming the withdrawal
of the fashionable élite from the political and social space of the public
playhouse. As early as 1777 R. B. Sheridan noted with concern 'the
number of private Plays at Gentlemen's seats' and the fact that the 'politer
Class of people' felt themselves to be 'excluded from our Theatres'.[3] He
argued the need for a third theatre on the grounds that the expansion of

---

[1] For military theatricals of the Peninsular War see Antony Brett-James, *Life in Wellington's Army* (London, 1972), 159–66. Prof. Rob Jordan of the University of New South Wales
is working on a study of garrison and convict theatre in Australia.

[2] Sybil Rosenfeld, *Temples of Thespis: Some Private Theatres and Theatricals in England
and Wales, 1700–1820* (London, 1978), 11.

[3] Sheridan, *Letters*, i. 118. For the development of London at this period see Langford,
Polite and Commercial People, 426.

the metropolis meant that the 'Politer streets', that is, areas such as the recently constructed Finsbury and Bedford squares and the new developments at Marylebone, were located at an inconvenient distance from the less salubrious environs of Drury Lane and Covent Garden. Sheridan perceived that the restriction of theatrical entertainment to the two patent houses was a blight on their long-term prospects: unless managements could adapt to the changing social geography of London they would lose the most influential sector of the audience—the fashionable élite.

Another drawback of the patent theatres in the eyes of the fashionable élite was the fact that they were socially heterogeneous spaces. As William Hazlitt pointed out in 1829 one of the major attractions of theatre-going was the accessibility of the rich and powerful to public view: once the élite decided that they no longer wished to exploit this kind of theatricality, a significant *raison d'être* of the patent theatres was removed.[4] The discomforting proximity of the lower orders was even more palpable in the provincial theatres, especially in those dominated by the will of the gallery. Playhouse entrepreneurs were careful to ensure the maintenance of strict demarcations between people of the 'politer Class' and those of the lowest rank, not only within the auditorium but also in the approaches to it. In 1799 separate entrances were proposed for the gallery and boxes of William Wilkins's new theatre in Norwich, while in 1813 the new lessee of the Birmingham theatre, Robert Elliston, felt compelled to reassure his potential patrons that the 'best company' of the city would be assembled there: 'all persons coming to the Theatre on the Friday would be . . . surrounded by those they might be pleased to meet.'[5] In addition to the fear of being confronted with one's servant or tradesman in their recreational moments, polite patrons of the provincial theatres were also repelled by the insanitary conditions of these public places. A Belfast playgoer complained that it was 'impossible for Ladies to go in full or half dress without chances of their cloathes being soiled or totally destroyed by the quantities of dirt and dust which are suffered to remain for

---

[4] The 'nobility and gentry no longer appearing in the open boxes, they have ceased to be the favourite resort of genteel and fashionable company; people no longer go for the chance of sitting in the next box to a prince or minister of state, of seeing how a courtier smiles on hearing a countess lisp, or with the hope of being mixed up in splendid confusion with the flower of the land': William Hazlitt, *The Complete Works of William Hazlitt*, ed. P. P. Howe (34 vols.; London, 1930–4), xx. 287. For a parallel phenomenon, the withdrawal of the élite to private concerts, see Simon McVeigh, *Concert Life in London from Mozart to Haydn* (Cambridge, 1993), 47.

[5] Quoted John E. Cunningham, *Theatre Royal: The History of the Theatre Royal Birmingham* (Oxford, 1950), 28. For Wilkins's proposal see David Thomas (ed.), *Restoration and Georgian England, 1660–1788* (Cambridge, 1989), 299.

months . . . The gallery is so ill ceiled that quantities of punch and other liquors fall in copious showers on the unoffending heads in the boxes.' In short, 'these faults act as so many effectual bars against the attendance of many a female party that would otherwise more generally grace the theatre with their presence'.[6]

The appeal of amateur dramatics as a retreat from the bustle of the patent theatres was articulated by a former commander of the British army, General Conway, in a prologue to a performance of Arthur Murphy's *The Way to Keep Him* at Richmond House in 1787:

> To modern Stages, too, in my conception,
> One fairly too might produce some just objection;
> 'Tis such a concourse, such a staring show!
> Mobs shout above, and Criticks snarl below . . .
> While here, in this fair Garden's calm retreat,
> At once the Virtues, and the Muse's seat;
> Where friendly Suns their kindest influence shed,
> Each tender Plant may dauntless raise its head.[7]

Far from indicating a rejection of theatricality, amateur dramatics represented an attempt by the élite to control it more absolutely, to limit their exposure to the gaze of 'the staring show'. Among the most popular plays to be performed were two satires on plebeian habits and pretensions, Foote's *The Mayor of Garratt* and *High Life Below Stairs* by James Townley.[8] The performance of these plays in the commercial theatre was often the occasion for the rehearsal of class tensions. A production of *High Life Below Stairs* in Edinburgh led to vociferous objections from a group of footmen who regarded the farce as an insult to the 'fraternity': peace in the theatre was only restored when the gentlemen of the boxes overpowered their servants in the gallery.[9] However, the performance of these plays within the confines of the great house effectively neutralized the possibilities of this kind of counter-theatre; the retreat from the public theatre to the 'private' domain of the great house thus enabled the élite to savour fully the pleasure of aping the lower orders. The political resonances of the élite's amateur theatricals could therefore be significant. For events which were supposedly 'private', they received as much, if not more, publicity than performances at the patent houses: newspapers and journals printed accounts of *bon ton* theatricals, including 'private' play-

---

[6] Quoted Clark, *Irish Stage*, 266.

[7] *Prologue and Epilogue to the Play of the Way to Keep Him, Performed at Richmond House, in April 1787, in a Private Society* [London, 1787?].

[8] See Rosenfeld, *Temples*, 169. [9] Jackson, *History*, 377–8.

bills; caricaturists lampooned the activities of amateur thespians; dramatists and novelists constructed narratives around them.[10] By refracting their performances through the medium of print culture the fashionable élite was thus able to exploit the political symbolism of theatricality without the drawbacks of a counter-theatre from the gallery; this not only represents a significant change in the attitudes of the upper class towards public culture but also indicates the emergence of the print media as a valuable tool in the shaping of public opinion. There were other, more specific, political benefits to be derived from private theatricals. Amateur acting provided a forum for the cementing of social and political relations within the élite and also allowed women an important mediatory role that was denied them in Westminster and other male dominated institutions. In April 1787, for example, a motion in the House of Commons was postponed on account of the fact that many parliamentarians were in attendance at the performance of *The Way to Keep Him* at Richmond House; those present included the Prince of Wales, Pitt, Fox, Sheridan, and the Duchesses of Richmond and Devonshire.[11] Many leading Whig families were identified as enthusiastic thespians; in this respect amateur acting can be regarded as part of a repertoire of behaviour—including libertine flamboyance, female exhibitionism, and the cultivation of public celebrity—that was used to define the Prince of Wales's party in defiance of the 'Farmer George' probity associated with the King.

Private theatricals were also an important element in the élite's paternalistic social role. Sponsorship of an amateur performance in a country house was one way of importing metropolitan culture to the provinces, reintegrating a great family with its servants and tenantry in the process and providing a useful stimulus to local economic and cultural development.[12] The private theatricals of the family of James Harris, for example, took place in the context of his general encouragement of theatre and

---

[10] For contemporary reports of private theatricals see Charles Burney, A Collection of Playbills, Notices and Press-cuttings Dealing With Private Theatrical Performances, 1750–1808, British Library. For plays about private theatricals see Dane Farnsworth Smith, *Plays About the Theatre in England, 1737–1800: or, The Self-Conscious Stage from Foote to Sheridan* (Cranbury, NJ, 1979), 132–47. The most significant novel to concern itself with the craze is of course Jane Austen's *Mansfield Park* (1814): see Sybil Rosenfeld, 'Jane Austen and Private Theatricals', *Essays and Studies*, 15 (1962), 40–51; Jonas Barish, *The Antitheatrical Prejudice* (Berkeley, Calif., 1981), 299–307; Joseph Litvak, 'The Infection of Acting: Theatricals and Theatricality in *Mansfield Park*', *ELH* 53 (1986), 331–55, which appears in a later version in his *Caught in the Act: Theatricality in the Nineteenth-Century English Novel* (Berkeley, Calif., 1992), 1–26.

[11] Rosenfeld, *Temples*, 38.

[12] See Paul Langford, *Public Life and the Propertied Englishman, 1689–1798* (Oxford, 1991), 383.

music in Salisbury and set an example for town notables as a whole.[13] That such an example was followed was to the benefit of not only the community but also of the noble family. The boredom of a sojourn in the country would be relieved by a more vital local culture; at the same time the publicity given to private theatricals in both the local and national press ensured that the aristocrat remained in the public eye even while 'in exile' in the country.

The temporary decline in upper-class theatricals which Sybil Rosenfeld traces to the 1790s was a reflection of the constraints and tensions of the period. Such conspicuous consumption and exhibitionism seemed out of place during a time of war, food riots, and political unrest. However, some of the leading exponents of the craze carried on regardless. The *Oracle* of 7 March 1795 noted how the Margravine of Anspach had 'commenced her THEATRICAL ENTERTAINMENTS for the season' with a performance which had been 'attended by persons of the first distinction'. On the same page the newspaper had also recorded that the patent theatres were suffering a decline in patronage: 'politics, the continuance of a war, and the pressure of taxes, stint the liberality of pleasure, and narrow the public munificence.' In such circumstances, playwrights, theatre managers, and actors came to regard private theatricals as a significant source of competition. Part of the plot of John O'Keeffe's comedy, *Wild Oats: Or The Strolling Gentlemen* involves a proposal of amateur theatricals by an aristocratic Quakeress, Lady Amaranth. Having discovered that her steward has wrongly evicted a poor tenant she inveighs against her decision to indulge in such amusements: 'I could chide myself that these pastimes have turned my eye from the house of woe. Ah! think, ye proud and happly affluent, how many, in your dancing moments, pine in want, drink the salt tear; their morsel, the bread of misery, and shrinking from the cold blast into their cheerless hovels.'[14] By aligning his critique of amateur theatricals with sentimentalist attacks on aristocratic mores, for example, in the plays of Inchbald or Holcroft, O'Keeffe was able to distance the commercial theatre from the proud and uncaring affluent.

The skirmishes between theatre professionals and aristocratic amateurs developed into a full-scale war when, in 1802, the Pic Nic Society was formed. Led by Colonel Henry Greville, the Pic Nics comprised a group of aristocratic thespians who established a subscription theatre in the

---

[13] Clive T. Probyn, *The Sociable Humanist: The Life and Works of James Harris 1709–1780* (Oxford, 1991), 230–4. See also Arnold Hare, *The Georgian Theatre in Wessex* (London, 1958), 120–40.

[14] John O'Keeffe, *Wild Oats: Or The Strolling Gentlemen* (London, 1794), 63.

concert rooms of Tottenham Street.[15] The Frenchman Anthony Le Texier, '*monolinguist, actor, violinist, manager, pyrotechnist*' and erstwhile associate of the Margravine of Anspach, was closely involved in the proceedings. He had made a career as an entertainment consultant to the titled and wealthy, and promoted events, such as dramatic monologues, in his own home in Lisle Street, Soho, which exploited public curiosity in the domestic amusements of the great.[16] It was this exploitation of the shady area between amateurism and professionalism, between private and public, which most alarmed R. B. Sheridan. No longer a supporter of the principle of a third theatre and anxious to protect his investment in Drury Lane, Sheridan mounted an extensive press campaign against the Pic Nic society exploiting the notoriety of female subscribers such as the Countess of Buckinghamshire who had been fined for illegal gambling in 1797. While the Pic Nics and their defenders stoutly asserted that no lady actually performed in public, the mud insinuated by Sheridan successfully adhered to the female subscribers of the society. Gillray's ambivalent caricature of the controversy, 'Blowing up the PIC NIC's;—or—Harlequin Quixotte attacking the Puppets', shows Sheridan leading a band of professional actors against the aristocratic amateurs. Sheridan's tricolour cockade insinuates an association with Revolutionary republicanism, while the professionals, including John Philip Kemble and Sarah Siddons, are carrying banners bearing the names of Otway, Rowe, Kotzebue, and Schiller. The leading banner, labelled Shakespeare, is significantly tattered and torn to indicate the dubious validity of the cause of the patent theatres. The depiction of the amateurs, who are performing Fielding's mock-heroic satire *Tom Thumb*, features the bare-breasted figure of the Countess of Buckinghamshire in the role of Dollalolla. In Gillray's representation, an artistically and politically bankrupt institution—Drury Lane—is quixotically tilting against the windmills of a morally dubious aristocratic alternative.[17]

Gillray's ambivalence indicates the difficulties faced by the patent houses in mounting an ideologically coherent resistance to the challenge of amateur theatricals by the élite. To invoke moral objections against acting *per se* or against female performers was to undermine the validity of its own practices: such criticisms had the effect of strengthening the cause

---

[15] See Henry Angelo, *Reminiscences of Henry Angelo* (2 vols.; London, 1828), i. 288–95.

[16] Philip H. Highfill Jr., Kalman A. Burnim, and Edward A. Langhans, *A Biographical Dictionary of Actors, Actresses, Musicians, Dancers, Managers & Other Stage Personnel in London, 1660–1800* (16 vols.; Carbondale, Ill., 1973–93), ix. 257. See also James Boaden, *Memoirs of the Life of John Philip Kemble* (2 vols.; London, 1825), i. 253–5.

[17] For further details of this caricature see George, *Satires*, viii. 107–9.

of the anti-theatricalists, while at the same time alienating those elements of society whose patronage Sheridan was ostensibly anxious to maintain. Of more fundamental and far-reaching significance was the fact that by establishing its own quasi-public entertainments in such a way, the élite had notified the patent theatres that it no longer needed their endorsement or the kinds of interaction with other classes of society that such institutions offered. Indeed, upper-class sponsors of the Pic Nic society went so far as to counter-attack Sheridan by asserting that the 'profligacy of public manners' was not to be found in the Tottenham Street concert rooms but in the various public tea gardens and taverns of the metropolis. A writer in the journal *Pic Nic* claimed that the entertainments of the 'mechanic' and the 'tradesman' were more 'dreadfully pernicious to the animal economy, and much more conducive to dissipation than a concerto of Haydn's'.[18] Such a strategy was designed to draw attention to the common threat faced by both the élite and the middling orders—a vital and expanding popular culture which was also a locus of ultra-radical activity.[19] The phenomenon of amateur theatricals was therefore part of a broader struggle for the definition and control of various kinds of sociability in late eighteenth-century Britain. As institutions based on the model of the centrality of theatre within public culture, the patent theatres had everything to lose in this struggle; the Pic Nic controversy served to confirm that there was in fact no homogeneous public culture to underpin the twin edifices of Covent Garden and Drury Lane.

Another significant dimension of late eighteenth-century amateur dramatics was the productions of the minor gentry and professional classes of the provinces. Typical of such occasions were the performances of *The Careless Husband*, *The Way to Keep Him*, and *Tom Thumb*, as described by Frances Burney, and the Austen family theatricals at Steventon rectory in the 1780s. Dorothea Herbert, who, like Jane Austen, was the daughter of a country rector, gave an account of an amateur theatrical performance in her *Retrospections* of her life in Carrick-on-Suir, Ireland:

The Old Garret the scene of most of our childish Pranks was our theatre—The Fair Penitent the play we chose—I had at once the laborious Tasks of painting the Scenes and fitting Myself for the formidable part of Calista—Otway acted Altamont—George Carshore Lothario—Miss Carshore Lavinia—and Tom the brave Horatio—We made the children act as Snobs, Stage Sweepers Guards Musicians and waiting Maids—All the Money we could rap or run was expended in Canvas, Whiting, Gambouge, Stone Blue and Oil for the Painter—and many a

---

[18] *Pic Nic*, 2 (1803), 164–5.   [19] See McCalman, *Radical Underworld*.

time the poor Boys denied themselves a halfpennyworth of Elecampane or Gingerbread to devote their little pocket Money to the Theatre—We got a friend to dig up a skull in the Church Yard and ransacked every place for Relicks to make the last Scene as dismal as possible—My Fathers old black Cassocks served for hangings, and his Wig converted Altamont into a venerable Sciolto—We had the whole Stage decorated with Pictures, flower pots Ribbons Shells Moss and Lobster Claws—Calista was dress'd in Virgin White with her beautiful golden Locks hanging in loose Ringlets and festoon'd with penny Rings and two penny Beads &c—Lavinia was dress'd in a Salmon Colour Stuff ornamented with Natural flowers—Great Interest was made by Captains Curtis and Perceval to be admitted as Snobs, but we limitted [*sic*] our Audience to the Carshores, Jephsons, Mr Rankin and some Others—Many were our failures and Mischances—Our Prompter not yet out of his spelling Book miscalled his Words or lost his place— The gallant gay Lothario grew sulky and refused to act his Part when the brave Horatio tilted him too roughly—The venerable Sciolto burst out laughing just in the act of introducing the lost Calista to the dead Body of her Lover—Calista and Lavinia fought desperately behind the scenes about change of Dresses—and finally the Candle snuffers set the Stage on fire.[20]

In contrast to highly publicized affairs such as the Margravine of Anspach's theatricals, the amateur productions of the provincial gentry were very much domestic occasions, rituals of family. The Herberts' production, for example, was one way in which the elder children of the family could confirm their status in relation to their younger siblings, confined to the roles of 'Stage Sweepers' or 'waiting Maids'. The enterprise of 'getting up' a play was also a means of strengthening links with trusted neighbouring families such as the Carshores, of possible long term importance to future alliances through marriage. In this latter context, the choice of play, Nicholas Rowe's *The Fair Penitent*, is significant. A 'shetragedy' of seduction and betrayal, Rowe's play was one of the most popular choices for amateur performance in the eighteenth century.[21] Apart from offering opportunities for histrionic excess, *The Fair Penitent* functioned as a vehicle for the negotiation of sexuality within the family and the definition of the gendered roles of boys and girls. In the case of the Herberts' performance, the allocation of roles is significant: Dorothea's brother Otway took the part of the betrayed husband Altamont, while George Carshore, the neighbour and 'outsider' in relation to the Herbert

[20] Dorothea Herbert, *Retrospections of Dorothea Herbert 1770–1806* (Dublin, 1988), 170–1.

[21] Rosenfeld, *Temples*, 169. Other frequently performed 'she-tragedies' were Thomas Otway's *Venice Preserv'd*, ed. M. Kelsall (London, 1969), and Nicholas Rowe's *Jane Shore*, ed. H. W. Pedicord (London, 1975).

family, played the role of the seducer Lothario. Dorothea, the chronicler of the event, was Calista, the tragic heroine who succumbs to the advances of Lothario. It was perhaps on account of the subject matter of the play that the performance was restricted to immediate family and neighbours: the two military men who showed 'Great Interest' in it, Captains Curtis and Perceval, may have been intrigued by the opportunity of witnessing a young girl in the role of an adult woman of dubious sexual morality. It is significant that the figure of authority in the Herbert household, Dorothea's father, is not mentioned directly but represented in terms of the emblems of his public role—the cassocks used as hangings and the wig which transforms Altamont into 'a venerable Sciolto' (the aggrieved father in Rowe's play). As in *Mansfield Park*, the theatricals at Carrick-on-Suir take place in an environment where patriarchal authority only seems to be in abeyance: such a dispensation allows for the expression of sexual and sibling tension, but temporarily, as the fact of the theatricals is predicated on the eventual restoration of the rule of the father.

The significance of family theatricals in the negotiation of a younger generation's 'entrance into the world' is also apparent in Frances Burney's account of a similar episode which took place during a visit to her cousin's home, Barborne Lodge, Worcestershire, in 1777. The plays performed were Arthur Murphy's genteel comedy, *The Way to Keep Him*, followed by a farce—Fielding's *Tom Thumb*. On this occasion male parental figures played a dominant role in the proceedings. Frances Burney was given advice and encouragement by her uncle, who seems to have supervised the production, while also present in the audience were two relative strangers to her, a Dr Wall and a militia officer, George Coussmaker. Being subject to such public (and male) scrutiny, Frances Burney suffered extreme self-consciousness and stage fright: 'When I came to be Painted, my Cheeks were already of so high a Colour, that I could hardly bear to have any added: but, before I went on, I seemed siezed [*sic*] with an Ague fit, & was so extremely Cold, that my Uncle, upon taking my Hand, said he thought he had touched ice or marble.'[22] Frances Burney was not the only member of the family to feel nervousness in this way: her cousin Edward was apprehensive about speaking the prologue which had probably been specially written for the occasion by his father. Other members of the family did not find acting such an ordeal, however. Cousin James played the part of the fop, Sir Brilliant Fashion, with 'such a satisfied, nay *insolent* assurance of success' that Frances, the object of his attentions in the role

---

[22] Fanny Burney, *The Early Journals and Letters of Fanny Burney*, ed. Lars E. Troide (2 vols.; Oxford, 1988), ii. 238.

of Mrs Lovemore, felt herself to be nearly overpowered: 'had I been entirely myself, & free from fear, he would have wholly disconcerted me: as it was, my flurry hardly admitted of encrease: yet I felt myself glow most violently.'[23] Later, in her scenes with her cousin Richard, playing the part of Mrs Lovemore, Frances noted how 'natural' and at ease he seemed in the role of husband. He performed his part 'admirably in character, & yet he seemed as if he *really could not help it*'.[24] With the exception of Edward, who seems to have had difficulties in speaking the words of his father, the younger male Burneys appear to have relished the performance of roles which anticipated their potential identities as adults. Whether as foppish man about town or the insouciant husband, it was always possible for eighteenth-century males to be 'in character', but as Frances Burney's account makes clear, the parts played by women—those of wife or daughter, subject to the supervision of husbands, fathers, and uncles—were not so readily adaptable to the public sphere. Her response to acting was not merely stage fright but a more fundamental recoil from the sexual and gender politics underlying this particular family ritual. The amateur theatricals at Barborne in effect initiated Frances Burney into the performance of womanhood, revealing that she was much more comfortable in a burlesque role such as that of Huncamunca in *Tom Thumb* (the 'extreme absurdity & queerness of my part contributed greatly to reviving me') than she was playing the more 'conventional' Mrs Lovemore.[25]

The amateur theatricals of the minor gentry were therefore important on a number of levels—they not only enacted and defined family relationships but also educated the younger generation in the gendered roles which they would perform as adults. For boys, the construction of 'manliness' also entailed the capacity to bond successfully in an institutional context—hence the fact that play-acting was an intrinsic part of the curriculum of public schools and military academies. Westminster School in London was well known for its annual production of a Greek or Latin play, often given prominent notice in newspapers and theatrical journals. The school also staged pieces from the English repertory such as *King John* and the ubiquitous *High Life Below Stairs*.[26] In 1805 part of the 'Annual Rhetorical Exercises of the Gosport Naval Academy' involved the performance of a tragedy entitled *Thermopylae or Repulsed Invasion*: 'Several striking stage pictures are happily introduced; such as a dying hero, transferring the untasted cup of water to a wounded soldier . . . the capture of Xerxes's royal standard—the crowning of the young king, as

[23] Burney, *Early Journals*, ii. 240.   [24] Ibid. 243.   [25] Ibid. 248.
[26] Burney, Collection of Playbills; see Baer, *Theatre and Disorder*, 170 n. 17.

the curtain falls upon the kneeling Spartans, &c.'[27] Such exercises in dramatic performance inculcated young men with the heroic ideals and *esprit de corps* necessary for future officers of Nelson's navy.

Beyond the naval academies and public schools there were the amateur acting societies or spouting clubs where lower ranking military men, artisans, and clerks staged their own theatrical entertainment. These clubs were independent of sources of authority—the schoolmaster, the captain, the father—and afforded young men the opportunity for conviviality and free association. The plays performed there included many of the pieces identified with dilettanti theatricals—farces and comedies such as *Bon Ton* and *The Heir at Law*. In addition, many aspiring actors would essay speeches from plays such as *Hamlet* and *Macbeth* that were collected in spouters' companions. On account of their independence from other forms of social and cultural control, spouting clubs were stigmatized as sites of vice and dissipation.[28] For William Oxberry, writing in the 1820s about such a club in Catherine Street, London, they were the haunts of a theatrical under-class and of dubious criminal types: 'we do verily believe that every notorious theatrical ruffian in London had assembled—fellows, illiterate and ragged, and whose looks were so expressive, that we instinctively kept our hands upon our watches and pockets.'[29] Amateur acting, therefore, was not the preserve of a particular rank or grouping but was to be found across the social spectrum. An indication of its considerable appeal, especially to hierarchical institutions such as the military, is to be found in an anecdote in the memoirs of Robert Dyer, a professional actor who gained his early experience in a Plymouth spouting club known as the Stonehouse Amateur Company. Dyer claimed that a corporal in the Marines had committed embezzlement in order to maintain his payments to the society and that as a result of his crime he had been flogged and demoted.[30] In this case, amateur acting was something for which the corporal was prepared to risk physical punishment as well as his career. For such men the spouting clubs were places where scenarios of social transformation could be enacted—an artisan could play Lord Duberley in *The Heir at Law*, for example, or a lowly corporal could strut the stage as Othello or Macbeth. Spouting was thus capable of articulating basic social aspirations, offering not simply a counter-theatre to the élite amateurs of

---

[27] *Hampshire Chronicle*, 22 Apr. 1805.

[28] John A. Thieme, 'Spouting, Spouting Clubs and Spouting Companions', *Theatre Notebook*, 29 (1975), 9–16.

[29] William Oxberry, *Dramatic Biography, and Histrionic Anecdotes* (5 vols.; London, 1825–6), v. 54.

[30] Robert Dyer, *Nine Years of an Actor's Life* (London, 1833), 4.

6. The 1814 Jubilee

7. Mrs Jordan as Little Pickle in *The Spoil'd Child*

8. The Patent Theatres attack fashionable theatricals

9. James Hadfield's attempted assassination of George III in Drury Lane

the Pic Nic society but an appropriation of the political language of the latter's performance.

Military Theatricals

Amateur theatricals were therefore an important means of rehearsing many of the central preoccupations of late Georgian society—the education of young people, the construction of gender, the political visibility of the élite, the theatricality of social behaviour, and in particular, the relations between public and private culture. In the next part of this chapter I want to examine the importance of amateur acting to the army and navy, an integral part of this broader cultural phenomenon. The military thespian was likely to have had experience of amateur theatricals in other, civilian contexts: he could have taken part in family dramatics (as in the case of Jane Austen's naval brothers); acted in performances at his public school or military academy; or participated in fashionable theatricals such as those of the Margravine of Anspach. If a mason, he may have indulged in theatrical performances at his lodge. The lower ranking soldier and sailor, on the other hand, may well have been a denizen of a spouting club such as the Stonehouse Amateur Company. The various political and social contexts of these activities bore significantly on the phenomena of military theatre, of which I want to distinguish two types at this point: first, performances in England, and secondly, shipboard theatre off the coast of England and elsewhere.

A typical example of the kind of military theatre which took place in England during the French wars is that described by the *Portsmouth Telegraph* on 24 November 1800:

WEYMOUTH THEATRICALS.—On Tuesday the two favourite farces of *Bon Ton* and *High Life Below Stairs* were performed by the Officers of the Somerset Militia, for the laudable purpose of applying the receipts of the House to relieve the distressed Poor of that Place. The principal parts were most ably supported by Sir Charles Bamfield, Major Prowse, Captain Barton, Lieut. Hudson, and Ensign Redmond. The House was a bumper. Among the fashionables were, Lady Shaftesbury and her beautiful daughter, Lady Taylor, and her amiable family, the Honourables Mrs. Bennet and Mrs. Fitzgerald, Mr. and Mrs. Sturt, Lord Lisle, &c. &c. &c.

This account shares many of the conventions of the reporting of other theatricals by the civilian élite—most notably a reluctance to enter into any serious criticism of the actors. The major significance of the performance was its status as a social occasion, as indicated by the reference by name to the military performers and their fashionable guests. On this occasion, as on many others, the audience was as much on show as the military actors. The location of the theatricals in the resort town of Weymouth was also significant: it was patronized by the King and Queen and by many noteworthy families, so the 'getting up' of a play there was likely to gain not only local but also national attention for the Somerset Militia. This kind of event can be linked with the cultural politics of élite theatricals as a whole—the desire to assert the hegemony of the fashionable while at the same time exerting control over the public space that it occupied. One military corps in particular was closely associated with amateur theatrical performances—the Brigade of Guards, recruited primarily from the higher echelons of society and well known for its exclusivity and fashionable pretensions. In March 1802 members of the Brigade of Guards performed Shakespeare's *King John* and Foote's *The Minor* at The Theatre, Rochester, before the Earl of Chatham and an audience of 'the first rank and fashion'.[31] Three years later the Rochester theatre was again the venue for a theatrical production by the officers of the Guards— the tragedy of *Douglas* by John Home, followed by another farce by Foote, *The Prize*.[32] Other fashionable regiments chose to emulate them: in March 1804 the Life Guards chose the home of the Pic Nic society, the Tottenham Street concert rooms, as a venue for the performance of *The Revenge* by Edward Young. The *Morning Post* noted the presence of that doyenne of amateur theatricals—the Margravine of Anspach with 'her usual party'.[33] In September 1804 officers of the Coldstream, Third Guards, West Norfolk, and West Yorkshire regiments collaborated in a production of *The Heir at Law* and *The Mayor of Garratt* at Coxheath Camp, for which a theatre was specially constructed. 'A more brilliant assemblage of fashion has never been witnessed', exclaimed the *Morning Post* in its report of the evening: 'present were the Earl and Countess of CHATHAM, Earl and Countess TEMPLE, Lord SOUTHAMPTON and family, the neighbouring Nobility, and the Officers of the camp.'[34] In December 1804 the Earl and Countess of Chatham were again the patrons of a private performance at Chatham: officers of the Coldstream and Third Guards and the Royal Artillery staged *The Merry Wives of Windsor*.[35]

The plays performed by these military actors represented the conventional fare of fashionable theatricals—farces such as *The Mayor of Garratt* and *Bon Ton* which enabled officers to indulge themselves in stereotypical

---

[31] *Monthly Mirror*, 13 (1802), 219–20.   [32] Ibid. 19 (1805), 201–2.
[33] *Morning Post*, 22 Mar. 1804.   [34] Ibid. 26 Sept. 1804.
[35] Ibid. 17 Dec. 1804.

'low life' roles. Mr Babington of the Third Guards achieved notable success as a stage Irishman in the performance of *The Heir at Law* at Coxheath in 1804. According to the *Morning Post*, 'his dialect was admirable; he sympathised in the distresses of *Caroline Dormer* with much feeling, and never lost sight of the duties of a faithful servant'.[36] Many reports of theatricals in newspapers and journals include cast lists suggesting that those in the fashionable world who knew the officers concerned were being encouraged to evaluate the appropriateness or otherwise of their roles, as was the custom in the commercial theatre. Officers performed tragedy and comedy to indicate their virtuosity: thus Mr Babington, the stage Irishman of *The Heir at Law* appeared as Lord Randolph in the performance of *Douglas* at Rochester in 1805, while the multi-talented Captain Braddyll played the eponymous role in *King John* in 1802 and, in the same evening, those of Swift and Smirk in the farce of *The Minor*. Other popular pieces were tragedies such as *The Revenge*, *Mahomet*, and *The Orphan of China* which offered possibilities for exotic display—of major importance to a military élite which defined itself through excessive costuming. In the case of the Guards' performance of *King John*, the costumes, specially made by 'Messrs. Brooks and Heath of Newport-street, were superb and characteristic almost beyond precedent', while a report of a production of *The Orphan of China* by the officers of the Ipswich and Colchester garrison commended 'the splendour and propriety of the Tartar and Chinese costumes'.[37] The military performers in the production of *Mahomet* at the Chichester theatre in February 1805 were decorated with the spoils of recent colonial adventures. According to the *Hampshire Telegraph*, Mahomet wore 'the robe of *Tippoo Sultan* and the sword of the *Dey of Tunis*; The matchless Oriental shawls which composed their dress were alone worth 300*l*. Nor were the other Turkish habiliments of farther inferiority than in gradation of rank. The turbans were particularly fanciful and elegant, and jewels to a large amount were worn in collars, bandeaus, belts &c.'[38]

Amateur play-acting thus had the dual function of gratifying the military's sense of its own theatricality as well as enhancing its public profile: as such, it was a logical extension of playgoing. It was especially significant to members of the military, such as the Guards, in that it reinforced their social links with the fashionable world and extended the cultural ambit of the camps. Lower-ranking officers and the common soldiery in particular

---

[36] Ibid. 26 Sept. 1804.
[37] *Monthly Mirror*, 13 (1802), 220; *Morning Post*, 25 Sept. 1806.
[38] *Hampshire Telegraph*, 18 Feb. 1805.

had no part to play in these entertainments which were notable for their social exclusivity. Unlike the theatricals of the Margravine of Anspach and other aristocratic families, military performance did not take place in country or town houses but in the commercial theatres, specially hired for the occasion. This practice enabled élite corps such as the Guards to select their own audience, which usually meant the exclusion of undesirable soldiers and civilians. In 1805 the officers playing *Douglas* at the Rochester theatre went so far as to alter the configuration of the auditorium, replacing the pit with boxes and raising the price of a gallery ticket from one to three shillings. Such practices can be regarded as an extension of the attempts of the officer class to assert their political presence within the commercial theatres; if they could not compel the gallery into submission, they would exclude it altogether. This appropriation of the commercial theatres was, if anything, more far-reaching in its implications than the retreat of the fashionable world to their own theatricals in so far as it signalled the power of the military to control a politically charged public space. As many disturbances customarily affirmed, playgoing was one of the inviolable rights of Englishmen, a right that was being denied when officers took over the theatre for their own performances.

Military theatricals had other political implications. While officers were displaying their histrionic talent in the theatres, those under their command were subjecting the civilian community to a different kind of performance. In February 1805 the *Hampshire Telegraph* noted that the 'Charity Play by the Military Officers at Chichester, will take place on Tuesday next . . . Tickets to nearly twice the contents of the Theatre have been disposed of.' The report went on:

We are sorry to be obliged to report the continued depredations of the soldiery in the neighbourhood of Lewes: Mr Peckham, music master of that town, was one night last week stopped at Northease, and forced into a field, by three men in soldiers' jackets, with every apparent symptom of impending ill usage, when the approach of a horseman relieved him, and occasioned the flight of the villains.[39]

Amateur theatricals need to be regarded in the context of a local community's experience of the military as a whole. Events such as the performance at the Chichester theatre were one way in which officers could distinguish themselves from the mass of men under their command. The discreet elegance of a 'private' entertainment at the theatre represented a very different image of the military to that of a villainous soldiery marauding the Sussex countryside. Such contrasts were hardly likely to assure

---

[39] *Hampshire Telegraph*, 11 Feb. 1805.

civilians of the unanimity of the armed forces, nor to promote confidence in a national army, united in the cause of patriotism.

The appropriation of the commercial theatres by the military inevitably involved some kind of relationship with theatre professionals. It was often an uneasy one. The patronage of the Earl and Countess of Chatham was undoubtedly welcome to managers such as Sarah Baker, who derived most of her custom in Rochester from the officers of the Chatham garrison. But her labours, and those of the people who worked for her, were generally treated with condescension by the military thespians. The social stigma associated with the professional theatre was such that young gentlemen were careful to distinguish their activities as strictly amateur: they did not wish to be tainted with the reputation of mere players. Thus it was customary for military performers not to employ any of the auxiliary staff of the theatres but to do everything themselves, ranging from scene construction and painting to costuming and music. The 'admirable band' of the Tyrone militia, for example, played the music before and between the acts of *Henry IV Part One*, performed by the gentlemen of the garrison at Clonmell, Ireland, in 1806, while the scenery was 'executed by an amateur artist of distinction'.[40] Problems inevitably arose in relation to the performance of female roles. Military amateurs were faced with the dilemma of either compromising their masculinity by playing female parts, or risking moral censure by too close involvement with professional actresses of dubious reputation. A compromise of sorts was achieved, whereby actresses were hired to perform female roles in mainpiece tragedies and comedies, while officers continued to play obviously burlesque female characters in farces. The delicacy surrounding the issue was such that the *Monthly Mirror*'s cast list for the performance of *King John* at Rochester does not include the name of Mrs Litchfield, a well-known professional actress who played the part of Constance. Her contribution is acknowledged at the very end of its account of the evening in a way that marginalizes her role and clearly distinguishes between her professionalism and the amateurism of the officers: 'We had almost forgotten to mention that Mrs Litchfield, of Covent-Garden theatre, performed *Constance* . . . A very handsome present has been made her, in a gold purse, as a compensation for her services on this occasion.'[41]

One way in which the military was able to deflect criticism of their use of the commercial theatres was by dedicating the proceeds of their performances to charity. The production of *Bon Ton* and *High Life Below*

[40] *Monthly Mirror*, 22 (1806), 279.   [41] Ibid. 13 (1802), 220.

Stairs at Weymouth was 'for the laudable purpose of applying the receipts of the House to relieve the distressed Poor of that place'.[42] The Guards' performance of *Douglas* and *The Prize* at Rochester was 'for the benefit of the poor in the vicinity': profits from the production of *Mahomet* at Chichester in 1805 were 'appropriated to the charity for supplying the poor with cheap coals'.[43] As such, the military was able to attach itself to one of the most significant forces in late Georgian society—that of local philanthropy, in which the theatre had always played an important role. Throughout the eighteenth century provincial managers had justified the existence of their theatres by allowing them to be used for charitable purposes.[44] Profits devoted to the poor countered criticism from the Church and other anti-theatricalists, especially during periods when the community as a whole was suffering from economic hardship. Philanthropy was a complex phenomenon which could articulate local independence and pride as well as promote class differentiation in terms of those who gave and those who received. Many charitable functions, such as theatre benefit nights, were not entirely altruistic: money raised on these occasions could prevent increases in the poor rates, likely to be more costly in the long run to the pockets of the beneficent.[45] Charitable activity also functioned as a way in which disenfranchised urban groups—professionals, retailers, small masters, dissenting intellectuals, artisans, women—could exert power and influence within the community: 'philanthropy could be appropriated as a badge of fashionable, genteel culture, bringing together town and county notables in a dazzling display of the enlightened munificence of wealth and rank which refracted on to even the most modest participants.'[46] Many provincial theatre managers, entrepreneurs of a consumer culture, belonged to these urban groups, and the dedication of their playhouses to charitable purposes was one way of asserting the civility of the stage and their own status within society. The theatre, moreover, was especially important as a forum in which charity could be seen to be done. Playbills proclaimed benefit nights and, indirectly, the generosity of their patrons: occasional prologues extolled the

---

[42] *Portsmouth Telegraph*, 24 Nov. 1800.

[43] *Monthly Mirror*, 19 (1805), 201; *Hampshire Telegraph, and Sussex Chronicle*, 4 Feb. 1805.

[44] Borsay, *English Urban Renaissance*, 119, 266.

[45] See Jewson, *Jacobin City*, 62, and *Oracle*, 5 Jan. 1795; also A. Temple Patterson, *Radical Leicester: A History of Leicester 1780–1850* (Leicester, 1954), 125.

[46] Kathleen Wilson, 'Urban Culture and Political Activism in Hanoverian England: The Example of Voluntary Hospitals' in *The Transformation of Political Culture: England and Germany in the Late Eighteenth Century*, ed. Eckhart Hellmuth (London, 1990), 177.

charitable instincts of theatre audiences and the social groups they represented. The exertion of philanthropy in this way shows the theatre to be
intimately involved in the construction and maintenance of power structures in Georgian provincial society. The fact that the military had recourse to it in order to justify its own theatricality is significant. Charity,
in the form of benefit performances, enabled elements of the officer class
to exercise a paternalistic role within society, one which overlapped with
their gentlemanly origins and identities. But the other context of philanthropy—its use by competing social groups as a means of demonstrating
a place in the community—is a reminder that the military, too, had to
struggle to assert its own position in a society which traditionally regarded
it with ambivalence.

Naval Theatricals

Military theatricals represented one of the ways in which the Georgian
army was 'within but distinct' from society as a whole. The appropriation
of such a culturally significant site as the commercial theatre for its own
'private' performances enabled officers to assert their own prestige and
exclusivity, while at the same time integrating themselves culturally and
politically with other urban groups and social practices. The amateur
theatricals of the navy, however, do not have the same kind of configuration as those of the army, due to the essentially different roles of the two
services. The most meaningful venue for naval theatricality was the ship
itself, a closely knit and complex fighting unit with its own rituals,
language, and costume. 'A lonely village', in the words of the naval
historian Michael Lewis, the ship of the Royal Navy was foreign to the
rest of society, a celebrated 'wooden world' of which most civilians knew
nothing.[47] Much more than was the case with the common soldier, sailors
on shore were a race apart, characterized by a distinctive dress, language,
and manner. Moreover, to the sailor himself, accustomed to a lifetime of
seafaring, civilian society could be an alien one: as I indicated previously,
the theatres of naval towns such as Portsmouth or Sheerness were important sites of cultural mediation between the familiar domain of the ship
and the strangeness of the world beyond.

Naval theatricals were therefore much more introverted and self-reflex-
ive affairs than those of the military élite. They bear analogies with the

[47] Michael Lewis, *A Social History of the Navy 1793–1815* (London, 1960), 243. See also
N. A. M. Rodger, *The Wooden World: An Anatomy of the Georgian Navy* (London, 1986), 15.

theatricals of the Herberts and the Burneys in that they were low-key events, designed for the entertainment of the shipboard community—the naval 'family'. As such they could enact the kind of familial tensions that I have described earlier in relation to the Burneys and the Herberts—conflicts of hierarchy, gender, and sexuality. While ships were homosocial environments, they were not exclusively so. Women were a significant presence, especially when ships were in port which amounted to more than half the time of their commission, even during wartime.[48] Some of these women were prostitutes, the 'defiled and defiling' according to one sailor, but others were wives of ratings and commissioned officers.[49] Children, the offspring of these women, or young boys sent to prepare themselves for a naval career, were also an integral part of the ship community. The sexual life of a Georgian ship could be a complex one, ranging from open heterosexual intercourse on the lower decks to difficult and dangerous homosexual encounters, punishable by death. Children and adolescent boys were early initiates into sexuality on board ship: 'courts-martial show quite numerous cases of child molesting by officers. In the first few months of 1808 alone, there were three such cases.'[50] Apart from active sexual practices, the close-knit nature of naval warfare also encouraged strong homosocial bonding, not necessarily of a sexual nature, but equally, if not more, significant to life on board ship.

The thoroughly sexualized environment of this Georgian 'wooden world' had to be strictly controlled, chiefly by ignoring the presence of women and thus the heterosexuality that they represented, and by enforcement of capital punishment for buggery. Executions for the latter increased dramatically after 1797, the year of the mutinies at the Nore and Spithead, a sign that the authorities regarded mutiny and sexual deviance as synonymous.[51] In addition to the potential for sexual tension on board ship there were the constant strains of maintaining the complex hierarchies of naval rank and social class which, as N. A. M. Rodger points out, were not necessarily synonymous. There was no clear-cut class barrier separating officers and gentlemen from the rest of a ship's crew:

In reality the company of every ship was divided in many overlapping, ambiguous and untidy ways, some ill defined by the regulations, and some not mentioned at

---

[48] Rodger, *Wooden World*, 38.

[49] Samuel Leech, *A Voice from the Main Deck*, quoted in Henry Baynham, *From the Lower Deck: The Old Navy 1780–1840* (London, 1969), 94.

[50] Brian Lavery, *Nelson's Navy: The Ships, Men and Organisation 1793–1815* (London, 1989), 210.

[51] See Gilbert, 'Sexual Deviance and Disaster' and 'Buggery and the British Navy'.

all . . . The formal system of ranks and ratings distinguished commissioned officers (who were also sea officers), warrant officers who were sea officers and those
who were reckoned only as inferior officers, petty officers with the status of
inferior officers, and others who were simply ratings, slightly superior to the rest
of 'the people', the common term for the ratings of the ship as a body . . . Across
all these boundaries, affecting them all but corresponding with none, lay the
invisible distinctions of social class, distributing gentlemen and tradesmen, noble-
men and artisans with careless impartiality among the ranks and ratings.[52]

The complicating factor of social class became even more significant after
the passing of the Quota Acts in 1795. Many of these impressed sailors
were Irishmen, some of them unsympathetic to the cause of Britannia: 25
per cent of the crew of the *Victory* who took part in England's finest hour,
the Battle of Trafalgar, were in fact Irish.[53] The subtly nuanced divisions
within a ship's company were also signified through territorial hierarchies:
every sailor had an allotted station, and a particular part of the ship where
he ate and slept. The territory of the captain—the quarterdeck—was
bounded by ritual and symbolism which stressed its significance as a site
of authority and privilege. The system of discipline on board ship was
inherently theatrical in so far that every act of punishment, ranging from
the ritual of a flogging to an admonition by word or look, was played out
before others with the potentiality of resistance.[54] There were thus distinct
similarities between the theatre and the ship of the line as social institutions. Both conjoined 'rulers' and 'ruled', allowing for many subtle kinds
of theatre and counter-theatre. Both were segregated spaces with highly
conscious and coded hierarchies. It is not surprising that sailors, whose
lives were determined by territorial space, felt 'at home' in the provincial
theatre. When on land the 'wooden world' of the high seas found its most
meaningful analogy in the small, intimate environment of the Georgian
playhouse.

Cultural life on board ship reflected the complex and ambiguous nature
of naval hierarchies, the 'untidiness' emphasized by N. A. M. Rodger.
Commissioned officers and the people associated in different parts of the
ship, but in such a small environment it was difficult to maintain the kind
of cultural distinctions that were apparent on land. As so much of a ship's
time was spent at anchor in the roads of the English Channel or in the
blockade of enemy ports, entertainment was an important means of dis-
pelling boredom, often the seed-bed of a more dangerous disaffection. It

---

[52] Rodger, *Wooden World*, 16.   [53] Wells, *Insurrection*, 82.
[54] For a more detailed discussion of this see Dening, *Mr Bligh's Bad Language*, esp.
81–3.

was therefore in a captain's interests to patronize and encourage the cultural interests of his crew. One sailor, Samuel Leech, claimed that but for the opportunity to sing or laugh together 'life in a man-of-war with severe officers, would be absolutely intolerable; mutiny or desertion would mark the voyages of every such ship'. Leech compared the singing of a ship's crew with that of the slave population of the American south: 'they do it . . . to drown in sensual gratification the voice of misery that groans in the inner man.'[55] Many ships maintained a band of musicians whose task was not only to maintain the morale of the crew but also to entertain visiting dignitaries, both naval and civilian. Dorothy Jordan, the most famous actress in the land after Sarah Siddons, was welcomed on board the *Victory* by the ship's band during a visit to Portsmouth in 1812. She claimed that she 'never was so astonished or so gratified by any sight in my life'.[56] These bands of musicians enabled captains and commissioned officers to exploit the ship as a venue for their social activities, thus maintaining their ties with local civilian élites. On a visit to Fiume in 1807 a Captain Campbell invited the English consul and 'a party of ladies and gentlemen' to a ball staged on the quarterdeck of his command, the *Unite*. The ship's company were permitted to watch the proceedings, but it is likely that they were equally on display to Captain Campbell's civilian friends as evidence of his naval authority.[57]

Another significant recreation on board ship was reading. Matthew Lewis, author of *The Monk* and *The Castle Spectre*, noted the activities of the crew of his merchant ship while on a visit to the West Indies in 1816: 'The carpenter was very seriously spelling a comedy; Edward was engaged with "The Six Princesses of Babylon;" a third was amusing himself with a tract "On the Management of Bees;" another had borrowed the cabin-boy's "Sorrows of Werter".'[58] The availability of forms of serial publication, especially of plays, ensured that literature could be cheaply bought and conveniently transported aboard ship, while enlightened captains, such as Sir Sidney Smith, maintained libraries which they encouraged their men to use. On some ships there were even printing presses capable of producing playbills and other material that would enhance the status of

[55] Leech, *Voice from the Main Deck*, in Baynham, *From the Lower Deck*, 95.

[56] Dorothy Jordan, *Mrs Jordan and her Family: Being the Unpublished Correspondence of Mrs. Jordan and the Duke of Clarence, Later William IV*, ed. A. Aspinall (London, 1951), 243.

[57] Robert Mercier Wilson, 'Journal 1805–1809' in *Five Naval Journals 1789–1817*, ed. H. G. Thursfield (London, 1951), 177.

[58] M. G. Lewis, *Journal of a West India Proprietor, Kept During a Residence in the Island of Jamaica* (London, 1834), 34.

the crew's cultural activities.[59] For some men of relatively low social status, the navy offered opportunities for self-improvement and possible advancement. Matthew Lewis's reference to the carpenter 'spelling a comedy' suggests that theatrical activity and progress in literacy were often linked. Acting and reading could function as the means whereby an intelligent sailor gained the attention, and patronage, of a sympathetic superior. An example of this is the case of Robert Hay, an uneducated weaver from Scotland who joined the navy because of lack of employment at home. He became servant to Edward Hawke Locker, the admiral's secretary on *HMS Culloden*, learnt to read and write, and eventually emulated his patron by composing a prologue for a play to be acted on board ship. It was rejected by the manager of the production on the grounds of Hay's poor spelling, to which the sailor responded: 'Whoever heard such nonsense! Had it been all good otherwise how, if it had been rightly spoken, were the audience to know whether or not it was rightly spelt . . . I began it with taking a view of the theatre and of the audience contrasting them with the metropolitan stages and audiences.'[60]

It is a measure of Hay's ambition (or presumption) that he should attempt to write a prologue, a privilege usually reserved within amateur theatricals for those in positions of prestige or authority—the father, a favourite son, a commissioned officer. In conjunction with playbills, prologues represent the main evidence for amateur acting within the navy. The former have survived in the personal papers of prominent naval men such as Captain Hardy of the *Victory*, while many of the latter were published in the *Naval Chronicle*, the journal of the senior service. The reporting of amateur performances on board ship differs significantly from the way in which military theatricals are represented in the pages of theatrical journals such as the *Monthly Mirror* and newspapers such as the *Morning Post*. Occasional prologues were composed for and spoken at military theatricals within Britain, but they were not deemed as important as cast lists, usually based on playbills circulated before and during a performance. As I have emphasized previously, for the military much of the social value of amateur acting lay in personal publicity and the reinforcement of links with fashionable society. Such self interest coincided with the print media's preoccupation with the activities of the *bon ton*,

[59] See Vanessa Histon Roberts, 'Publishing and Printing on Board Ship', *Mariner's Mirror*, 74 (1988), 329–34.

[60] Robert Hay, *Landsman Hay: The Memoirs of Robert Hay 1789–1847*, ed. M. D. Hay (London, 1953), 129.

hence the importance of identifying both actors and members of the audience. In contrast, naval theatricals were primarily designed for the entertainment of the ship's company and, occasionally, interested observers. Moreover, their location, in ships anchored in the roads of the English Channel or in the war zone of the Mediterranean, restricted their accessibility to both fashionable society and journalists. In these conditions of geographical, social, and cultural isolation, the opportunities given by the prologue for self-definition and justification assumed a considerable importance.

Before I discuss some examples of prologues spoken before performances on board ship, I would like to consider the significance of playbills, prologues, and epilogues within late Georgian theatre practices and culture as a whole. They were integral to the ritual of theatre-going in this period but because of their dubious cultural status they have been largely ignored by literary critics and historians. As printed texts, they cannot be so readily accommodated within privileged literary genres. Prologues and epilogues, for example, occupy a literary no man's land somewhere between the kind of occasional verse recuperated by Roger Lonsdale in the *New Oxford Book of Eighteenth Century Verse* and the canon of dramatic literature. Whether or not they are included as part of the printed text of a play can reveal a great deal about its literary status: if included, the play will be historicized, often in relation to a specific performance, a practice that many editors would reject. An additional problem is that because prologues and epilogues reflect the collaborative nature of work in the theatre, they may not be by the same author, or as Shirley Strum Kenny has emphasized 'have nothing to do with the contents of the play'.[61] In Kenny's terms, the inclusion of prologues and epilogues carries the risk of diminishing the integrity of not only the authorial voice but also the literary content of the play itself.

This neglect of the prologue and epilogue is to be regretted on a number of grounds. In dramatic terms, they were important vehicles for the distinctive self-consciousness that characterized the Georgian theatre. Many a lachrymose comedy is framed by a sceptical prologue or epilogue, while actors exploited their conventions in order to establish their stage personae. Audiences found themselves mirrored, mocked, and flattered within them, while playwrights and managers used the prologue and epilogue in order to advance their own programme for the theatre, cajoling and sometimes hectoring a recalcitrant

[61] Shirley Strum Kenny, 'The Playhouse and the Printing Shop: Editing Restoration and Eighteenth-Century Plays', *Modern Philology*, 85 (1987–8), 412.

public.[62] Most represented the audience more deferentially, as the 'masters' to whom the 'servants' of the theatre paid their nightly respects. The performance of the prologue and epilogue was thus a rehearsal of customary obligations based on an ideology which regarded the actor as socially, politically, and morally subject to his or her 'betters' in the audience. Their gradual disappearance from nineteenth-century practice was due not only to the rise of naturalistic performance conventions but also to social and political changes that made the actor less inclined to maintain this show of servility. Prologues and epilogues were also important in registering the temporality of a particular theatrical event—that is, actual performance time, the 'here and now' of a group of actors preparing to play before an audience, as opposed to the various levels of temporal signification operating within the play itself.[63] Once printed, rather than enunciated from the stage, prologues and epilogues inscribe this temporality: thus the most famous prologue of the eighteenth century, written by Samuel Johnson to inaugurate the new dispensation of the English Roscius, has the title 'Spoken by Mr. Garrick at the Opening of the Theatre Royal, Drury Lane, 1747'. The emphasis within the prologue and epilogue on performance time is a factor in their political significance—the 'here and now' encompassed the world outside the theatre as well as what was happening on stage. The politicization of certain performances, especially of old plays, was often achieved most successfully in a prologue which explicitly related the occasion of the performance to topical events.

Like the prologue and epilogue, the playbill was an integral part of the experience of Georgian theatre-going. Without one, claimed Leigh Hunt, 'no true play-goer can be comfortable'.[64] Charles Lamb claimed that the casual sight of an old playbill, dating from 1799, had led him to remember how important they were to the theatrical event, how playgoers had spelled out 'every name, down to the mutes and servants of the scene' in a kind of litany.[65] Sold both inside and outside the patent theatres, or touted by strolling players in country towns, playbills had a distinctive set of rhetorical and typographical conventions, so familiar to the public that

[62] For collections of prologues and epilogues see Mary E. Knapp, *Prologues and Epilogues of the Eighteenth Century* (New Haven, Conn., 1961), and Pierre Danchin (ed.), *The Prologues and Epilogues of the Eighteenth Century, A Complete Edition* (Nancy, 1990).

[63] For temporal levels in the dramatic text see Keir Elam, *The Semiotics of Theatre and Drama* (London, 1980), 118.

[64] Leigh Hunt, *Dramatic Criticism 1808–1831*, ed. L. H. Houtchens and C. W. Houtchens (London, 1950), 232.

[65] Lamb, *Works*, ii. 132.

they were often parodied for political purposes. A broadside from the invasion scare of 1803 begins:

> Theatre Royal, England
> In rehearsal, and meant to be speedily *attempted*,
> A FARCE
> In One Act, called THE
> Invasion of England
> Principal Buffo, Mr BUONAPARTE
> Being his FIRST (and most likely his Last) Appearance on this Stage[66]

Amateur actors on Nelson's flagship used the conventions of the playbill in a similar way when they declared themselves to be the 'Theatre Royal Victory', an assertion of their importance within the national polity.[67] This suggests that the ritualistic aspects of the theatrical event—the distribution of playbills, the composition and performance of the prologue, even phrases such as 'getting up a play'—were capable of conveying a powerful sense of community, affirming the significance of an amateur performance as a distinctively British social occasion. For military men the temporality of the prologue, epilogue, or playbill could also be highly significant; the heightened sense of time conveyed by such practices paralleled a soldier or sailor's perception of the distinctiveness of time at war. The prologue not only commemorated the specificity of a performance but also the specificity of the military community itself—its temporal and geographical place in the continuum of conflict. Publication of prologues in the *Naval Chronicle* introduced a further dimension in that the theatrical event thereby acquired the status and 'permanence' of the printed text, entering the historical record of the navy. One such prologue, spoken on board *HMS Britannia* during the blockade of Cadiz in 1805, begins by defining the audience:

> My *Lord* and *Gentlemen*—alas! off Cadiz,
> How hard it is we can't address the *Ladies*!
> For 'if the *brave* alone deserve the *fair*,'
> BRITANNIA's Sons should surely have *their* share!
> But, since their valour, tho' upon record,
> Like other merits, is its own reward;
> Tho' *female* charms inspire us not—again
> We welcome *you*—my *Lord* and *Gentlemen*!

[66] 'Theatre Royal, England' in Broadsides etc. Relating to the Expected Invasion of England by Bonaparte, British Library.

[67] 'Theatre Royal Victory', MS playbill, Captain Hardy's papers, National Maritime Museum, Greenwich.

You, too, brave fellows! who the *back ground* tread,
Alike we welcome—jackets *blue* or *red*![68]

The 'Lord' was the Earl of Northesk, rear-admiral and patron of the theatrical entertainment on board the *Britannia*: the gentlemen were the flagship's officers; the 'brave fellows' in the 'back ground' the company of sailors and marines. The prologue refers to the conventions of its equivalent in the commercial theatre—in particular the chivalrous acknowledgement of the power of the ladies—but in a way that defines what is different about the 'theatre' of the *Britannia*. Here the hierarchies of pit, box, and gallery take the form of the distinctions of naval rank, with the Earl of Northesk at the apex. The gesture to the absent ladies marks the shipboard theatre as a masculine domain, while rendering invisible any lower-class women who may have been present with the 'brave fellows' in the background. This emphasis within the prologue on the gendered nature of the theatricals also extends to the actors. One address, spoken on board the *Albion* in February 1808 before a performance of *Douglas* and *The Padlock*, apologizes for the deficiencies of the female characters:

> But most our females your indulgence claim,
> If they should fail, 'tis nature you must blame;
> She, from the tone of their organization,
> Will suffer but a cold representation;
> Hoping to please, they willingly come forth,
> Well knowing failure cannot taint their worth;
> For in their bosoms still, a sacred flame
> Burns emulative of a Nelson's fame.
> Under each plaid, we trust, you'll find a heart
> That fain would act a more important part . . .[69]

This suggests that rather than compromising their masculinity in the performance of female roles, the sailors will in fact reinforce it. Failure as women only affirms rather than taints their worth which, as the last two lines imply, is linked with martial prowess and achievement. The 'important part' which the sailors play in war is, in a basic sense, their masculinity.

The conventions of the prologue were thus reinscribed in ways which defined shipboard theatre as a predominantly 'manly' environment and replaced the social distinctions encoded by theatrical space with naval hierarchy—the 'place' accorded to the 'Lord', 'Gentlemen', and others. This reinscription is also apparent in the way that the naval prologues

---

[68] *Naval Chronicle*, 15 (1806), 69.   [69] Ibid. 21 (1809), 56.

represent patriotism. In the commercial theatre the sailor was often the addressee of the prologue, the idealized 'gallant tar' whose loyalty and steadfastness were implicit. Even though the soldier and sailor were an important element of the audience, they were often referred to as if they were absent on the high seas or in the 'tented field' of battle: as I have noted in the previous chapter, this sense of the military as unproblematic and passively heroic was a bulwark of patriotism at this period. Naval prologues are interesting because of the way they show these instruments of patriotic feeling speaking for themselves. While affirming the navy's steadfastness in defending Britain's cause, many of them also reveal levels of anxiety and circumspection. Another *Albion* prologue, dating from 1808 and possibly by the same author, develops the trope of the actor's humility before an audience:

> We strive to please—not to draw plaudits forth,
> Success or failure cannot change our worth:
> We may succeed, but yet by fears oppress'd,
> Expect you have endurance at the best;
> And, dreading failure, to prevent our shame,
> We own our weakness, and indulgence claim:
> If, as we fear, our strength should prove too small,
> Let interposing pity break our fall.
> If we succeed, there's but one wish behind,—
> The fervent wish of each true British mind:
> From war's alarms may Britain soon be free,
> Her commerce flourish, and her name still be,
> 'The world-envied sovereign of the sea'.
> But when the sword is drawn in her dear cause,
> Still may th'event prove tragic to her foes:
> Her sons, in this deep drama, all unite;
> And may the Albions yet throw in their mite.
> Firm and undaunted, then, each swelling heart
> Will eager strive to take a foremost part:
> Deem themselves blest in meeting wat'ry graves,
> Proclaiming to the world that—*Britain rules the waves.*[70]

The speaker begins by claiming that success or failure as an actor cannot diminish the integrity of the sailors of the *Albion*, in the same way as the performance of female roles could not taint their masculinity. Nevertheless he cannot shake off the trope of the actor's servility—'dreading failure, to prevent our shame, | We own our weakness, and indulgence

---

[70] *Naval Chronicle*, 21 (1809), 57.

claim'—suggesting a more fundamental anxiety about the meaning of acting within the 'deep drama' of war itself. Success on that particular stage is equated with death, the 'wat'ry graves' that, like the prologue, declare a sailor's patriotism.

It is rare for prologues in the commercial theatre to articulate the meaning of patriotism in terms of personal sacrifice. This suggests that apart from affirming the hierarchical and gendered identity of the 'wooden world', an important function of the prologue was the mediation, and possibly exorcism, of the deepest anxieties of a ship's community—the fear of death, or a sense of alienation from home, whatever that meant to the varied experiences and ethnicities within the navy. The *Britannia* prologue of 1805, for example, offers assurance by envisaging the 'future destinies' of the crew:

> '*Your grateful country*' shall her arms extend,
> To greet your glad return with conscious pride,
> And in her bosom bid your cares subside!

A particularly poignant prologue was that spoken on board the *Superb* on a cold New Year's Eve during the blockade of New London in 1814. Advising his audience that the 'spouting group' will perform a comedy, the speaker declares that 'No mournful tragedy . . . should chill, | By murdering scenes, and deadly deeds of ill, | A night like *this*!' The prologue goes on to contemplate wistfully the ship's situation 'still upon a foe's rude coast, | In hostile vigilance' while Europe celebrates peace: although the speaker declares the crew's 'firm resolve' to fight on, the impression persists of a group of cold, homesick sailors cheerlessly welcoming the New Year of 1815.[71] This frank acknowledgement of the collective loneliness of the *Superb* emphasizes the inward-looking dynamic of shipboard performances, in contrast to that of the military theatricals described previously.

Unfortunately, there are no accounts of the theatricals accompanying the prologues that were published in the *Naval Chronicle*; in some cases the titles of the plays performed are not even given. For a detailed account of an amateur performance on board ship we have to turn to Tate Wilkinson, manager of the Yorkshire circuit of theatres, who was guest upon the *Bedford* in March 1791 when members of the crew staged Rowe's *The Fair Penitent* and the farce of *Who's the Dupe?* by Hannah Cowley. In concluding this chapter, I would like to discuss Wilkinson's account of this performance in some detail.

[71] Ibid. 35 (1816), 168.

Tate Wilkinson was present on board the *Bedford*, then preparing to sail to Botany Bay with a consignment of convicts, as guest of Lieutenant Bennett, a relation of Mrs Esten of Covent Garden. As manager of the Yorkshire circuit of theatres, Wilkinson was the leading figure in the provincial theatre of his time with considerable celebrity status.[72] He had just performed a benefit in the Portsmouth theatre to what he claimed was a 'crammed house . . . superior in the receipt to any one during the whole season' (*WP* iii. 170). His visit to the *Bedford* can be seen as a *coup* for Lieutenant Bennett, who like other officers seems to have used the ship as a venue for his social activities. However, it was the lower ranks of the ship's company and not the officers who were to perform for the Yorkshire manager. According to Wilkinson

the carpenter, his mate, the boatswain, in short a great number of the sailors, were amateurs of the drama, and had acted two or three plays, with great applause from their officers, and in the higher degree of fame than usual from all the sailors and their wives, many of whom, with their children, were then on board . . . Captain Bennett and the officers judged it would be a great treat to Wilkinson, the veteran actor, to see their royal company of actors, who might justly be called the *King's Servants*. On the hint, the performers were engaged to prepare and shew their abilities (*WP* iii. 178).

Handwritten playbills were circulated, exploiting the conventions of their equivalent in the professional theatre by declaring the company to be 'His Majesty's Servants'. Wilkinson later reproduced one in *The Wandering Patentee* (*WP* iii. 180). A stage, consisting of 'a painted flat and two side canvas wings', was constructed on the middle deck (*WP* iii. 181). In terms of the territorial divisions of the ship, the middle deck was identified with the lower ranks and the ship's people, while remaining subject to the authority of the captain and his officers. Part of the ritual of the performance involved the formal invitation of the officers of the quarterdeck to the domain of those they commanded. The play thus represented an occasion on which the ship's company could temporarily suspend the divisions of rank and class in an act of social integration, a 'holiday' from the normal pattern of shipboard life. Wilkinson was impressed by the image of community offered by his audience:

I do suppose there were not less than 400 persons at this play, and I do aver, I thought it then the finest sight I ever had beheld, or ever should. Only, reader,

[72] In addition to *The Wandering Patentee* see Tate Wilkinson, *Memoirs of his Own Life* (4 vols.; York, 1790). There is no book-length biography of Wilkinson but see Charles Beecher Hogan, 'One of God Almighty's Unaccountables: Tate Wilkinson of York', in *The Theatrical Manager in England and America*, ed. Joseph W. Donohue, Jr. (Princeton, NJ, 1971), 63–86.

figure to your imagination 400 persons, all belonging to his Majesty, then engaged to fight the enemies of their country; not one drunken person, not one ill-humoured, and what was more extraordinary, there actually was not one dirty face to be seen, every countenance appeared to the best in their power, and every one also from the commander to the lowest sailor in the ship, looked so honourably and so regardfully attached to each other, as made the sight wonderful (*WP* iii. 181–2).

After the performance, the normal life of the ship was resumed and 'all parties retired to their different quarters; *we*, the quality-part of the audience to regale at a supper ready on the table'. The actors, however, were given the privilege of a space to themselves, a tent 'where they only for that evening presided and regaled', apart from both their fellows and the officers commanding them (*WP* iii. 185).

The significance of this theatrical holiday is complex. It is clear from Wilkinson's account that amateur acting on ships was not confined to the officers and higher ranks, as was the case with the theatrical activities of military élites within England. In addition to Wilkinson, there is the evidence of the playbill from the papers of Captain Hardy of the *Victory* declaring the performance on board ship of Elizabeth Inchbald's *Animal Magnetism* by lower ranking sailors, probably sometime between 1803 and 1805.[73] As noted previously, there were spouting clubs existent in the naval towns of Plymouth and Portsmouth, indicating the popularity of amateur acting amongst ordinary seamen. William Oxberry claimed that it was 'well known that our tars have all a *penchant* for theatricals, which, in long voyages, is frequently indulged'.[74] This activity, however, could not be conducted on ship without the knowledge, and at least tacit permission, of superior officers and captains. Why did they give it? In the case of the *Bedford*, the performance of *The Fair Penitent* and *Who's the Dupe?* was in honour of the famous York manager, to the credit of Lieutenant Bennett. Wilkinson claimed that the boatswain and the carpenter organized the performance at the suggestion or 'hint' of the Lieutenant, but it is not clear how imperative this 'hint' actually was. It is possible that part of the attraction of the theatricals for the officers of the *Bedford* lay in the comic possibilities of hardened seamen of lowly origins playing the roles of gentlemen and ladies in a mainpiece tragedy and a genteel farce. Like the crew of the *Unite* who acted as audience for Captain Campbell's ball, the crew of the *Bedford* was on display for Tate Wilkinson, again as a means of impressing a civilian outsider. While the *Bedford* performance

---

[73] Theatre Royal Victory'.   [74] Oxberry, *Dramatic Biography*, i. 144.

temporarily elevated the actors to positions of privilege on the ship, it involved no real challenge to authority. In this sense it can be seen as an exercise in paternalism, comparable to the family theatricals of the Burneys and the Herberts; like Dorothea Herbert's father or Frances Burney's uncle the 'fathers' of the *Bedford* had allowed their 'children' to perform, temporarily suspending their authority, if only, ultimately, to reinforce it.

There is, however, another dimension to this aspect of the performance. As Wilkinson makes clear, those involved included the carpenter, his mate, and the boatswain, all important figures in the ship's community. The boatswain and carpenter were, in the words of Michael Lewis, 'bred-in-the-bone seamen', whose lives were completely identified with their ship.[75] Responsible for the sails and the rigging and for general discipline, the boatswain was often one of the most feared figures on board, while the carpenter, who ensured that the ship was seaworthy, usually commanded more respect. Both came from comparatively lowly levels in civilian society and would have risen through the ranks: they were required to be literate. The carpenter on the *Bedford*, a Mr Woodward, had constructed the stage and was one of the actors. Wilkinson claimed that he was contented with a minor part in the tragedy, but when he played the part of Old Doiley in the farce 'it is impossible to describe the enthusiastic love and partiality that was shewn on the appearance of [the audience's] friend the Carpenter' (*WP* iii. 185). It would seem, then, that the paternalism governing the shipboard community had a number of dimensions. In terms of the *Bedford*'s hierarchy, the carpenter and the boatswain were subordinate to Lieutenant Bennett who had commanded them to act, but it is also clear that the performance celebrated their own authority and value to others on the ship—a different kind of paternalistic relationship, possibly more meaningful to the ship's people as a whole.

I would now like to consider the appropriateness in this context of Rowe's *The Fair Penitent*. As we have seen earlier, it was one of the most popular choices for amateur performance in the eighteenth century: using the example of the Herberts, I argued its particular relevance for patriarchal and gender politics within the family.[76] Part of the appeal of this play and other 'she-tragedies' to amateur performers lay in the way that they theatricalized the domestic. By this I mean that watching *The Fair*

---

[75] Lewis, *Social History*, 264.

[76] See also M. G. Lewis's account of the performance of the fourth act of *The Fair Penitent* by slaves in Jamaica: *Journal*, 56.

Penitent implied a public act of complicity in the 'private woes' of the protagonists. As Christina Marsden Gillis points out, this complicity is the result of Rowe's exploitation of stage space as a metaphor for both public and private interiorized space. The stage direction at the beginning of Act V reveals a room 'hung with black' and the body of Lothario, Calista's murdered lover, on a bier; at a further remove, the heroine is 'discovered' within the scene, 'her hair hanging loose and disordered'.[77] According to Marsden Gillis, 'when Calista "comes forward" on the stage, she detaches herself from the abysmal scene, becomes spectator as well as participant in the tragedy, observing her own scene as an object in the moral lesson'.[78] In this way, the boundaries between private and public space are confused; the domestic interior space is theatricalized, made an object of public scrutiny.

The themes and dramatic structures of *The Fair Penitent* would thus seem to have a direct relationship to the contexts in which it was played by amateur actors—rooms such as the Herberts' garret or the middle deck of the *Bedford* which, by the performance of the play within them, were made simultaneously public and private. The ship, in particular, was a domain in which the usual distinctions between the domestic and the public did not apply. I have earlier referred to the complex sexual life of the Georgian navy—the open practice of heterosexuality; the identification of the ship as a predominantly 'manly' environment in ways which rendered invisible both women and homosexual relations between sailors. Wilkinson's account of the performance emphasizes the female presence on board the *Bedford*, as well as that of children. He notes the ease with which the officers placed the children at the front of the audience, an attention that was also paid to some of the 'pretty lasses and wives' of the sailors. Discreetly baulking at this evidence of droit de seigneur, Wilkinson expresses his hope that 'the strict virtue of the brave lads' wives and sweethearts, and the chastity of the officers, will not permit any insinuation of mine to let in a sly suspicion that is not strictly conformable to the nicest ideas'. 'But such things have been,' he adds, 'and perhaps

[77] Nicholas Rowe, *The Fair Penitent*, ed. M. Gold (London, 1969), 61.

[78] Christina Marsden Gillis, 'Private Room and Public Space: The Paradox of Form in *Clarissa*', *Studies on Voltaire and the Eighteenth Century*, 176 (1979), 165–6. Antony Kubiak has claimed that 'the apparent retreat into familial and sentimental dramas in the romantic theatre does not represent a withdrawal of theatre into more private spaces, but indicates instead the publication of the family—its forces, relations, and activities—as an artifact of culture created as performance': *Stages of Terror: Terrorism, Ideology, and Coercion as Theatre History* (Bloomington, Ind., 1991), 184 n. 19. The *Bedford* performance exemplifies this process.

may happen again' (*WP* iii. 182). There is a certain appropriateness of such behaviour in the context of a play that dealt with adultery. Many of the women in the audience of *The Fair Penitent* would have understood the price of illicit sexual relations; some may have sympathized with Calista when she declares, 'How hard is the condition of our sex, | Through ev'ry state of life the slave of man!'[79] Although the playbill reproduced by Wilkinson makes it clear that the minor female roles of Lavinia and Lucille in *The Fair Penitent* were played by two women, Mrs Harrendine and Mrs Greengrass, the central role of the heroine was performed by a man, Mr Bowen, who also took the part of Elizabeth Doiley in *Who's the Dupe?* Wilkinson claimed that the 'fair male Calista . . . sunk to her bed of death with all imaginable decorum, without the least indecency of informing whether the frail penitent was a Sans Culotte or not' (*WP* iii. 182–3).

We have seen earlier how military actors in amateur theatricals resorted to professional actresses, rather than compromise their masculinity by playing female roles in mainpiece drama. This recourse was not readily available to the performers of the *Bedford* and there were important reasons why the women aboard were disqualified as actresses. The involvement of the wives of the officers would probably have made the production too obviously immoral. But there is another overriding reason why Calista was not performed by a woman. The travestying by a male of the central female role of *The Fair Penitent* reflects the gender politics of the shipboard community as a whole—the invisibility of women and their exclusion from the network of paternal relations dominating the ship. In this sense *The Fair Penitent* was an appropriate choice for performance. According to Vaska Tumir, the 'world of familial relations' in Rowe's play is transformed 'into an arena of power-play: more specifically, into a territory of irrational and intensely ambivalent "homoerotic" competition for mastery, dominated by strong father figures'.[80] Tumir interprets the play as a metaphor for the recasting of Stuart autocracy after 1688:

[it] provides irreproachable authority for England's rejection of autocracy, while simultaneously reclaiming for its élite the Son's paternally approved right to rule. The play's fragmentation and duplication of son figures in Altamont and Horatio, and the latter's multiple roles of father, brother, and friend of Sciolto's principal heir—he himself being another—may be seen as a . . . redistribution of masculine authority. The exclusive paradigm of patriarchy remains in place, but its

[79] Rowe, *Fair Penitent*, 34.

[80] Vaska Tumir, 'She-Tragedy and Its Men: Conflict and Form in *The Orphan* and *The Fair Penitent*', *SEL* 30 (1990), 417.

coerciveness can now be safely deplored in representations of female figures whose struggle for autonomy and equality leads to tragic ends. And precisely because such insubordination is bound by tragedy, it can be allowed a fully sympathetic portrayal.[81]

This assessment of the politics of Rowe's play is also applicable to the wooden world of the *Bedford*; it was a society dominated by a number of competing 'father figures', bound together by ties of obligation, duty, and affection that excluded the women of the ship, who were spectators, as well as the necessary focus, of this exclusive 'paradigm of patriarchy'.

So far I have referred to Wilkinson's account as if it were transparent to the event it describes. However, the York manager was not an objective observer but an equal player in the performance; the narrative constructs a meaning for what he sees, that is in turn shaped by existing discourses, in particular, the discourse of patriotism and the role of the navy within it. Wilkinson was an important figure in provincial culture, but as a theatre manager and actor he was still subject to the stigmatization that was associated with his profession. During his Portsmouth trip he had been invited to dine on *HMS Matilda*, only to arrive to find the captain engaged elsewhere, 'incivility and rudeness in the extreme' that could not 'admit of any palliation' (*WP* iii. 175). Wilkinson was not only sensitive to social slights: when he arrived at the *Bedford* he insisted on demonstrating his manliness by climbing up the side of the ship, in spite of an injured leg, rejecting the offer of a seat that had been used by Mrs Bennett. However, the most significant evidence of Wilkinson's actual status in society is his response to an appeal for help from a former servant, who had committed a crime and was awaiting transportation to Botany Bay. Wilkinson's narrative of their meeting off Portsmouth is indebted to a trope of sentimental discourse—the theatricalized act of charity which refines the feelings of the giver more than the receiver. He even quotes from Elizabeth Inchbald's sentimental drama *Such Things Are* in defining the difference between justice and mercy. However, there is no satisfactory resolution to the encounter because in contrast to other narratives in which charity defines the man of feeling, such as Sterne's *A Sentimental Journey*, Wilkinson is powerless. He has no contacts with great men and does not even know who is in charge of the transportation of prisoners from Portsmouth. While he perversely enjoys the role imputed to him by his former servant and the latter's sympathetic captain, his part as a philanthropist is no more than that, an act of role-

---

[81] Ibid. 425.

playing which conceals his ineffectuality. As an actor, he has no access to the sources of power in his society.

This particular episode casts a significant light on Wilkinson's role as observer of the theatricals on board the *Bedford*. His narrative represents the ship's community in a similar way to that of the provincial theatre of the period—as a band of gallant tars, commanded by noble officers. Writing in the context of the Revolutionary war, Wilkinson saw fit to declare, 'if officers and sailors on board every man of war are like those of the Bedford, we need never fear or doubt victory were *little* Great Britain only opposed to the malignity of France, our common enemy' (*WP* iii. 178). In common with the representation of sailors by other theatrical autobiographers such as John Bernard and John O'Keeffe, he describes the *Bedford* crew as 'devoid of art either in their countenances, their inclinations, or their honest noble hearts' (*WP* iii. 184). This emphasis on naval naïvety was integral to the ideological construction of the senior service as passive, non-individuated guardians of the nation. Wilkinson even represents the language of the sailors in terms of the patois to be heard everywhere in the provincial theatres. 'Dam'ee, Jack,' one of them is heard to say, 'I had like to have been out in that there speech to Calistar, but tack'd about and got to the right, and don't think that Mr. York Actor found me out' (*WP* iii. 185).

However, this construction of the *Bedford* as an image of unanimity, resonant ultimately of the tight little island of state, is later undermined by Wilkinson's account of his return journey to Portsmouth. Accompanied by a very drunk Lieutenant Bennett, the actor was rowed by a group of sailors from the *Bedford*, an arduous task in any circumstances. According to Wilkinson, Lieutenant Bennett

called on the sailors repeatedly for their opinion, whether there were such a fine set of fellows in his Majesty's navy, and insisted on an answer from them; but after a pause they only minded their duty as to rowing. I said it was not fair to ask such a question, though the truth might not be doubted. The Lieutenant then said if they did not say they were the best sailors in his Majesty's navy, he should not mind chucking them over-board;—yet not any answer more than 'Jack, dam'ee, steer more to the right' (*WP* iii. 188).

Wilkinson later asked one of the sailors why they had refused to accept Lieutenant Bennett's compliment to which he replied, 'what our Master Bennett says as to our being fine fellows, is true, and we all knows it; but vy should he say as how he would chuck a man into the sea' (*WP* iii. 189). It is significant that this incident took place on the sea between the ship and Portsmouth, a no man's area where the sailors felt they could resist their commanding officer and where Wilkinson was not so clearly identified as the interloper, nor with the 'quality part' of the ship. It shows that like many eighteenth-century social institutions, the naval community operated on the basis of customary rights and privileges. Although Lieutenant Bennett was complimenting his men, he had expressed it in a way that demanded an acknowledgement of his power over them. This was regarded by the sailors as negating the respect due to his rank and they had refused to show him deference. While Lieutenant Bennett was too drunk to press the matter further, in other circumstances such an incident could have led to open defiance, even mutiny.

This epilogue to Wilkinson's visit to the *Bedford* suggests that the image of unanimity promoted by the amateur theatricals masked a finely balanced and complex matrix of power relations on the ship, involving nuances of class, naval rank, and gender. As author of *The Wandering Patentee* and leading figure in the provincial theatre, Tate Wilkinson was involved in the promotion of this masque/mask of unanimity. However, as revealed by the encounter with his former servant, in other ways Wilkinson was politically powerless. It is significant that when he arrived in Portsmouth he 'judged it right' to give the sailors 'a trifle as a reward', as if in acknowledgement of the wrong done to them by Lieutenant Bennett (*WP* iii. 189). As an actor, Wilkinson was accustomed to the benefit system whereby performers solicited financial acknowledgement from their patrons, a sign of the theatre's roots in pre-commercial culture. For the sailor, his reward was the knowledge that he was acting in the service of his country; he was not supposed to be fighting for mercenary reasons. Wilkinson's act of giving the sailors money can be interpreted as an attempt to replace an economy of service and deference with the lateral relationships of a commercial transaction; it was a recognition of mutual powerlessness, of their bond as 'actors' in a theatre of war.

7

Littoral Rites: Military Theatre and Empire

TATE WILKINSON was one of the most successful and respected figures in the provincial theatre, yet his account of the performance of *The Fair Penitent* suggests that he had to struggle to assert his professional and personal respectability. This was because the façade of the dominant theatrical culture in Britain, that of the patent houses in London and the provinces, concealed another kind of theatre, the underworld of itinerant players who made their living performing in the barns, the fairground booths, and in the open-air. The theatre of Tate Wilkinson—urban, commercialized, 'legitimate'—was constantly shadowed by that of the strolling player—predominantly rural-based and unrespectable. It was only in 1788 that there was a change in the law classifying all actors, including Wilkinson, as craftsmen, rather than rogues and vagabonds. As a profession, acting retained the stigma of immorality and criminality. Even after 1788 strollers were still regarded with suspicion by magistrates and some local notables.

As we have seen in the previous chapter, military thespians within Britain aligned themselves with the dominant theatrical culture in order to enhance their position 'within but distinct' from society as a whole. Elements of the officer class chose to perform in public theatres because of the powerful position of such institutions within urban culture. What did it mean, however, when soldiers performed outside these contexts on the battlefields and in the garrisons of the empire? As I indicated in the introduction, Britain's wars had an important global dimension. The struggle against the armies of the Revolution, and later Napoleon, was also a struggle for colonial mastery and world power. What relevance, if any, do amateur theatricals have in this context? The scope of this book precludes a comprehensive account of military theatricals outside Britain. Instead I want to examine examples of military theatre in three particular contexts—the American War of Independence, the British administration of the Cape of Good Hope between 1796 and 1803, and the War of 1812 between Britain and the United States.

The export of its culture, in particular drama, was one of the most significant ways in which British colonial power was reinforced. Accustomed to a peripatetic existence, actors were natural colonists, eager to bring Shakespeare, Otway, and Rowe to the West Indies, North America, and India.[1] Drama was also the channel by which the colonists' experience was conveyed to the public in Britain. A well-known early example of the theatre's participation in colonial exchange is the feathered dress obtained by Aphra Behn in Surinam which, according to her account in *Oroonoko*, later became the costume of Dryden's Indian queen.[2] In the vanguard of these colonizing actors were the soldier-strollers. The establishment of civilian, professional theatre companies was often preceded by the activities of military amateurs who charted the territory for drama in these new worlds.

The military had many reasons for wanting to stage theatrical performances in Britain's expanding empire. As we have seen in earlier chapters, amateur acting was an expression of the importance of theatricality within military culture as a whole and was of particular importance to the ideology of a war of élites. In some contexts, such as North America or the Cape Colony where the already established European settlers had a strong tradition of anti-theatricalism, the performance of plays by the military was a means of rehearsing the ideological and political differences between the antagonists. The American Congress banned theatrical performances in 1774, so the persistence of British officers in staging plays in Boston, New York, and Philadelphia was a calculated affront to the rebels. At a more mundane level acting also served as a useful military exercise. The organization of a performance, in some cases involving the construction and maintenance of a theatre building, was one way of occupying both officers and men during periods when they were not fighting, thus maintaining morale and preventing indiscipline. The imitation of the practices of the Georgian theatre, including the production and distribution of prologues and playbills and the replication of the hierarchy of 'box, pit, and gallery', enabled the military to define itself in relation to the alien environment of the battlefield or garrison and also, perhaps more significantly, in relation to those for whom they were fighting. As in the case of

---

[1] See e.g. Richardson Wright, *Revels in Jamaica 1682–1838* (New York, 1969); Errol Hill, *The Jamaican Stage, 1655–1900: Profile of a Colonial Theatre* (Amherst, Mass., 1992): S. K. Mukherjee, *The Story of the Calcutta Theatres 1753–1980* (Calcutta, 1982); Laurence W. Levine, *Highbrow/Lowbrow: The Emergence of Cultural Hierarchy in America* (Cambridge, Mass., 1988).

[2] See Laura Brown, 'The Romance of Empire: *Oroonoko* and the Trade in Slaves' in *The New 18th Century: Theory Politics English Literature*, ed. Felicity Nussbaum and Laura Brown (New York, 1987), 52. For a later theatrical mediation of a colonial encounter, O'Keeffe and De Loutherbourg's *Omai or a Trip Round the World*, see Dening, *Mr Bligh's Bad Language*, 269–76.

naval theatricals, the act of 'getting up a play' became a rite of British identity, a way of asserting a relationship with the homeland. But the very fact that this rite took place outside Britain, in radically different social, political, cultural, and geographical situations, ensured that military theatricals did not represent an uncomplicated nostalgia. Like the culture of the camps, the performance of plays was a way of registering difference—the fact that 'this', whatever or whenever 'this' was in terms of time or place, was not the Britain that the soldiers knew but that nevertheless, they were still compelled to perform 'Britain' in their roles as defenders of the nation. Those who were ideologically central to the security of Britain—the 'brave boys' on the battlefield or on the high seas without whom the homeland would not survive—now found themselves on the littoral of the empire, conscious that while they might be celebrated in some quarters at home, they were also regarded with distrust and suspicion by large sections of the civilian population and even by the government that had sent them out to fight. Thus, whereas in Britain military thespians sought to identify themselves with the legitimate arm of the theatre, the military actor overseas adopted the marginal status and practices of the unrespectable, itinerant theatre. The soldier became the empire's stroller.

True vagrants of the Thespian race

As is the case with naval theatricals, prologues are a useful source of information about how military actors saw themselves. Some important examples survive from the theatrical campaigns of the British army during the American War of Independence. They indicate the significance of these performances as political events, occasions on which the role of the British in America could be enacted, not only before an audience of rebellious Yankees beyond the walls of the theatre but also in relation to a distant audience at home in Britain. In the prologue to the performance of *Zara* in Boston in 1775, General Burgoyne compared the crisis in the colonies to the English Civil War. Beset by factionalism, 'Freedom', represented as female, had destroyed herself, in the process vanquishing the 'liberal art' of the stage:

> IN Britain once (it stains th'historic page)
> Freedom was vital-struck by party rage:
> Cromwell the fever watch'd, the knife supplied,
> She madden'd, and by suicide she died.
> Amidst the groans sunk every liberal art.

> That polish'd life, or humaniz'd the heart;
> Then fell the stage, quell'd by the bigot's roar . . .[3]

Burgoyne is suggesting that the mission of the soldier is a curative one, the theatre, and by extension conflict itself, being the medicine necessary to purge the disease of party division in the American colonies. The role of the soldier is thus elevated beyond the realm of the political to that of disinterested duty. Moreover, by representing the concept that the soldier is defending—'Freedom'—as a victimized female, Burgoyne is able to suggest that freedom too is a matter of chivalric duty, not factional politics. In this context the mainpiece play that was to be performed, Aaron Hill's she-tragedy *Zara*, is significant in so far as the eponymous heroine personifies the feminized 'Freedom' that the officers claimed to be defending. Indeed, the actions of the male actors are made synonymous with the integrity of Hill's heroine. At the end of the prologue Burgoyne claims that the good intentions of the performers, like the virtue of Zara, will outface their critics:

> When the heart's right, the action can't be wrong.
> Behold the test, mark at the curtain's rise
> How Malice shrinks abash'd at Zara's eyes.[4]

The importance of gender in the ideological construction of the theatricals is apparent in other prologues such as the one written for the opening of the 'Theatre Royal' in New York in January 1778. It represents the purpose of the performance as a feminine ministering to the sufferings of the community; the soldiers would relieve 'the brow of care' and 'wake to pity, and with soft control | Melt into tender sympathy the soul'. The same prologue also articulates an awareness of how the exploits of the army were being received in Britain:

> O Britons! (and your generous thirst of fame
> Has fully prov'd you worthy of the name),
> Tho' scowling faction's interested band
> At home asperse us, and with envious hand
> Our well earn'd laurels tear, the public weal
> Bids us not murmur whatso'er we feel . . .[5]

These lines imply that it is the soldiers in the audience who are the 'true' Britons, not those politicians at home who criticize the conduct of the war,

---

[3] John Burgoyne, *The Dramatic and Poetical Works of the Late Lieut. Gen. J. Burgoyne* (2 vols.; London, 1808), ii. 238.

[4] Ibid. 239.   [5] Quoted Dunlap, *History*, 52.

suggesting the importance of the prologue (and the performance as a whole) as a mechanism of self-defence and self-justification. Significantly, the speaker acknowledges that it is not the soldier's place to question authority—'the public weal | Bids us not murmur whatso'er we feel'— but the very act of stating this was itself a complaint. It was only in the highly conventionalized realm of the theatrical performance that dissension could be spoken and even then only indirectly.

The British soldier's sense of his beleaguered position, caught between the rebellious colonists on the one hand and a critical public at home, is also evident in a prologue spoken at the New York theatre on 9 January 1779. It represents the playhouse as a battlefield in which the actor must reluctantly confront his opponents, the audience. Developing the trope of the actor's subservience before the superior judgement of his patrons, the prologue describes the audience as 'unerring marksmen at an actor's fault'. The critic of the pit is 'the foe in the ravine'. The orchestra pit is the 'upper ground and palisades' defending the player from the assaults of 'missile pippins' from the 'heights' of the gallery. '*Vivat Rex*, none come behind the scene' suggests that the soldier-actor's last protection is his 'manager', the king. As in the case of Burgoyne's Boston prologue, the actor's defence is his Zara-like virtue, the purity of his motives in performing. The prologue suggests that acting, like warfare, involves self-exposure, rendering the soldier vulnerable to attack: 'Unarmed we appear in ev'ry part— | And least of all protected at the heart.'[6]

This suggestion of the actor-soldier's 'feminine' vulnerablity is then developed in an elaborate conceit which reinterprets the legend of the rape of the Sabine women in terms of fashionable adultery:

> Can censure raise a dart against our scene
> When *charity* extends her hand between?
> Thus when on Latia's shore the *Sabine* host
> ('Twas then the fashion) rag'd for spouses lost;
> Lest bloodshed should ensue each *gentle* woman,
> With condescension, took her fav'rite *Roman*:
> Nor less compliant, to appease the strife,
> Each *Sabine* in *true ton*, gave up his wife.

So, the prologue goes on to claim, charity 'interposes like the Sabine dames' to effect a treaty between the performers and their critics:

> *Critic* and *Actor*, in the middle field
> Shall meet and parley—shall relent and yield;

[6] Quoted Seilhamer, *History*, ii. 40.

Give but the fair, the treaty shall prevail—
We will like *Romans* use the lady well.[7]

The reconfiguration of rape in terms of the 'condescension' of fashionable adultery is a sign of how the theatrical performances of the military represented a sublimation of the violence of war. The conflict was here travestied in terms of a fashionable diversion, a theatre war. It is not surprising that many American Revolutionaries were affronted by this.[8] The British officers were probably fully aware of how the prologue was likely to be received beyond the boundaries of the theatre. In that sense the prologue was functioning as a weapon in the war for the hearts and minds of both the British and their opponents. At another level, however, it is possible to recognize in it evidence of an ideology in crisis. The reference to the Sabine women suggests that the British desperately needed to justify their actions, not only as amateur performers, but as soldiers fighting the war. Their defence is the code of chivalric honour that was also in evidence at the 'Mischianza', their assurance to the critics, both in America and in Britain, that they will 'use the lady well'. However, it is a measure of their sense of the weakness of their position that the feminine virtue of Charity becomes an ideological shield, like the Sabine women, interposing between the stage of the war and the hostile audience beyond.

We have seen already how military élites in Britain used philanthropy as an excuse for their appropriation of the public theatres. I argued in Chapter 6 that their insistence on the charitable purpose of the performance was a sign of the military's need to prove its worth to a society which traditionally regarded it with ambivalence. In the context of the American War, and especially an awareness that the conduct of the army was under scrutiny at home, the need for self-justification was even more pressing. By constantly stressing the philanthropic spirit of the theatricals, principally in support of the wives and children of the dead and wounded, the officers were also reminding themselves and others of their amateur status. This was essential to a sense of themselves as gentlemen first and soldiers second. (It also conveniently obscured the fact that, contrary to their protestations, officers were pocketing the profits from the theatricals.)

---

[7] Ibid. 40–1.

[8] For the response of the American Revolutionaries, significantly in terms of a counter-theatricality, see Norman Philbrick (ed.), *Trumpets Sounding: Propaganda Plays of the American Revolution* (New York, 1972), and Jeffrey H. Richards, *Theater Enough: American Culture and the Metaphor of the World Stage, 1607–1789* (Durham, NC, 1991).

The significance of charity as an ideological and ethical lifeline for the military is suggested by one of the most famous prologues from the American War, that written for the opening of the John Street theatre in New York in 1777 which begins:

> Once more ambitious of theatric glory,
> Howe's strolling company appears before ye.
> O'er hills and bogs, through wind and weather,
> And many a hair-breadth 'scape, we've scrambled hither;
> For we, true vagrants of the Thespian race,
> While summer lasts ne'er know a settled place.
> Anxious to prove the merits of our band,
> A chosen squadron wanders through the land;
> How beats each Yankee bosom at our drum!
> 'Hark, Jonathan! zounds, here's the strollers come.'[9]

The prologue represents the opening of the theatre as marking the return of the soldier-strollers—'true vagrants of the Thespian race'—to a winter residency in the town. The differentiation between the country and the city, so essential to the construction of British civility, is recast in terms of this particular theatre of war, New York taking the place of the metropolitan centre, a London, while the rebellious Yankees, caricatured as the Jonathans and Tabithas who come to gawp at the stroller army, are suitably located in the country. By using this conceit, the prologue writer is able to represent the conflict in America as one between two different standards of intellectual, cultural, and political development—the British 'city' and the American 'country'. He is also able to suggest that wherever the British are, even when they are on the move in time of war, is the centre. As soldier-strollers, they perform the values of the city for the barbarous Americans in the same way as the actors of the patent theatres brought 'culture' to the provinces:

> Wing'd with variety our moments fly,
> Each minute tinctur'd with a different dye.
> Balls we have plenty and *al fresco* too,
> Such as Soho or King street never knew;
> Did you but see sometimes how we're array'd
> You'd fancy we designed a masquerade;
> 'Twould tire your patience were I to relate here,
> Our routs, drums, hurricanes and *fêtes champêtres*.[10]

---

[9] Quoted Seilhamer, *History*, ii. 27.   [10] Ibid.

These lines suggest that the reinvention of urbanity that typified the culture of Coxheath and Warley—the construction of miniature Ranelaghs and Vauxhalls, the taverns made of boughs—was carried beyond Britain to underpin the ideology of warfare itself. The camp and the battlefield were conceived by these officers as simulacra of élite metropolitan culture, the worlds of the masquerade, the ball, and the theatre endlessly reproduced. The conceptualization of the army as a group of strolling players was important in this respect because it was able to express the idea of warfare as the export of metropolitan values to the margins. Like the strolling company, the military forces of Britain roamed unconfined; in a sense they exceeded metropolitan culture in their capacity to perform the values of the centre. The very world was their theatre. 'Let Ranelagh still boast her ample dome', declared the prologue, 'while heaven's our canopy the earth's our room.'[11]

As in the 'Sabine women' prologue, the construction of war as the military's recreation or entertainment was also directed at the audience of rebellious Yankees. The prologue suggests that no matter how much 'old vaunting Saddler's Wells' should boast of 'her tight ropes and ladder dancing', Cunningham 'in both excels'.[12] This was a reference to the Provost-Marshal of New York, the administrator of martial law and notorious for his brutality. His 'tight ropes' were not those of the acrobat or pantomime artist but a sign of his stock-in-trade, the hangman's noose. Like the 'Mischianza's' re-enactment of war in terms of a chivalric joust, such an allusion was politically significant in that it showed that the British did not need to take war seriously. The ropes were in their hands. However, the reference to Cunningham in the prologue is immediately followed by a change of tack, suggesting that even the writer was conscious that this calculated levity had perhaps gone too far. The prologue begs the condescension of the audience:

> But soft! a word or two before I go.
> Benevolence first urged us to engage,
> And boldly venture on a public stage;
> To guard the helpless orphan's tender years,
> To wipe away th' afflicted parent's tears . . .
> This our design—and sure in such a cause,
> E'en error's self might challenge some applause.
> With candour then our imperfections scan,
> And where the actor fails absolve the man.[13]

[11] Ibid. 28.   [12] Ibid.   [13] Ibid.

The prologue moves from the provocative irony of its reference to Cunningham to a plea that the benevolent intentions of the actors will extenuate their 'imperfections'. Once more the resort to philanthropy as a moral defence suggests the anxieties involved in performing the role of soldier in late eighteenth-century culture. Theatricals were more than the self-indulgence of a group of dilettanti officers but a way of enacting what it meant for the soldier to expose himself on the stage of war, conscious that his actions were being scrutinized by an audience that was complicitous but at the same time able to project the responsibility for violence on to him. In its plea to 'absolve the man' if the actor fails, the John Street prologue can be regarded as a secular prayer, a request for forgiveness, like Prospero's epilogue to *The Tempest*. This suggests that the anti-theatricalists' suspicion that the theatre was an inverse church was to some extent justified: performance was the military's sacrament and the prologue its *mea culpa*.

'The African Theatre'

In 1800–1 a series of reports appeared in both *The Times* and the *Monthly Mirror* in relation to the founding of a theatre in the British colony at the Cape of Good Hope in southern Africa. Substantial amounts had been spent on a building and professional actors were said to be preparing to leave England in support of the endeavours of the colonists.[14] However, in 1803, as part of the Peace of Amiens, the Cape was returned to Holland (then under French control) in exchange for Trinidad and Ceylon.[15] Although the British later retook the Cape after the collapse of the Peace of Amiens, the theatrical project does not seem to have been revived. The revels ended almost as soon as they had begun.

The reporting of such events in the London newspapers and journals was a sign of the importance attached to theatre in Georgian culture, an importance that soldiers and colonists were only too willing to exploit in order to gain publicity for themselves at home. The spread of theatre to the far-flung corners of the globe, such as the penal colony of New South Wales, allowed many domestic readers to assume the enlightening influence of British culture. A theatre automatically implied urbanity and civilized values: it did not matter if these 'theatres' were sometimes only

[14] *The Times*, 11 July 1801; *Monthly Mirror*, 10 (1800), 407.
[15] See Richard Elphick and Hermann Giliomee, *The Shaping of South African Society, 1652–1840*, 2nd edn. (Middletown, Conn., 1989), 324–5.

temporary, improvised structures, existing in conditions that were very different from those, for example, of Tunbridge Wells. Colonists, however, were reluctant to disabuse a domestic audience of its misconceptions. Like the diaries, letters, and travel accounts of this period, prologues and playbills were part of a circulating colonialist discourse that worked to reinforce the idea of the civilizing influence of British culture. If a domestic audience wanted to see the world in terms of a global Tunbridge Wells, then the actors of the garrisons and colonies were only too ready to confirm them in this view.

The prologues that survive from the shortlived 'African Theatre' of the Cape of Good Hope therefore have the status of documents of empire. They were written mainly by the wife of the military physician of the colony, Eliza Somers, who seems to have been a motivating force in the founding of the theatre. The British were relative newcomers to the Cape of Good Hope which had been a Dutch colony since 1652. Throughout the eighteenth century the influence of the Dutch East Indies Company, the administrators of the colony, had been in decline: when Holland was overrun by French Revolutionary forces in 1794, the Prince of Orange allied himself with George III and ordered his representatives in the Cape to cede control to the British forces. While the governor of the colony agreed, there was considerable resistance to what was regarded as surrender to a competing power, a resistance that was eventually crushed at the Battle of Muizenburg in 1795. The British had every reason for wanting to replace the Dutch as the dominant influence on the Cape, which was of prime strategic importance to the route to India. The colony was also logistically significant as a place where the fleet could be provisioned and maintained and where soldiers and sailors could recuperate after a frequently arduous voyage from England. Southern Africa was regarded as a useful 'middle station', enabling soldiers to accustom themselves to a different climate and terrain before they encountered India.[16] There was thus a large transient population at the Cape with its attendant manifestations of drinking, brothels, and disorderliness. In addition to the large number of Dutch settlers who remained resentful of the British presence, there was also a considerable slave population, brought from Ceylon, the East Indies, and Mozambique, as well as the indigenous inhabitants, the Khoikhoi (or, as they were known by the British, the Hottentot), and the San.

The Cape of Good Hope was therefore a very diverse, complex com-

---

[16] Bayly, *Imperial Meridian*, 105.

munity that was riven with racial, political, class, and gender differences. Many of the dominant white population regarded it as a place of only temporary residence and were incapable of identifying the colony as 'home'. By its very nature, life as a military man or colonial administrator was subject to the control of a central authority that could move one at any time. The Earl Macartney, the Irishman who in 1793 had led the first British embassy to China, spent less than two years in the Cape as governor between 1797 and 1798.[17] People who were lower on the ladder such as the Somerses were fully aware that their time at the Cape was likely to be brief. The 'African Theatre' of 1800–2 thus emerged in this context of impermanence and instability as a way of defining first, the colonists' position in an alien land, and secondly, the more inward-looking dynamic of relations within the colonizing community itself.

One of the most striking aspects of the British theatricals at the Cape was the dominant role played in them by a woman, Eliza Somers. Because of the status of the Cape as a garrison, the 'African Theatre' was military in character. Its audience consisted mainly of officers of both the army and the navy who also took part as actors. Military theatricals elsewhere, as we have seen, tended to be dominated by men. While acting appears to have relaxed the boundaries of gender, allowing soldiers and sailors to express the 'femininity' of their position as instruments of civilian society, theatricals still very much represented men addressing other men. Women were present in the role of the decorative 'fair ones' legitimating the chivalric endeavours of the actors, or rendered invisible if they were the lower-class followers of the army and navy. Eliza Somers's dominating role in the theatricals at the Cape was therefore unusual and needs to be regarded in the context of the internal politics of the British community at the Cape. As the wife of the army physician, Mrs Somers was not among the first rank of the British and was looked down upon by Lady Anne Barnard, the wife of Andrew Barnard, the Secretary of the Colony, who had important political connections, including the Earl Macartney and Henry Dundas. In her correspondence with the latter, Barnard implied that the Somerses were presumptuous in their refusal to call their quarters, where the first performance was held, a hospital. She claimed that had the Governor been content to stage private performances at his own house instead of planning a public subscription theatre, she would have been quite willing to participate: 'as to acting on any theatre where money was to be paid for admission, or any theatre except one in his house, I

---

[17] See J. L. McCracken, 'The Cape of Good Hope 1796–98' in *Macartney of Lisanoure 1737–1806: Essays in Biography*, ed. Peter Roebuck (Belfast, 1983), 266–77.

whispered my fixed refusal.' Nevertheless, Lady Barnard did supply 'an old shilling Paris-plaster horse' to act 'the equestrian statue of Marcus Aurelius' in a farce by Foote, as well as a 'large bronze Venus in paper'.[18]

Like the Margravine of Anspach and numerous other Georgian women, such as Mary Robinson and Mary Anne Clarke, Eliza Somers used the theatre as a means of gaining access for herself to the public sphere. If both class and gender inhibited her capacity to act within the British community at the Cape, then she would create her own stage. In the prologue to the first performance at the Somers's residence, Sea Lines, entitled 'ON THE INTRODUCTION OF THEATRICALS AT THE CAPE OF GOOD HOPE', she alluded to the question of whether the performers were amateurs or professionals by declaring: '*Our* merits librate on this modest plea, | A corps of Volunteers—you have our service *free.*'[19] She also claimed that the actors were 'untrain'd to Buskin, or the Sock', but yet were prepared to 'arm for these boards', the stage of not only the Somers's residence but of the colony as a whole. This emphasis on the actors/ soldiers as a 'corps of Volunteers', enthusiastic amateurs in the service of Britain, was making an important political point on behalf of the Somerses and their peers in the British community. In the same way as a soldier was not supposed to fight for financial reward—to do so was to become a mercenary and to lose one's British identity—so for Eliza Somers and her husband to describe themselves as volunteers in the service of the crown was to claim their place with people such as Lady Anne Barnard and the Earl Macartney. The performance at Sea Lines was an attempt to appropriate the moral and political authority of élite theatricals, the right of the upper class to determine the kind of sphere it wished to occupy. Lady Anne Barnard realized that to go along with Eliza Somers's scheme was to concede to her a kind of equality in the governing of the colony. The theatricals were therefore a power game that tested many of the barriers defining the hierarchies within the British community—the barriers of male and female, private and public, amateur and professional.

Nor was the political significance of the theatricals directed at the upper echelon of Cape society alone. The performances were also a way for the Somerses to define themselves in relation to the mass of the soldiery. Lady Anne Barnard claimed that the Governor had planned that the new theatre would consist of boxes only: 'no pit, each box to cost 24*l.* a year, and

---

[18] W. H. Wilkins (ed.), *South Africa a Century Ago: Letters Written from the Cape of Good Hope (1797–1801) by the Lady Anne Barnard* (London, 1901), 297–8.

[19] Eliza Somers, occasional prologue, 'On the Introduction of Theatricals at the Cape of Good Hope', Miscellaneous Letters, Cuttings Etc. 1792–1802, British Library.

to hold six subscribers, for twelve nights only; consequently it is on too dear a plan to suit the pockets of subalterns.'[20] As in the theatre in Britain, pricing was used to determine the kind of audience that the Somerses wanted, a very limited one which excluded the lowest ranking officers and certainly the mass of ordinary soldiers and sailors. For this small fraction of the population of the Cape, Eliza Somers sought to establish the theatre as:

> . . . a *moral* school,
> Where *scenic* mirth, and *Attic choice* shall rule.
> To *form a taste yet new* in Afric's clime,
> That haply shall Bellona's sons incline
> To study of *Belles Lettres* and the *Nine*.[21]

Eliza Somers's purpose was the feminization of war, suggesting a desire to establish a place for herself in a theatre which normally did not allow a role for women. Her authority is the code of neo-Hellenism which redeems Africa with civilized values. The address which opened the 'African Theatre' at Cape Town on 12 October 1801 was given by Dr Somers 'IN THE CHARACTER OF APOLLO'S HIGH PRIEST' and begins by hailing the occasion as '*Our* Temple rites!'. (Lady Anne Barnard commented caustically that the address was above the capacities of the audience '& seem'd rather an index of pretty learning'.)[22] The prologue goes on to enunciate a history of human endeavour which places the stage in the vanguard of progress:

> From parent East, in Egypt cradled long,
> The sciences were rear'd to wing more strong.
> Thence, into Greece, the Migrants took their flight,
> And spread a morn of philosophic light . . .
> Rude was society, still *unrefin'd*!
> 'Till stroller Thespis, in his far fam'd cart,
> With mask and pipe, first taught the scenic art . . .
> Wherever civilization *yet* has spread
> To *bless* mankind, it is *the Stage* has led;
> Daughters of Greece, with *her* last liberty,
> Borne by the Zephyrs of th' Aegean sea,
> She fled—with Athenais—to Italy,
> Together seen, and walking *hand* in *hand*,
> *Mark*! *where* they've travers'd Europe's happy land . . .

---

[20] Wilkins, *South Africa*, 296.
[21] Somers, 'On the Introduction of Theatricals'.
[22] Dorothea Fairbridge, *Lady Anne Barnard at the Cape of Good Hope 1797–1802* (Oxford, 1924), 289.

Not cherished *wide* in vast of western bound,
Atlantic's bosom buoys them to *this* sound.
Thus retrograded, Afric, to thy shores,
Let them not shipwreck near their ancient towers.
Protect the *strangers*, give them welcome here;
They'll smoothe the brow of *war* to aspect clear,
And draw the social *charities* more *near!*[23]

Eliza Somers represents the coming of the British to the Cape as a return of civilization to its ancient origins in African Egypt. Like the 'Howe's strolling company' prologue, the address reveals an attempt to reconceptualize the relationship between the centre and the periphery, suggesting the need for the agents of empire to think of themselves as bearing the authority of the centre. In this case, Eliza Somers was able to use her 'index of pretty learning' in order to imply that the arrival of the British represented more than the imposition of alien civilization upon a barbarous country but the completion of a cycle of history that had begun with the scientists of Egypt. The fact that she should use such an argument suggests the extent of her desire to legitimate not only British imperialism but also the unrespectable arts of the theatre and, ultimately, her own position in the cultural and political life of the colony.

As in the case of the American prologues, the rituals of theatre are used to articulate the anxieties of the soldier-stroller. Eliza Somers's address is not just the customary gesture of the actor towards a potentially hostile audience but a plea that the 'true vagrant race'—the British soldier—might find a resort in an alien environment. Thus, she expresses the hope that Africa will 'protect the strangers', a curious way of representing a military power that was more than capable of exerting its own will in the colony. These anxieties become even clearer in the address 'WRITTEN AND SPOKEN BY MRS SOMERS' for the final performance at the 'African Theatre', before the British were due to withdraw from the Cape as a result of the signing of the Peace of Amiens. The address was the epilogue not only to the performance but also to what Eliza Somers believed was the end of British rule in southern Africa:

FAIR Dames—and Gents—ere yet the Curtain falls,
Ere yet lone Echoes claim these vacate walls,
One parting word I pray: I'm hither sent
Our Green-room little Squad to represent . . .
. . . now we take our leave,

---

[23] Eliza Somers, 'An Occasional Address Upon the Opening of the African Theatre, Cape Town', Miscellaneous Letters, British Library.

> Ne'er more to meet you *here* at sprightly Eve;
> No more in Buskin'd pride—these boards to tread;
> Th' *Enchanter's* Wand is *broke*—Illusion's fled![24]

The allusion to *The Tempest* in these lines suggests that theatricality could function not only as a reinforcement of British military power overseas but also as a sign of the fragility or insubstantiality of that power, its embeddedness in a historical moment that would not last. As the empire's strollers, the soldiers of the Cape would, by necessity, be moving on. The world was their circuit but they remained itinerants within it. However, in claiming that the departure of the British would leave nothing but 'echoes' within the 'vacate walls' of the colonial theatre, Eliza Somers was effectively ignoring the presence of other actors at the Cape—the slaves, the indigenous Africans, the Dutch, even the ordinary British soldier and sailor. Her theatre, which represented itself as a *theatrum mundi*, left out more than it included, indicating the power of amateur theatricals, not only as a form of aggrandizement but also as a way to 'protect the strangers' from what they would not or could not know.

The Theatre of the Isle Dauphine

The significance of theatre as a framework in which the anxieties of empire could be articulated is also clear in the final example of military theatricals that I wish to discuss—the performances by a group of soldiers and sailors on an island in Mobile Bay on the Gulf Coast of North America during the War of 1812 between Britain and the United States. Analogies with *The Tempest*, which I have been suggesting in this chapter so far, are even more pertinent in this case, although they were never explicitly articulated by the participants in the theatricals. The Isle Dauphine was, to European eyes at least, a kind of paradise, populated by exotic birds such as humming-birds, pelicans, and parakeets. Like Caliban's island, it merged the realms of both earth and water with its marshes, its sandy reaches, and its shoreline covered with oyster beds.[25] The 'Prospero' of the Isle Dauphine was an Irishman, a Mr Cooney (or Rooney in one account) who had been in the service of the United States navy, but had been banished to the island for an unspecified misdemeanour. Cooney was the *de facto* ruler of the island, which was also the home

---

[24] Eliza Somers, 'A Farewell Epilogue', Miscellaneous Letters, British Library.

[25] Captain John Henry Cooke, *A Narrative of Events in the South of France, and of the Attack on New Orleans, in 1814 and 1815* (London, 1835), 278–9.

of a number of black slaves who had escaped from plantations on the mainland. After their defeat at the Battle of New Orleans on 8 January 1814, the British forces planned an offensive against Mobile with the intention of recapturing New Orleans by an overland route. First, they had to attack Fort Bowyer which guarded access to Mobile from the sea. The Isle Dauphine, which was situated on the opposite side to the entrance to Mobile Bay, served as a British encampment. The attempt on Fort Bowyer was successful and the British were preparing to attack Mobile when they were informed that a treaty had been signed between the Americans and the government in London, ending the War of 1812.

Like the Cape of Good Hope, the history of the Gulf Coast of North America was a palimpsest of colonial activity in the region. Its indigenous inhabitants were the Creek Indians, whose territory had been contested by the Spanish, the French, the British, and the United States throughout the eighteenth century. The Gulf Coast was strategically significant because of its proximity to Cuba and the West Indies. Whoever controlled it would also have access to the North American interior via the Mississippi. By 1812, as a result of the Peninsular War and insurrections in the colonies of South America, Spain was a declining influence in the region. Both the British and the United States attempted to exploit the vacuum that this created, the British encouraging Indian grievances against the Americans with the long term goal of establishing an Indian buffer state that would protect the West Indies.[26]

After they received news that the war was over, the British forces in Mobile Bay experienced an hiatus while they waited for the treaty to be signed, prisoners to be exchanged, and preparations made for embarkation to England. The army and the navy were thus effectively marooned on the Isle Dauphine for a two-month period. Initially, officers occupied their time by organizing sham fights as a way of keeping their men active and also to maintain levels of military readiness. Captain John Henry Cooke, who was an observer of the proceedings, claimed that the participants treated these mock contests 'with as much zeal and anxiety as if the fate of a capital city was to be decided'. The warriors went so far as to issue mock orders and dispatches 'for this petty war', some of which Cooke kept as souvenirs.[27]

The logical extension of the theatricality of the sham fight was the staging of plays, but there was no substantial building on the island which

---

[26] Frank Lawrence Owsley Jr., *Struggle for the Gulf Borderlands: The Creek War and the Battle of New Orleans 1812–1815* (Gainesville, Fla., 1981), 6–17.

[27] Cooke, *Narrative*, 283.

could serve as a theatre. The regiments on the Isle Dauphine thus went about constructing a playhouse of their own, what Cooke described as 'a pastoral theatre'. They fixed on a site behind the encampment where pine trees and undergrowth were cut down to leave four trees 'so exactly opposite one another and at a given distance (both as to the wished-for breadth and length of the intended erection), that they formed the angles and the four corners of the gable ends of the contemplated transatlantic place of amusement'.[28] Tree trunks were driven into the ground as support for the benches of the theatre and the 'walls' were created by the weaving of branches in a wickerwork effect. Two mainsails from one of the naval vessels anchored off the island formed the roof of the construction, while ship's canvas also served as scenery. According to Benson Earle Hill, an artillery officer whose acting experiences in the army led him to take up a career in the professional theatre, the company of the Isle Dauphine was faced with a problem when it came to painting the scenery:

our sandy isle produced neither red nor yellow ochre; the neighbouring sea was unconscious of sepia: neither Sienna nor Cologne could be visited to procure their precious earths; of Indigo, although an American produce, we were without a morsel; vermillion could not be extracted from the jackets of our soldiers, for they now resembled Spanish brown.[29]

Hill claimed that the solution arrived at by the soldiers was to use the material that they carried with them everywhere—gunpowder and pipe-clay. (The latter was used for the whitening of breeches.) The scenery, which represented the columns and arches of a proscenium, 'a street' and 'a chamber', resembled 'an Indian ink drawing on an enormous scale', indicating a resourcefulness which Hill claimed the scene-painters at the patent theatres, Stanfield and the Grieves, would have been at a loss to emulate.[30]

The ingenuity of the soldier-actors was also evident in their choice of costume. Hill claimed that the resources of the island were adapted in all sorts of ways:

Ostrich feathers, ingeniously cut out of silver paper; green plumes, from the young shoots of the pine tree; a shirt cut in half made two well-sized aprons; whilst

---

[28] Cooke, *Narrative*, 304.

[29] Benson Earle Hill, *Recollections of an Artillery Officer: Including Scenes and Adventures in Ireland, America, Flanders and France* (2 vols.; London, 1836), ii. 67. For Hill's theatrical career see his *Playing About: Or Theatrical Anecdotes and Adventures* (2 vols.; London, 1840) and *Home Service: Or, Scenes and Characters from Life, At Out and Head Quarters* (2 vols.; London, 1839).

[30] Hill, *Recollections*, ii. 67–8.

the sleeves, stuffed with dry moss, and tied with red tape from the adjutant's desk, were converted into becoming turbans; small fir-cones, and the dried berries of a shrub, name unknown, were drilled for necklaces; fans, of palm grass; gold paper cut into brooches, earrings, and eye-glasses; these and a thousand other substitutes were resolved on, rather than evince a lack of zeal in the cause.[31]

The actors' wardrobe was later augmented by a consignment of costumes from a Spanish theatrical troop which had been captured by an English cruiser in the Gulf but allowed to go free in exchange for their finery. Cooke claimed that 'these flimsy green-room dresses of transparent texture of male and female attire were deposited in bundles in the *Isle Dauphin*' and were 'all ready made for both sexes, or, more properly speaking, for the transmogrifying of males into the flounces and other female trappings'.[32] As in the case of other military theatricals, the question of who would play the female roles was of crucial importance. Benson Earle Hill's account suggests that there were some women on the island, followers of the soldiery, who lent some of their dresses as costume for which they were financially rewarded. However, there was no question of these women performing in the theatre. As in the case of the performance on board *HMS Bedford*, part of the appeal of the theatricals was that they enabled the travestying of female roles. Hill claimed that one of the highlights of the performance occurred when 'our fair Melissa, Kitty, and the Mesdames Gadabout and Trippet' (all played by men) entered the stage in Foote's *The Lying Valet*. The shouts of the audience 'rent the air'.[33]

For the first night of the theatricals on the Isle Dauphine a wing was added to the building in order to accommodate the actors. Hill claimed that it was 'in truth, a *green* room'.[34] An orchestra, formed of the various regimental bands on the island, provided the music and trusted non-commissioned officers were stationed at the door to receive tickets from patrons. Like the 'African Theatre' of the Cape, the pastoral theatre of the Isle Dauphine was exclusive, admitting only subscribers whose rank was reflected in the configuration of the auditorium. Areas within the theatre were demarcated by finer wickerwork than that of the walls and 'dignified by the name of "stage boxes" '.[35] They were for the use of senior officers. The common soldiery, whose labour had helped construct the building, were kept outside. Hill claimed that once the auditorium was full, part of the sail roof was lifted to allow the soldiers, perched on the trees outside the theatre, to look inside and observe the officers at play.[36]

[31] Ibid. 68–9. [32] Cooke, *Narrative*, 305. See also Ibid. 73.
[33] Hill, *Recollections*, ii. 69–70. [34] Ibid. 69. [35] Ibid. 66–7. [36] Ibid. 69.

The first play to be performed was Foote's *The Lying Valet*, taken from a volume of farces in the possession of one of the officers. It was followed by *The Honey Moon*, a comedy by John Tobin, and another farce by Foote, *The Mayor of Garratt*. Situated as they were on the margins of North America with no access to a town or city, the choice of the players as to what they would perform was determined by the personal libraries of the participants, so it is unwise to read much into the repertory of the Isle Dauphine theatre. However, it is significant that the officers chose to perform farces, in particular that favourite of military thespians in Britain and overseas, *The Mayor of Garratt*. One probable reason why farce was preferred by amateur performers was that it did not require subtle acting skills, unlike high tragedy which presumed some level of competence if it was not to appear ludicrous. But it is more likely that plays such as *The Mayor of Garratt* and *High Life Below Stairs* appealed to military thespians because their comic effect was based on the reversal of normal social hierarchies. As I indicated in my discussion of the performance on board *HMS Bedford*, transgressive role-playing within the strictly defined limits of a theatrical event could be highly significant in communities for which hierarchy was everything.

The accounts of the pastoral theatre on the Isle Dauphine by Cooke, Hill, and by another military observer, William Surtees, all suggest the transformatory quality of the event.[37] The performances took place at the very edge of America, on an island which was itself on the margins of land and sea. Adapting the practices of the strolling theatre, the British forces constructed a playhouse that was improvised and impermanent. It belonged more to the natural world than it did to the world of towns and cities: its gable ends were rooted trees, its walls a lattice of branches permeable to light, its roof moved with the breeze. The costumes represented the point at which the natural was transformed into the civilized, fir-cones becoming necklaces, palm grass a lady's fan. The very *matériel* of a soldier's life—his gunpowder and pipe-clay—was transformed into scenic images of the world he had left behind. Gender too was indeterminate: as John Henry Cooke suggested, male was 'transmogrified' into female by the flimsy insubstantiality of the costumes of a theatrical troop that the actors had never seen. Not only were the boundaries of gender and geography uncertain, a temporal transition from war to peace was also being marked. American officers, who only a few weeks before had been fighting the British, were present at the performances and commended

---

[37] William Surtees, *Twenty-Five Years in a Rifle Brigade* (Edinburgh, 1833), 391–400.

their former foes on the quality of the building which, they claimed, the Indians would have envied.[38]

In marking the uncertainties of war in this way the pastoral theatre could not be permanent. Benson Earle Hill claimed that an officer had the idea of burning down the theatre to represent the descent of Don Juan into hell, but it was decided to leave the 'huge basket' to the elements.[39] Presumably it returned to the natural world out of which it had been created. The building was in many respects more important than the performances that took place within it and the attention given to its construction in the accounts of both Cooke and Hill testifies to this. This was because the theatre was not only symbolic of the transformatory possibilities of war, it also represented what the officers thought they were doing in this corner of the world—erecting a model of British identity, hence Benson Earle Hill's comparison of the theatre with the distant patent houses of Stanfield and the Grieves with their stage boxes and green rooms. However, this reference to the metropolitan centre also had the effect of registering what was different about the Isle Dauphine. The additional accommodation built for the actors was 'in truth, a *green* room', the 'in truth' highlighting just how outlandish the theatre was, in the same way as the green taverns of Warley and Coxheath were a measure of how the camps were a simulacra of civilized London.

The significance of these military theatricals was therefore manifold. In their insubstantiality they marked the distinctiveness of the experience of war, the way in which it placed the normal categories of identity—time, place, rank, gender—in a condition of flux and uncertainty. They also functioned as cultural events in which the British forces could test their sense of national identity, projected in terms of the rites of theatre, against the alienating realities of war and empire. What did it mean to 'act' Britain in this way? It is clear, from the Isle Dauphine and other examples of military theatre discussed here, that acting Britain meant excluding certain groups from the country's 'theatre'. Whereas the Isle Dauphine theatricals were highly fluid in certain of their practices, this fluidity was constrained within the boundaries of military rank, social class, gender, and above all, race. Who was entitled to enter the theatre, both as actors and as members of the audience, was clearly demarcated. The common soldiery were excluded, as were the women of the encampment. It is not clear whether Mr Cooney, the erstwhile Briton who had joined the enemy, was a participant. Certainly none of the accounts make any reference

[38] Ibid. 400.   [39] Hill, *Recollections*, ii. 82.

to the presence of either the Indians or the escaped black slaves on the island, some of whom had been recruited by the British to fight the Americans. Presumably their place was on the very fringes of the audience, beyond the soldiery in the trees, if they were allowed a place at all. Although the British had made use of the slaves as soldiers, for the same reasons as they had exploited Indian grievances, when the plantation owners arrived on the Isle Dauphine to reclaim their property, every assistance was given to them. Benson Earle Hill claimed that the resort of his black servant had been to 'adopt invisibility', hiding in the wilds of the island until the plantation owners had gone.[40] This condition of invisibility reflected the status of black and indigenous people within the military theatre of Britain as a whole.

Postscript

A contemporary historian of the war on the Gulf Coast, A. Lacarrière Latour, remarked that the British army and its black regiments in particular suffered in the period immediately following the declaration of peace. As they prepared for embarkation to England, the British forces, he claimed, were subject to the diseases that infested the sub-tropical island. There were up to two thousand sick and wounded men in the fleet: 'it is impossible to ascertain correctly the number of the victims of disease, from the 19th of January until the end of March, the time of evacuation by the army. Judging from the number of graves around their camps, it certainly was considerable.'[41] The accounts of the theatricals by Hill, Cooke, and Surtees make no mention of the dying that was going on around them. This suggests that the performances created a defensive palisade, not only against those who might threaten the British theatre, but also against death itself, the ultimate shadowy actor in the theatre of war.

---

[40] Hill, *Recollections*, 80.

[41] A. Lacarrière Latour, *Historical Memoir of the War in West Florida and Louisiana in 1814–15* (orig. edn. 1816; Gainesville, Fla., 1964), 226.

8

Conclusion: 'A Strange Metamorphosis'

THE final defeat of Napoleon at the Battle of Waterloo was an inauspicious event for the British theatre. After 1815 the commercial and artistic fortunes of playhouses in both London and the provinces suffered considerably: there were no more victories to be triumphantly staged before a public eager for news of the war, while the reduction in the peacetime establishment meant that there were fewer soldiers and sailors thronging the galleries and fewer officers parading themselves in the boxes and the pit. Some provincial theatres such as Samuel Jerrold's in Sheerness never recovered from the decline in patronage while metropolitan stages such as Astley's and Sadler's Wells survived by revisiting the war in the form of spectacular re-enactments of the battles of Trafalgar and Waterloo and by elaborating forms such as nautical melodrama.[1] This crisis is a reflection of what I have been stressing throughout this book—the fact that war and theatre were mutually sustaining, not only in material terms but also culturally, ideologically, and politically. In this final chapter I would like to consider some of the implications of the reflexivity of acting and soldiering in late Georgian Britain.

One sign of this relationship was the fact that the very language of the acting profession was militaristic—an actor-manager was a 'general', his performers his 'troops', London was their 'winter quarters', the acquiescence of a local magistrate to a performance was known as 'taking the town'. Examples of this kind of language are too numerous to outline in detail here, but one puff from the *Monthly Mirror* will stand for the many:

Having sacked the town, and made a rich booty, the Astleys are preparing to re-cross the bridge at Westminster, and to commence on Easter Monday, as usual, their spring campaign. The success of this storming the pockets of the citizens is principally owing to the ingenious plans of action, drawn out by Mr. Astley, junr. all of which have been put into execution by his crack company, with an effect rarely unparalleled. At the head of the muster-roll we place Mrs Astley, who is a

[1] For this post-war decline see Dibdin, *Memoirs*, 119, and *Gentleman's Magazine*, 87 (1817), 270.

host herself. She is indeed a sort of *Joan of Arc*; success sits perched upon her banners.[2]

The military metaphors were particularly apt in this case, as Philip Astley senior, the founder of the dynasty, had himself been a soldier. He had perfected his horsemanship as a sergeant in the 15th Dragoons during the Seven Years War and never completely renounced his military background, even after establishing himself as the leading circus entrepreneur.[3] When war was declared in 1793, he volunteered at the age of fifty-one and later produced two military textbooks, *A Description and Historical Account, of the Places now the Theatre of War in the Low Countries* (1794) and *Remarks on the Profession and Duties of a Soldier* (1794).[4] The former, which made no reference to Astley's theatrical career, was a guide to the battlefields and fortified towns of the Low Countries, based on the author's experiences during the Seven Years War. His military knowledge of the fortifications of Valenciennes was later incorporated into his re-enactment of the siege that had taken place there. A sign of the inseparability of war and theatre for Philip Astley was the fact that military *matériel* was part of the very fabric of his theatres. As I indicated previously, a cannon that had been captured at Valenciennes was used to enhance the verisimilitude of the representation of the siege.

There are a number of reasons why the identities of the actor and the soldier should have been interchangeable in late Georgian society. First, as I have suggested before, acting and soldiering were peripatetic activities, often amounting to a renunciation of family and local ties. To those who had never gone beyond their parish or village, the departure of a young man (or woman) for the army, navy, or the stage often meant that they never saw them again, or, if they did return, that they were changed utterly by the experience. By the same measure the visits of recruiting parties and strolling players to the countryside represented the incursion of an outside world that was attractive but also potentially threatening. Both kinds of 'invasion' used the appeal of exoticism in order to attract custom, the recruiting officer by exerting his showmanship, the 'general' of a strolling company by proclaiming the attractions of his troop. Significantly, both kinds of 'theatre' deployed similar strategies: it was customary for the theatrical manager to beat a drum on entering a town, a practice

[2] *Monthly Mirror*, NS 3 (1808), 274–5.

[3] For Astley see Highfill *et al.*, *Biographical Dictionary*, i. 149.

[4] Philip Astley, *A Description and Historical Account, of the Places now the Theatre of War in the Low Countries* (London, 1794) and *Remarks on the Profession and Duty of a Soldier* (London, 1794).

that was also followed by the army. Local inhabitants were often confused as to whether the drum signalled the arrival of a strolling company or a recruiting party.[5] The metaphor of 'taking the town' in theatrical journalism reflected the fact that staging a play in the country occasionally involved a struggle with the local authorities who were resistant to theatre on moral and political grounds. Similarly, the military was often made unwelcome in towns and villages because of its justified reputation for disorderliness and the fear that it might be used by the authorities against the local inhabitants. No less important was the fact that actors and soldiers represented a sexual threat to their host community, leaving broken relationships and unwanted pregnancies in their wake.

To become a soldier in late Georgian society was therefore to take on the identity of the actor (and vice versa)—stigmatized, dislocated, and exotic. As Carolyn Steedman suggests, the soldier's story was 'a social myth, a drama of alienation, journeying and arrival' and in numerous autobiographies published after the Revolutionary and Napoleonic Wars this 'drama' was repeatedly re-enacted.[6] A trope of these soldiers' stories is formed by their accounts of when they first realized that they had, in fact, become soldiers. For Thomas Jackson this moment occurred when he joined the militia: 'I now saw myself a new figure—my head being trimmed to order, and crimped with hot irons; my blood red coat, white small-belows, with black leggings; belted and armed; and with a long leather cue, or tail, fashioned to my pole. A strange metamorphosis, thought I, of myself, since the day before.'[7] The transformatory power of military experience is highlighted by Jackson's capacity to stand back and regard himself in 'a new figure', as if he were his own mirror, or indeed, an actor playing a role. That the army could have this disjunctive effect on the individual is suggested by the recurrence of the term 'metamorphosis' in John Shipp's account of his first days in the military: 'I was . . . paraded to the tailor's shop, and deprived of my new clothes,—coat, leathers, and hat,—for which I received, in exchange, red jacket, red waistcoat, red pantaloons, and red-foraging cap. The change, or metamorphosis, was so complete, that I could hardly imagine it to be the same dapper little fellow.'[8] For both Jackson and Shipp the word 'metamorphosis' marks their realization that entering the army should amount to such a radical

[5] On the use of the drum see Lawrence, *Old Theatre Days*, 11–21.

[6] Carolyn Steedman, *The Radical Soldier's Tale: John Pearman, 1819–1908* (London, 1988), 37.

[7] Jackson, *Narrative*, 5.

[8] John Shipp, *Memoirs of the Extraordinary Military Career of John Shipp* (3 vols.; London, 1829), i. 31–2.

alteration in their identities. Becoming a soldier was thus, at a fundamental level, a theatrical experience. It meant the realization of a capacity to take on another identity, to perform the military or naval role. In late Georgian culture going for a soldier also implied that one was lost to civilian society in the same sense as joining the stage implied estrangement from the respectable norm. In the *Journal of a Soldier of the Seventy-First*, the decision of the author to join the army was represented as a direct result of his interest in theatricals. He was so ashamed at his family's revulsion on the news that he wanted to become an actor that the only way he could make 'atonement', as he describes it, was to go for a soldier, serving his country as a penance for his sense of personal failure.[9] By becoming a soldier he projected himself even further into the marginal status he had assumed when he first performed on stage, so far in fact, that he was unable to reconcile himself to returning to Scotland, his birth place. There is no resolution to this soldier's story, only an assertion of permanent alienation and itinerancy.

John Shipp, the young man who had experienced the 'metamorphosis' of a uniform, had no family to object to his decision to join the army. His father, who had himself been a soldier, was dead, as was his mother, while his brother had been impressed and never seen again. His first encounter with the military occurred sometime in the 1790s when, a workhouse boy alone in a frozen turnip field near Saxmundham in Suffolk, he heard a military band playing 'Over the Hills and Far Away'. Fired by enthusiasm, he eventually joined the army at the age of twelve, seeing service in Guernsey, the Cape of Good Hope, and India, where he spent most of his career. Intelligent and resourceful, he rose through the ranks to become a lieutenant by the age of 20 and, after selling his commission to pay off debts, achieved the feat of being promoted by merit for a second time. While in India he took part in military theatricals at Cawnpore, playing the roles of Lord Duberley in *The Heir at Law* and Lord Minikin in *Bon Ton*. In his account of the theatricals, Shipp revealed that his commanding officer, the Marquis of Hastings, had praised his performance, especially in the role of Lord Duberley. Shipp was then informed that he had been appointed baggage-master to the left division of the army, a significant promotion. He went on to comment, 'Had I known this good news before, I would have thrown all the life and soul of a baggage-master into the character of Lord Duberley', suggesting that he conceived his role in the

---

[9] *Journal of a Soldier of the Seventy-First, or Glasgow Regiment, Highland Light Infantry, from 1806 to 1815* (Edinburgh, 1819), 12.

army as an act, commensurable with his successful performance as a lord in Colman's genteel comedy.[10]

In 1823, however, Shipp's career in the military was cut short when he was court-martialled for making allegations against a superior officer, a Major Browne, whom, he claimed, had suggested that Shipp was a swindler. He returned to London where he attempted to establish a career as a writer. He published two plays, *The Shepherdess of Arranville* (1826) and *The Maniac of the Pyrenees; or, The Heroic Soldier's Wife* (1829), but he achieved most success with his *Memoirs*, published in 1829. According to a later edition, published in 1843, the *Memoirs* had been written with the assistance of an unnamed 'gentleman', to whom Shipp had submitted the manuscript for revision.[11] In 1969 the *Memoirs* were published in an edition which further revises the 1829 text, removing much of the style that the editor, C. J. Stranks, considered as too Victorian and 'keeping the good, plain writing which was probably characteristic of Shipp when he let himself be natural'.[12] The 'probably' suggests that Stranks did not have access to the manuscript from which the 1829 *Memoirs* had been written, but was in fact producing his own version of a literary style appropriate to a former workhouse boy. Shipp's imaginative literature, which does not seem to have been mediated by editors or interpreters, may well be a more authentic record of his military experiences. *The Maniac of the Pyrenees* concerns a former soldier, Colonel De Bovre, and his wife who have been betrayed by the Colonel's brother and forced into exile in the Pyrenees. They are attacked by banditti, the Colonel is killed and as a result of a number of plot machinations, involving scenes in which the Colonel's wife goes spectacularly mad, revenge is exacted upon the brother. In its preoccupation with states of alienation and despair and its representation of society in terms of a disintegrating family, the piece can be compared with earlier and better known examples of Gothic drama, such as Charles Maturin's *Bertram*. *The Maniac of the Pyrenees* could be said to be a representation of Shipp's own sense of rejection by the military brotherhood that had once celebrated him, an alienation that was political in its scope. The play explicitly questions the basis of authority: at one point Colonel De Bovre declares to his wife: 'How sweet the humble crust, my

---

[10] Shipp, *Memoirs*, ii. 238.

[11] John Shipp, *Memoirs of the Extraordinary Military Career of John Shipp. A New Edition. To Which is Added, A Continuation of the Memoir, Until the Death of Mr. Shipp* (London, 1843), 330.

[12] John Shipp, *The Path of Glory: Being the Memoirs of the Extraordinary Military Career of John Shipp Written by Himself*, ed. C. J. Stranks (London, 1969), xiii.

beloved, when the heart knows it is not the stolen bread of oppression, the spoliation of despotism, or obtained by the coercive hand of power.'[13] In his *Memoirs* Shipp was highly critical of the practice of flogging, claiming that it not only brutalized the soldier but, once administered, ensured that the private would never rise above his rank or social station: 'in all professions, in whatsoever sphere we move, we all expect to rise above our first apprenticeship; but the moment you touch a soldier's back, it writes opposite his name ... "A private you are, and a private you must remain".'[14] Shipp advocated 'less coercive means' of punishment, including solitary confinement and the docking of pay. His arguments against flogging were subsequently extracted from the *Memoirs* and published in the form of a pamphlet addressed to Sir Francis Burdett who was able to use Shipp's text as a soldier's testimony. Shipp later received £60 from Burdett as an acknowledgement of his contribution.[15] In 1829 he was recruited in the newly formed Metropolitan Police as Inspector in the Stepney division. He then moved to Liverpool where he was made Superintendent of the Night Watch and, later, Governor of the Workhouse at a salary of £300 a year. Shipp died at the age of 49 in April 1834. Throughout the latter stages of his career, he continued to write, publishing stories about India in Liverpool newspapers. However, according to the 1843 edition of his *Memoirs*, 'his propensity for literary composition never interfered with his responsible duties as an officer'.[16]

The army could be said to have been good for John Shipp. The workhouse boy whose future was as bleak as the frozen turnip field in which he had first heard the call of the military had been elevated to a position of authority, respectability, and comparative wealth. A comparable figure to John Shipp is Robert Hay, the illiterate weaver's son who left the navy with an education and also produced an autobiography. Like Shipp, part of Hay's 'education' involved participation in amateur theatricals. The services condemned many a poor boy to degradation or death but for some they could act as catalysts for social transformation. Going for a soldier or going to sea was *the* formative experience for a large proportion of the male population of Britain in the late eighteenth and early nineteenth centuries. (The wars also influenced the lives of many women, but in

<hr>

[13] John Shipp, *The Maniac of the Pyrenees: or, The Heroic Soldier's Wife; A Melo Drama in Two Acts* (Brentford, 1829), 3.

[14] Shipp, *Memoirs*, iii. 204.

[15] John Shipp, *A Voice from the Ranks; or A Letter to Sir Francis Burdett, on the Barbarous and Degrading System of Flogging Soldiers and Sailors* (London, 1831); see also Dinwiddy, 'Flogging', 310.

[16] Shipp, *Memoirs. A New Edition*, 333.

different ways.) The army and the navy schooled the nation's manhood in all forms of education, both formal and informal, introducing young men and boys to experiences that were unimaginable from the vantage point of the farm, the village, or the borough. The dislocating effect of becoming a soldier or sailor was such that it often generated other forms of change. If joining the army or navy represented such a profound alteration, an assumption of a different identity, then other kinds of metamorphoses were possible, creating the Shipp who wrote his plays and memoirs, but also the Cobbetts, the Wedderburns, the Despards, the James Hadfield who entered Drury Lane with the intention of killing the King. The very theatricality which made men soldiers and sailors in the first place was also capable of making them something else which explains why civilian society was profoundly wary of the forces that it was compelled to celebrate as the nation's true defenders.

A Foucauldian interpretation of the careers of men such as Shipp and Hay would suggest that theatricality was part of the disciplinary apparatus that ensured that becoming a soldier did not truly emancipate but instead subordinated these men even more completely within existing structures of power. In his advocacy of solitary confinement and his later career in the Metropolitan Police and as Governor of the Liverpool Workhouse, Shipp could be said to exemplify the internally disciplined Foucauldian subject, so completely shaped by the discourses and apparatuses of power that he not only polices himself but also the working class out of which he emerged. By describing the ordinary soldier as an apprentice in a profession, Shipp revealed himself to have imbibed the ideology behind the move to 'de-civilianize' the military that I discussed in Chapter 2, by which the recalcitrant theatricality of the Volunteers was replaced by a disciplined career structure in which men would be, rather than act, the soldier. The ways in which this ideology functioned in practice are highlighted by John Shipp's own career and, in particular, his participation in the theatricals at Cawnpore, a symbolic enactment of what the profession of a soldier might mean for a workhouse boy. The equation of Shipp's performance as Lord Duberley with his promotion to baggage-master suggests that success in the army was, in effect, an aping of his betters. His actual career suggests that his superiors in the military were prepared to allow Shipp to progress in the ranks on the basis of merit, so long as his emulation of those in positions of power and authority did not go too far. In other words, his rise through the ranks was supervised in the same way as the Marquis of Hastings had monitored his performance as Lord Duberley. Like the staging of *The Fair Penitent* on board *HMS Bedford*, the Cawnpore theatricals exemplify the paternalistic ethos that governed the services as a whole, an ethos that was flexible enough to allow Shipp to think that he could progress in the career of a soldier, but also ruthless in the maintenance of the barriers that an aspiring workhouse boy could not cross. Shipp was a successful military actor for as long as he did not transgress the hierarchies that the performance encoded. When he challenged authority, significantly on the grounds of an insult to a gentlemanly prerogative, his 'honour', he discovered the actual limitations of his role—he could 'act' but never 'be' the officer. In this respect, Shipp's career is paradigmatic of the British response to the experience of the Revolutionary and Napoleonic Wars, and, in particular, to the ideology of the nation-at-arms. The Volunteer Movement, the attempt to emulate the *levée en masse*, had been shown to be politically and logistically unmanageable. However, in the post-Revolutionary context, the conduct of Britain's wars could not be left to an effete band of gentlemen amateurs who fought and played in their own, rather than the nation's, interests. Shipp was exactly the type of lower-class male to whom the defence of Britain could be trusted without endangering the existing social order. Theatricality, in the form of the military band, the attractions of a blood-red uniform, seduced such men into believing that the army was the place for them; in the form of events such as the Cawnpore theatricals, it also made clear how circumscribed this 'place' really was.

Shipp's capacity to shape his own destiny was thus severely limited, in the same way as when he attempted to write for a living he was ventriloquized by other anonymous voices—the gentlemen who re-wrote his manuscript and commented on his life for the 1843 edition of the *Memoirs*, not to mention C. J. Stranks in 1969. His attempts to become one of the literati were thwarted by the same social forces that had ended his military career. However, in spite of the condescension of the literary establishment, Shipp persisted in writing, in the same way as having identified the injustice done to him by Major Browne, he did not remain silent but challenged his superior officer in the latter's own terms. Once he had been 'metamorphosed' by war, he could not be replaced in the world from which he had come. Having become an actor, he continued to perform, challenging the limits of a theatre that had given him a role and a voice. He would tell his story, in the same way as James Hadfield's actions in entering Drury Lane on 15 May 1800 were an attempt to tell his. Significantly, both men gave accounts of the wounds they had received in battle as testimonies of their service. Shipp claimed to have suffered six wounds from matchlock balls, one of which had damaged his sight, while another had injured his skull, giving him severe headaches for the rest of his life.[17] The depictions of James Hadfield in contemporary prints treating the assassination attempt made much of his scarred condition. Later in his trial the wounds that he had received in battle were used to justify an assessment of him as insane, thus preventing him from going to the hangman and, also, depoliticizing his actions.[18] After Hadfield was apprehended at Drury Lane he was interviewed by Sheridan, the Prince of Wales, and the Duke of York. He addressed the latter in the following terms:

I know your Royal Highness—God bless you. You are a good fellow. I have served with your Highness, and (pointing to a deep cut over his eye, and another long scar on his cheek) said, I got these, and more than these, in fighting by your side. At Lincelles I was left three hours, among the dead, in a ditch, and was taken prisoner by the French. I had my arm broken by a shot, and eight sabre wounds in my head; but I recovered, and here I am.[19]

Like Shipp's *Memoirs*, Hadfield's actions represented an assertion of his presence, in both a physical and political sense, in the theatre of war. As it had been throughout the eighteenth century, Drury Lane was the most powerful symbol of that other theatre where Hadfield had fought on behalf of those he was now confronting. His statement to the Duke of York was an apotheosis which not only made it clear that war had failed to destroy him but also amounted to a realization that his attempt to kill the King was the final performance in which all the suffering made sense. Neither Hadfield nor Shipp can be said to have transcended the metamorphoses that had led from the moment that they first became soldiers, but neither can they be said to have been completely subjected by the experience of war. Theatricality moulded and controlled them, but it also enabled them to speak as actors, to say 'I recovered, and here I am'.

[17] Shipp, *Memoirs*, iii. 281–2.
[18] For Hadfield's acquittal see Roy Porter, *Mind-Forg'd Manacles: A History of Madness in England from the Restoration to the Regency* (Cambridge, Mass., 1987), 116–17.
[19] *Monthly Mirror*, 9 (1800), 314.

Select Bibliography

1. Manuscript sources and printed ephemera

BRITISH LIBRARY

A Collection of Cuttings from Newspapers containing Memoirs of Lord Nelson.
Broadsides etc. Relating to the Expected Invasion of England by Bonaparte.
Charles Burney, A Collection of Playbills, Notices and Press-cuttings Dealing
  With Private Theatrical Performances, 1750–1808.
Collection Relating to Sadler's Wells.
Eliza Somers, Miscellaneous Letters, Cuttings Etc. 1792–1802.

LINENHALL LIBRARY, BELFAST

W. J. Lawrence, 'The Annals of "The Old Belfast Stage"', typescript dated 1897.

NATIONAL MARITIME MUSEUM, GREENWICH

Captain Hardy's papers.

PUBLIC RECORD OFFICE, NORTHERN IRELAND

Drennan Letters.

THEATRE MUSEUM, LONDON

Playbills Drury Lane and Covent Garden.

2. Newspapers and periodicals

Cobbett's Weekly Political Register
E. Johnson's British Gazette, and Sunday Monitor
Indicator
Gentleman's Magazine
Hampshire Chronicle
Hampshire Telegraph, and Sussex Chronicle
Monthly Mirror
Morning Chronicle
Morning Post
Naval Chronicle
Oracle
Pic Nic
Portsmouth Telegraph
Public Advertiser

Sheffield Courant
Statesman
The Times
Thespian Magazine
Thespian Review
Tribune

3. Contemporary books, pamphlets, autobiographies, correspondence etc.

AIKIN, J., *A Description of the Country from Thirty to Forty Miles Round Manchester* (London, 1795).

ALBANICUS, *Letters on the Impolicy of a Standing Army, in Time of Peace* (London, 1793).

ALEXANDER, ALEXANDER, *The Life of Alexander Alexander*, ed. John Howell (2 vols.; Edinburgh, 1830).

ANGELO, HENRY, *Reminiscences of Henry Angelo* (2 vols.; London, 1828).

ANTON, JAMES, *Retrospect of a Military Life, During the Most Eventful Periods of the Last War* (Edinburgh, 1841).

ASTLEY, PHILIP, *A Description and Historical Account, of the Places now the Theatre of War in the Low Countries* (London, 1794).

—— *Remarks on the Profession and Duty of a Soldier* (London, 1794).

The Battle of Waterloo, 4th edn. (London, 1815).

Bell's British Theatre (20 vols.; 1776–8).

BERNARD, JOHN, *Retrospections of the Stage* (2 vols.; London, 1830).

BESSBOROUGH, EARL of (ed.), *Georgiana: Extracts from the Correspondence of Georgiana, Duchess of Devonshire* (London, 1955).

BOADEN, JAMES, *Memoirs of the Life of John Philip Kemble* (2 vols.; London, 1825).

BURGOYNE, JOHN, *The Dramatic and Poetical Works of the Late Lieut. Gen. J. Burgoyne* (2 vols.; London, 1808).

BURKE, EDMUND, *The Writings and Speeches of Edmund Burke*: viii, *The French Revolution*, ed. L. G. Mitchell (Oxford, 1989).

BURNEY, FANNY, *The Early Journals and Letters of Fanny Burney*, ed. Lars E. Troide (2 vols.; Oxford, 1988).

BUTT, JOHN, MACK, MAYNARD, *et al.*, *The Twickenham Edition of the Poems of Alexander Pope*, iii, part 2, ed. F. W. Bateson (London, 1951).

The Camp Guide: In A Series of Letters from Ensign Tommy Toothpick, to Lady Sarah Toothpick, and from Miss Nelly Brisk, to Miss Gadabout (London, 1778).

CHART, D. A. (ed.), *The Drennan Letters* (Belfast, 1931).

CLARE, JOHN, *The Prose of John Clare*, ed. J. W. and Anne Tibble (London, 1951).

COBBETT, WILLIAM, *The Autobiography of William Cobbett: The Progress of a Plough-Boy to a Seat in Parliament*, ed. William Reitzel (London, 1967).

COBBIN, INGRAM, *Stage Playing Immoral Vain and Dangerous in its Tendency*

(London, 1802).

COMBE, WILLIAM, *The Letters of Valerius* (London, 1804).

COOKE, CAPTAIN JOHN HENRY, *A Narrative of Events in the South of France, and of the Attack on New Orleans, in 1814 and 1815* (London, 1835).

COWPER, WILLIAM, *The Letters and Prose Writings of William Cowper*, ed. James King and Charles Ryskamp (5 vols.; Oxford, 1979–86).

Coxheath-Camp: a Novel in a Series of Letters by a Lady (2 vols.; Dublin, 1779).

CUMBERLAND, RICHARD, *Memoirs of Richard Cumberland 1806*, ed. Henry Flanders (orig. edn. London, 1856, New York, 1969).

The Death of Captain Cook, A Grand Serious-Pantomimic Ballet, in Three Parts (Hull, 1789).

DECASTRO, J., *The Memoirs of J. Decastro, Comedian*, ed. R. Humphreys (London, 1824).

DENT, JOHN, *The Bastille* (London, 1789).

A Description of the Defeat of the French Army . . . Now Exhibiting in Barker's Panorama, Strand, Near Surry-Street (London, 1816).

DIBDIN the ELDER, CHARLES, *The Professional Life of Mr Dibdin* (4 vols.; London, 1803).

DIBDIN the YOUNGER, CHARLES, *Professional and Literary Memoirs of Charles Dibdin the Younger*, ed. George Speaight (London, 1956).

DIBDIN, THOMAS, *The Reminiscences of Thomas Dibdin* (2 vols.; London, 1827).

DILLON, HENRY AUGUSTUS, *A Commentary on the Military Establishments and Defence of the British Empire* (2 vols.; London, 1811).

DUNLAP, WILLIAM, *A History of the American Theatre During the Revolution and After* (New York, 1832).

DYER, ROBERT, *Nine Years of an Actor's Life* (London, 1833).

EVERARD, EDWARD CAPE, *Memoirs of an Unfortunate Son of Thespis* (Edinburgh, 1818).

FAIRBRIDGE, DOROTHEA, *Lady Anne Barnard at the Cape of Good Hope 1797–1802* (Oxford, 1924).

FARINGTON, JOSEPH, *Diary*, ed. Kenneth Garlick, Angus Macintyre, and Kathryn Cave (16 vols.; New Haven, Conn., 1984).

FRANKLIN, ANDREW, *A Trip to the Nore* (London, 1797).

GOLDONI, CARLO, *Memoirs of Goldoni*, trans. John Black (2 vols.; London, 1814).

GOWER, LORD GRANVILLE LEVESON, *Lord Granville Leveson Gower (First Earl Granville): Private Correspondence, 1781–1821*, ed. Castalia, Countess Granville (2 vols.; London, 1916).

HAY, M. D. (ed.), *Landsman Hay: The Memoirs of Robert Hay 1789–1847* (London, 1953).

HAZLITT, WILLIAM, *The Complete Works of William Hazlitt*, ed. P. P. Howe (34 vols.; London, 1930–4).

HERBERT, DOROTHEA, *Retrospections of Dorothea Herbert 1770–1806* (Dublin, 1988).

HILL, BENSON EARLE, *Home Service: Or, Scenes and Characters from Life, At Out and Head Quarters* (2 vols.; London, 1839).

—— *Playing About: Or Theatrical Anecdotes and Adventures* (2 vols.; London, 1840).

—— *Recollections of an Artillery Officer: Including Scenes and Adventures in Ireland, America, Flanders and France* (2 vols.; London, 1836).

HILL, ROWLAND, *A Warning to Professors: Containing Aphoristic Observations on the Nature and Tendency of Public Amusements*, 2nd edn. (London, 1805).

HUDDESFORD, GEORGE, *The Second Part of Warley: A Satire* (London, 1778).

—— *Warley: A Satire* (London, 1778).

HUNT, LEIGH, *Dramatic Criticism 1808–1831*, ed. L. H. Houtchens and C. W. Houtchens (London, 1950).

JACKSON, JOHN, *The History of the Scottish Stage* (Edinburgh, 1793).

JACKSON, THOMAS, *Narrative of the Eventful Life of Thomas Jackson* (Birmingham, 1847).

JERROLD, BLANCHARD, *The Life and Remains of Douglas Jerrold* (Boston, Mass., 1859).

JORDAN, DOROTHY, *Mrs Jordan and her Family: Being the Unpublished Correspondence of Mrs Jordan and the Duke of Clarence, Later William IV*, ed. A. Aspinall (London, 1951).

Journal of a Soldier of the Seventy-First, or Glasgow Regiment, Highland Light Infantry, from 1806 to 1815 (Edinburgh, 1819).

LAMB, CHARLES, *The Letters of Charles and Mary Lamb*, ed. Edwin W. Marrs (3 vols.; Ithaca, NY, 1975–8).

—— *The Works of Charles and Mary Lamb*, ed. E. V. Lucas (7 vols.; London, 1903–5).

LATOUR, A. LACARRIÈRE, *Historical Memoir of the War in West Florida and Louisiana in 1814–15* (orig. edn. 1816; Gainesville, Fla., 1964).

LEE, HENRY, *Memoirs of a Manager: or, Life's Stage with New Scenery* (2 vols.; Taunton, 1830).

LEWES, CHARLES LEE, *Memoirs* (4 vols.; London, 1805).

LEWIS, M. G., *Journal of a West India Proprietor, Kept During a Residence in the Island of Jamaica* (London, 1834).

Mars's Holiday: or, a Trip to the Camp (London, 1792).

McGRIGOR, JAMES, *The Autobiography and Services of Sir James McGrigor, Bart.* (London, 1861).

MILMAN, HENRY HART, *Annals of S. Paul's Cathedral*, 2nd edn. (London, 1869).

The Naval Songster, or Jack Tar's Chest of Conviviality, for 1798 (London, 1798).

O'BRIEN, R. B., *The Autobiography of Theobald Wolfe Tone* (2 vols.; Dublin, 1893).

O'KEEFFE, JOHN, *Recollections of the Life of John O'Keeffe* (2 vols.; London, 1826).

—— *Wild Oats: Or The Strolling Gentlemen* (London, 1794).

OLD HUBERT [JAMES PARKINSON], *The Village Association or The Politics of Edley* (London, 1793).

OTWAY, THOMAS, *Venice Preserv'd*, ed. M. Kelsall (London, 1969).

OXBERRY, WILLIAM, *Dramatic Biography, and Histrionic Anecdotes* (5 vols.;

London, 1825–6).

PAINE, THOMAS, *The Writings and Speeches of Thomas Paine*, ed. Moncure Daniel Conway (4 vols.; London, 1894–6).

PILON, FREDERICK, *The Invasion; or, a Trip to Brighthelmstone* (London, 1778).

PINDAR, PETER, *The R—l Showman or the R—t's Gala* (London, 1814).

—— *The R—t's Fair, or Grand Galante-Show!!* (London, 1814).

PRENTICE, ARCHIBALD, *Historical Sketches and Personal Recollections of Manchester* (London, 1851).

Prologue and Epilogue to the Play of the Way to Keep Him, Performed at Richmond House, in April 1787, in a Private Society [London, 1787?].

Report from the Select Committee on Dramatic Literature: with the Minutes of Evidence, House of Commons, 2 Aug. 1832.

ROWE, NICHOLAS, *The Fair Penitent*, ed. M. Gold (London, 1969).

—— *The Tragedy of Jane Shore*, ed. H. W. Pedicord (London, 1975).

RYLEY, S. W., *The Itinerant: or Memoirs of an Actor* (9 vols.; London, 1808–27).

SARGENT, WINTHROP, *The Life and Career of Major John Andre, Adjutant-General of the British Army in America* (New York, 1902).

SHERIDAN, RICHARD BRINSLEY, *The Dramatic Works of Richard Brinsley Sheridan*, ed. Cecil Price (2 vols.; Oxford, 1973).

—— *The Letters of Richard Brinsley Sheridan*, ed. Cecil Price (3 vols.; Oxford, 1966).

—— *The Speeches of the Right Honourable Richard Brinsley Sheridan* (3 vols.; London, 1842).

SHIPP, JOHN, *A Voice from the Ranks; or A Letter to Sir Francis Burdett, on the Barbarous and Degrading System of Flogging Soldiers and Sailors* (London, 1831).

—— *Memoirs of the Extraordinary Military Career of John Shipp* (3 vols.; London, 1829).

—— *Memoirs of the Extraordinary Military Career of John Shipp. A New Edition. To Which is Added, A Continuation of the Memoir, Until the Death of Mr Shipp* (London, 1843).

—— *The Maniac of the Pyrenees: or, The Heroic Soldier's Wife; A Melo Drama in Two Acts* (Brentford, 1829).

—— *The Path of Glory: Being the Memoirs of the Extraordinary Military Career of John Shipp Written by Himself*, ed. C. J. Stranks (London, 1969).

Songs, Naval and National of the Late Charles Dibdin (London, 1841).

SOUTHEY, ROBERT, *The Life of Nelson* (London, 1909).

STEDMAN, CHARLES, *The History of the Origin, Progress, and Termination of the American War* (2 vols.; London, 1794).

STYLES, JOHN, *An Essay on the Character, Immoral and Antichristian Tendency of the Stage* (Newport, Isle of Wight, 1806).

SURTEES, WILLIAM, *Twenty-Five Years in a Rifle Brigade* (Edinburgh, 1833).

THELWALL, JOHN, *The Trident of Albion* (Liverpool, 1805).

WALPOLE, HORACE, *Correspondence*, ed. W. S. Lewis (48 vols.; New Haven, Conn., 1937–83).

WARD, THOMAS ASLINE, *Peeps into the Past* (London, 1909).

WILKINS, W. H. (ed.), *South Africa a Century Ago: Letters Written from the Cape of Good Hope (1797–1801) by the Lady Anne Barnard* (London, 1901).

WILKINSON, TATE, *Memoirs of his Own Life* (4 vols.; York, 1790).

—— *The Wandering Patentee* (4 vols.; York, 1795).

WILSON, ROBERT MERCIER, 'Journal 1805–1809' in *Five Naval Journals 1789–1817*, ed. H. G. Thursfield (London, 1951).

WINSTON, JAMES, *The Theatric Tourist* (London, 1805).

4. Secondary sources

ALDRIDGE, ALFRED OWEN, *Man of Reason: the Life of Thomas Paine* (Philadelphia, Pa., 1959).

ALTICK, RICHARD D., *The Shows of London* (Cambridge, Mass., 1978).

ARUNDELL, DENIS, *The Story of Sadler's Wells 1683–1964* (London, 1965).

ASHTON, JOHN, *Social England under the Regency* (London, 1899).

BACKSHEIDER, PAULA R., *Spectacular Politics: Theatrical Power and Mass Culture in Early Modern England* (Baltimore, Md., 1993).

BADDELEY-CLINTON, V. C., *All Right on the Night* (London, 1954).

BAER, MARC, *Theatre and Disorder in Late Georgian London* (Oxford, 1992).

BARISH, JONAS, *The Antitheatrical Prejudice* (Berkeley, Calif., 1981).

BATE, JONATHAN, *Shakespearean Constitutions: Politics, Theatre, Criticism, 1730–1830* (Oxford, 1989).

BAYLY, C. A., *Imperial Meridian: The British Empire and the World 1780–1830* (London, 1989).

BAYNHAM, HENRY, *From the Lower Deck: The Old Navy 1780–1840* (London, 1969).

BECKETT, IAN F. W., *The Amateur Military Tradition, 1558–1945* (Manchester, 1991).

BENNETT, BETTY T. (ed.), *British War Poetry in the Age of Romanticism: 1793–1815* (New York, 1976).

BINDMAN, DAVID, *The Shadow of the Guillotine: Britain and the French Revolution* (London, 1989).

BOHSTEDT, JOHN, *Riots and Community Politics in England and Wales 1790–1810* (Cambridge, Mass., 1983).

BOOTH, ALAN, 'Popular Loyalism and Public Violence in the North-West of England, 1790–1800', *Social History*, 8 (1983), 295–313.

BOOTH, MICHAEL R., *English Melodrama* (London, 1965).

—— *Victorian Spectacular Theatre 1850–1910* (London, 1981).

BORSAY, PETER, '"All the Town's a Stage": Urban Ritual and Ceremony 1660–1800' in *The Transformation of English Provincial Towns 1600–1800*, ed. Peter Clark (London, 1984), 228–58.

BORSAY, PETER, *The English Urban Renaissance: Culture and Society in the Provincial Town, 1660–1770* (Oxford, 1989).

BRATTON, J. S., 'British Heroism and the Structure of Melodrama' in *Acts of Supremacy: The British Empire and the Stage, 1790–1830*, ed. J. S. Bratton, Richard Allen Cave, Breandan Gregory, Heidi J. Holder, and Michael Pickering (Manchester, 1991), 18–61.

BRETT-JAMES, ANTONY, *Life in Wellington's Army* (London, 1972).

BREWER, JOHN, *Party Ideology and Popular Politics at the Accession of George III* (Cambridge, 1976).

—— *The Sinews of Power: War, Money and the English State, 1688–1783* (London, 1989).

BROWN, JARED A., 'British Military Theatre in New York in 1780–81', *Theatre Survey*, 23 (1982), 151–62.

—— ' "Howe's Strolling Company": British Military Theatre in New York and Philadelphia, 1777 and 1778', *Theatre Survey*, 18 (1977), 30–43.

BROWN, LAURA, 'The Romance of Empire: *Oroonoko* and the Trade in Slaves' in *The New 18th Century: Theory Politics English Literature*, ed. Felicity Nussbaum and Laura Brown (New York, 1987), 41–61.

CARLSON, JULIE A., *In the Theatre of Romanticism: Coleridge, Nationalism, Women* (Cambridge, 1994).

CARRETTA, VINCENT, *George III and the Satirists from Hogarth to Byron* (Athens, Ga., 1990).

CASE, SUE-ELLEN, and JANELLE REINELT (eds.), *The Performance of Power: Theatrical Discourse and Politics* (Iowa City, Ia., 1991).

CASTLE, TERRY, *Masquerade and Civilization: the Carnivalesque in Eighteenth-Century Culture and Fiction* (London, 1986).

CLAEYS, GREGORY, *Thomas Paine: Social and Political Thought* (Boston, 1989).

CLARK, W. S., *The Irish Stage in the County Towns 1720 to 1800* (Oxford, 1965).

COLLEY, LINDA, 'Radical Patriotism in Eighteenth-Century England' in *Patriotism: the Making and Unmaking of British National Identity*, ed. Raphael Samuel (3 vols.; London, 1989), i. 169–87.

—— 'The Apotheosis of George III: Loyalty, Royalty and the British Nation 1760–1820', *Past and Present*, 102 (1984), 94–129.

—— 'Whose Nation? Class and National Consciousness in Britain 1750–1830', *Past and Present*, 113 (1986), 97–117.

—— *Britons: Forging the Nation 1707–1837* (New Haven, Conn., 1992).

CONOLLY, L. W., *The Censorship of English Drama, 1737–1824* (San Marino, Calif., 1976).

COOKSON, J. E., 'The English Volunteer Movement of the French Wars, 1793–1815: Some Contexts', *The Historical Journal*, 32 (1989), 867–91.

—— 'The Rise and Fall of the Sutton Volunteers, 1803–4', *Historical Research*, 64 (1991), 46–53.

CORVISIER, ANDRÉ, *Armies and Societies in Europe, 1494–1789*, trans. Abigail T. Siddall (Bloomington, Ind., 1979).

Cox, Jeffrey N., 'The French Revolution in the English Theater' in *History & Myth: Essays on English Romantic Literature*, ed. Stephen C. Behrendt (Detroit, Mich., 1990), 33–52.

Crary, Jonathan, *Techniques of the Observer: On Vision and Modernity in the Nineteenth Century* (Cambridge, Mass., 1990).

Cunningham, Hugh, 'The Language of Patriotism, 1750–1914', *History Workshop*, 12 (1981), 8–33.

Cunningham, John E., *Theatre Royal: The History of the Theatre Royal Birmingham* (Oxford, 1950).

Danchin, Pierre (ed.), *The Prologues and Epilogues of the Eighteenth Century, A Complete Edition* (Nancy, 1990).

Dann, John C. (ed.), *The Nagle Journal: A Diary of the Life of Jacob Nagle, Sailor, from the Year 1775 to 1841* (New York, 1988)

Davidoff, Leonore, and Catherine Hall, *Family Fortunes: Men and Women of the English Middle Class 1780–1850* (London, 1987).

Davis, Jim, 'British Bravery, or Tars Triumphant: Images of the British Navy in Nautical Melodrama', *New Theatre Quarterly*, 4 (1988), 122–43.

Davis, Tracy C., *Actresses as Working Women: Their Social Identity in Victorian Culture* (London, 1991).

De Castro, J. Paul, *The Gordon Riots* (London, 1926).

Dening, Greg, *Mr Bligh's Bad Language: Passion, Power and Theatre on the Bounty* (Cambridge, 1992).

Dibdin, James C., *The Annals of the Edinburgh Stage: With an Account of the Rise and Progress of Dramatic Writing in Scotland* (Edinburgh, 1888).

Dinwiddy, J. R., 'The Early Nineteenth-Century Campaign against Flogging in the Army', *English Historical Review*, 97 (1982), 308–31.

Donohue Jr., J. W., *Dramatic Character in the English Romantic Age* (Princeton, NJ, 1970).

Dozier, Robert R., *For King, Constitution, and Country: The English Loyalists and the French Revolution* (Lexington, Ky., 1983).

Dugaw, Dianne, *Warrior Women and Popular Balladry, 1650–1850* (Cambridge, 1989).

Eastwood, David, 'Robert Southey and the Meanings of Patriotism', *Journal of British Studies*, 31 (1992), 265–87.

Elam, Keir, *The Semiotics of Theatre and Drama* (London, 1980).

Elphick, Richard, and Hermann Giliomee, *The Shaping of South African Society, 1652–1840*, 2nd edn. (Middletown, Conn., 1989).

Emsley, Clive, 'Political Disaffection and the British Army in 1792', *Bulletin of the Institute of Historical Research*, 48 (1975), 230–45.

—— 'The Military and Popular Disorder in England 1790–1801', *Journal of the Society for Army Historical Research*, 61 (1983), 10–21, 96–112.

—— *British Society and the French Wars, 1793–1815* (London, 1979).

Epstein, James, 'Understanding the Cap of Liberty: Symbolic Practice and Social Conflict in Early Nineteenth-Century England', *Past and Present*, 122 (1989),

75–118.

FAHRNER, ROBERT, *The Theatre Career of Charles Dibdin the Elder (1745–1814)* (New York, 1989).

FORREST, ALAN I., *Conscripts and Deserters: The Army and French Society during the Revolution and Empire* (New York, 1989).

—— *The Soldiers of the French Revolution* (Durham, NC, 1990).

FOUCAULT, MICHEL, *Discipline and Punish: The Birth of the Prison*, trans. Alan Sheridan (Harmondsworth, 1977).

FREY, SYLVIA, *The British Soldier in America: a Social History of Military Life in the Revolutionary Period* (Austin, Tex., 1981).

FRITZ, PAUL S., 'The Trade in Death: The Royal Funerals in England, 1685–1830', *Eighteenth-Century Studies*, 15 (1982), 291–316.

—— 'From "Public" to "Private": the Royal Funerals in England, 1500–1830' in *Mirrors of Mortality: Studies in the Social History of Death*, ed. Joachim Whaley (London, 1981), 61–79.

FULLER, J. F. C., *British Light Infantry in the Eighteenth Century* (London, 1925).

GALPERIN, WILLIAM H., *The Return of the Visible in British Romanticism* (Baltimore, Md., 1993).

GEORGE, M. DOROTHY, *Catalogue of Political and Personal Satires Preserved in the Department of Prints and Drawings in the British Museum* (vols. 5–11; London, 1935–54).

—— *English Political Caricature 1793–1832: A Study of Opinion and Propaganda* (2 vols.; Oxford, 1959).

GILBERT, ARTHUR N., 'Buggery and the British Navy, 1700–1861', *Journal of Social History*, 10 (1976), 72–98.

—— 'Sexual Deviance and Disaster During the Napoleonic Wars', *Albion*, 9 (1977), 98–113.

GILLIS, CHRISTINA MARSDEN, 'Private Room and Public Space: The Paradox of Form in *Clarissa*', *Studies on Voltaire and the Eighteenth Century*, 176 (1979), 153–68.

GLEN, GEORGE D., '"Nautical Docudrama" in the Age of the Kembles' in *When They 'Weren't' Doing Shakespeare: Essays on Nineteenth-Century British and American Theatre*, ed. Judith L. Fisher and Stephen Watt (Athens, Ga., 1989).

HACKER, BARTON C., 'Women and Military Institutions in Early Modern Europe: A Reconnaissance', *Signs*, 6 (1981), 643–71.

HADLEY, ELAINE, 'The Old Price Wars: Melodramatizing the Public Sphere in Early-Nineteenth-Century England', *PMLA*, 107 (1992), 524–37.

HARE, ARNOLD, *The Georgian Theatre in Wessex* (London, 1958).

HARRISON, MARK, *Crowds and History: Mass Phenomena in English Towns, 1790–1835* (Cambridge, 1988).

HAY, DOUGLAS, 'War, Dearth and Theft in the Eighteenth Century: The Record of the English Courts', *Past and Present*, 95 (1982), 117–60.

HERBERT, BRIGADIER CHARLES, 'Coxheath Camp, 1778–1779', *Journal of the Society for Army Historical Research*, 45–6 (1967), 129–48.

HIGHFILL JR., PHILIP H., KALMAN A. BURNIM, and EDWARD A. LANGHANS, *A Biographical Dictionary of Actors, Actresses, Musicians, Dancers, Managers & Other Stage Personnel in London, 1660–1800* (16 vols.; Carbondale, Ill., 1973–93).

HILL, ERROL, *The Jamaican Stage, 1655–1900: Profile of a Colonial Theatre* (Amherst, Mass., 1992).

HODGKINSON, J. L., and REX POGSON, *The Early Manchester Theatre* (London, 1960).

HODGSON, NORMA, 'Sarah Baker (1736/7–1816) "Governess-General of the Kentish Drama"' in *Studies in English Theatre History in Memory of Gabrielle Enthoven* (London, 1952), 65–83.

HOGAN, CHARLES BEECHER, 'One of God Almighty's Unaccountables: Tate Wilkinson of York', in *The Theatrical Manager in England and America*, ed. Joseph W. Donohue Jr. (Princeton, NJ, 1971), 63–86.

—— *The London Stage 1660–1800: A Calendar of Plays, Entertainments and Afterpieces Together with Casts, Box-Receipts and Contemporary Comment Compiled from the Playbills, Newspapers and Theatrical Diaries of the Period, Part 5: 1776–1800* (3 vols.; Carbondale, Ill., 1968).

HONE, J. ANN, *For the Cause of Truth: Radicalism in London 1796–1821* (Oxford, 1982).

HOULDING, J. A., *Fit for Service: The Training of the British Army, 1715–1815* (Oxford, 1981).

HOWSON, GERALD, *Burgoyne of Saratoga: A Biography* (New York, 1979).

HUBBACK, J. H., and EDITH C. HUBBACK, *Jane Austen's Sailor Brothers: Being the Adventures of Sir Francis Austen G.C.B., Admiral of the Fleet and Rear-Admiral Charles Austen* (London, 1906).

HUDSON, ANN, 'Volunteer Soldiers in Sussex during the Revolutionary and Napoleonic Wars, 1793–1815', *Sussex Archaeological Collections*, 122 (1984), 165–81.

HUNT, LYNN (ed.), *The New Cultural History* (Berkeley, Calif., 1989).

—— *Politics, Culture, and Class in the French Revolution* (Stanford, Calif., 1984).

HYDE, RALPH, *Panoramania! the Art and Entertainment of the 'All-Embracing' View* (London, 1988).

JEWSON, C. B., *The Jacobin City: A Portrait of Norwich in its Reaction to the French Revolution 1788–1802* (Glasgow and London, 1975).

JONES, STANLEY, *Hazlitt: A Life; from Winterslow to Frith Street* (Oxford, 1989).

JORDAN, GERALD, 'Admiral Nelson as Popular Hero: The Nation and the Navy, 1795–1805' in *New Aspects of Naval History: Selected Papers from the 5th Naval History Symposium*, ed. The Department of History US Naval Academy (Baltimore, Md., 1985), 109–19.

JORDAN, GERALD, and NICHOLAS ROGERS, 'Admirals as Heroes: Patriotism and Liberty in Hanoverian England', *Journal of British Studies*, 28 (1989), 201–24.

KENNY, SHIRLEY STRUM, 'The Playhouse and the Printing Shop: Editing Restoration and Eighteenth-Century Plays', *Modern Philology*, 85 (1987–8), 408–19.

KLINGBERG, F. J., and S. B. HUSTVEDT (eds.), *The Warning Drum, the British Home*

Front Faces Napoleon: Broadsides of 1803 (Berkeley, Calif., 1944).

KNAPP, MARY E., *Prologues and Epilogues of the Eighteenth Century* (New Haven, Conn., 1961).

KUBIAK, ANTONY, *Stages of Terror: Terrorism, Ideology, and Coercion as Theatre History* (Bloomington, Ind., 1991).

LANGFORD, PAUL, *A Polite and Commercial People: England 1727–1783* (Oxford, 1989).

—— *Public Life and the Propertied Englishman, 1689–1798* (Oxford, 1991).

LAVERY, BRIAN, *Nelson's Navy: The Ships, Men and Organisation 1793–1815* (London, 1989).

LAWRENCE, W. J., *Old Theatre Days and Ways* (London, 1935).

LEVINE, LAURENCE W., *Highbrow/Lowbrow: The Emergence of Cultural Hierarchy in America* (Cambridge, Mass., 1988).

LEWIS, MICHAEL, *A Social History of the Navy 1793–1815* (London, 1960).

LITVAK, JOSEPH, 'The Infection of Acting: Theatricals and Theatricality in *Mansfield Park*', *ELH* 53 (1986), 331–55.

—— *Caught in the Act: Theatricality in the Nineteenth-Century English Novel* (Berkeley, Calif., 1992).

LIU, ALAN, *Wordsworth, the Sense of History* (Stanford, Calif., 1989).

LOFTIS, JOHN, *Sheridan and the Drama of Georgian England* (Oxford, 1976).

LONSDALE, ROGER (ed.), *The New Oxford Book of Eighteenth Century Verse* (Oxford, 1984).

MALLET, DAVID, *The Plays of David Mallet*, ed. Felicity A. Nussbaum (New York, 1980).

MALONE, DIANE B., 'A Survey of Early Military Theatre in America', *Theatre Survey*, 16 (1975), 56–64.

McCALMAN, IAIN (ed.), *The Horrors of Slavery and Other Writings by Robert Wedderburn* (Edinburgh, 1991).

—— *Radical Underworld: Prophets, Revolutionaries and Pornographers in London, 1795–1840* (Cambridge, 1988).

McCRACKEN, J. L., 'The Cape of Good Hope 1796–98' in *Macartney of Lisanoure 1737–1806: Essays in Biography*, ed. Peter Roebuck (Belfast, 1983), 266–77.

McGUFFIE, T. H., 'Early Barrack Life', *Army Quarterly*, 54 (1947), 65–8.

McNEIL, DAVID, *The Grotesque Depiction of War and the Military in Eighteenth-Century Fiction* (Newark, NJ, 1990).

McVEIGH, SIMON, *Concert Life in London from Mozart to Haydn* (Cambridge, 1993).

MEISEL, MARTIN, *Realizations: Narrative, Pictorial and Theatrical Arts in Nineteenth-Century England* (Princeton, NJ, 1983).

MIDDLEKAUFF, ROBERT, *The Glorious Cause: The American Revolution 1763–1789* (New York, 1982).

MONOD, PAUL, 'Pierre's White Hat: Theatre, Jacobitism and Popular Protest in London, 1689–1760' in *By Force or By Default? The Revolution of 1688–1689*, ed. Eveline Cruickshanks (Edinburgh, 1989), 159–89.

MORLEY, MALCOLM, *Margate and its Theatres 1730–1965* (London, 1966).

MORRISS, ROGER, *The Royal Dockyards During the Revolutionary and Napoleonic Wars* (Leicester, 1983).

MUKHERJEE, S. K., *The Story of the Calcutta Theatres 1753–1980* (Calcutta, 1982).

NEWMAN, GERALD, *The Rise of English Nationalism: A Cultural History, 1740–1830* (New York, 1987).

NEWTON, ROBERT, *Eighteenth Century Exeter* (Exeter, 1984).

NICHOLSON, W., *The Struggle for a Free Stage in London* (Boston, Mass., 1906).

NICOLL, ALLARDYCE, *The Garrick Stage: Theatres and Audience in the Eighteenth Century* (Manchester, 1980).

O'BRIEN, R.B., *The Autobiography of Theobald Wolfe Tone* (2 vols.; Dublin, 1893).

OWSLEY JR., FRANK LAWRENCE, *Struggle for the Gulf Borderlands: The Creek War and the Battle of New Orleans 1812–1815* (Gainesville, Fla., 1981).

OZOUF, MONA, *Festivals and the French Revolution*, trans. Alan Sheridan (Cambridge, Mass., 1988).

PALMER, ROY (ed.), *The Rambling Soldier: Life in the Lower Ranks, 1750–1900, Through Soldiers' Songs and Writings* (Gloucester, 1985).

PARKINSON, C. N., *Portsmouth Point: The British Navy in Fiction 1793–1815* (Cambridge, Mass., 1949).

PATTERSON, A. TEMPLE, *Radical Leicester: A History of Leicester 1780–1850* (Leicester, 1954).

PEDICORD, HARRY WILLIAM, *'By Their Majesties' Command': The House of Hanover at the London Theatres, 1714–1800* (London, 1991).

PEEL, FRANK, *Spen Valley: Past and Present* (Heckmondwike, 1893).

PHILBRICK, NORMAN (ed.), *Trumpets Sounding: Propaganda Plays of the American Revolution* (New York, 1972).

PORTER, ROY, *English Society in the Eighteenth Century* (Harmondsworth, 1982).

—— *Mind-Forg'd Manacles: A History of Madness in England from the Restoration to the Regency* (Cambridge, Mass., 1987).

POSTLEWAIT, THOMAS, and BRUCE A. MCCONACHIE (eds.), *Interpreting the Theatrical Past: Essays in the Historiography of Performance* (Iowa City, Ia., 1989).

PROBYN, CLIVE T., *The Sociable Humanist: The Life and Works of James Harris 1709–1780* (Oxford, 1991).

REINELT, JANELLE G., and JOSEPH R. ROACH (eds.), *Critical Theory and Performance* (Ann Arbor, Mich., 1992).

RICHARDS, JEFFREY H., *Theater Enough: American Culture and the Metaphor of the World Stage, 1607–1789* (Durham, NC, 1991).

ROBERTS, VANESSA HISTON, 'Publishing and Printing on Board Ship', *Mariner's Mirror*, 74 (1988), 329–34.

ROBINSON, C. N., *The British Tar in Fact and Fiction* (London, 1909).

RODGER, N. A. M., *The Wooden World: An Anatomy of the Georgian Navy* (London, 1986).

ROE, NICHOLAS, *Wordsworth and Coleridge: The Radical Years* (Oxford, 1988).

ROSENFELD, SYBIL, 'Jane Austen and Private Theatricals', *Essays and Studies*, 15 (1962), 40–51.

—— *Georgian Scene Painters and Scene Painting* (Cambridge, 1981).

—— *Strolling Players & Drama in the Provinces 1660–1765* (Cambridge, 1939).

—— *Temples of Thespis: Some Private Theatres and Theatricals in England and Wales, 1700–1820* (London, 1978).

ROSTRON, DAVID, 'Contemporary Political Comment in Four of J. P. Kemble's Shakespearean Productions', *Theatre Research*, 12 (1972), 113–19.

RULE, JOHN, *Albion's People: English Society, 1714–1815* (London, 1992).

RUSSELL, GILLIAN, 'Playing at Revolution: the Politics of the O. P. Riots of 1809', *Theatre Notebook*, 44 (1990), 16–26.

SARGEANT, H., 'A History of Portsmouth Theatres', *Portsmouth Papers*, 13 (1971), 3–25.

SAXON, A. H., *Enter Foot and Horse: A History of Hippodrama in England and France* (New Haven, Conn., 1968).

SEILHAMER, GEORGE O., *History of the American Theatre* (3 vols.; Philadelphia, 1888–91).

SILVERMAN, KENNETH, *A Cultural History of the American Revolution: Painting, Music, Literature, and the Theatre in the Colonies and the United States from the Treaty of Paris to the Inauguration of George Washington 1763–1789* (New York, 1976).

SMITH, BERNARD, *European Vision and the South Pacific*, 2nd edn. (Sydney, 1985).

SMITH, DANE FARNSWORTH, *Plays About the Theatre in England, 1737–1800: or, The Self-Conscious Stage from Foote to Sheridan* (Cranbury, NJ, 1979).

STALLYBRASS, PETER, and ALLON WHITE, *The Politics and Poetics of Transgression* (London, 1986).

STEEDMAN, CAROLYN, *The Radical Soldier's Tale: John Pearman, 1819–1908* (London, 1988).

STEVENSON, JOHN, 'The London "Crimp" Riots of 1794', *International Review of Social History*, 16 (1971), 40–58.

STONE JR., GEORGE WINCHESTER (ed.), *The Stage and the Page: London's 'Whole Show' in the Eighteenth-Century Theatre* (Berkeley, Calif., 1981).

STRAUB, KRISTINA, *Sexual Suspects: Eighteenth-Century Players and Sexual Ideology* (Princeton, NJ, 1992).

SULERI, SARA, *The Rhetoric of English India* (Chicago, 1990).

SUMMERSON, JOHN, *The Life and Work of John Nash Architect* (London, 1980).

THIEME, JOHN A., 'Spouting, Spouting Clubs and Spouting Companions', *Theatre Notebook*, 29 (1975), 9–16.

THOMAS, DAVID (ed.), *Restoration and Georgian England, 1660–1788* (Cambridge, 1989).

THOMPSON, E. P., 'Patrician Society, Plebeian Culture', *Journal of Social History*, 7 (1974), 382–405.

—— *The Making of the English Working Class*, 2nd edn. (Harmondsworth, 1968).

TRUSTRAM, MYNA, *Women of the Regiment: Marriage and the Victorian Army*

(Cambridge, 1984).

TUMIR, VASKA, 'She-Tragedy and Its Men: Conflict and Form in *The Orphan* and *The Fair Penitent*', *SEL* 30 (1990), 411–28.

VIRILIO, PAUL, *War and Cinema: the Logistics of Perception*, trans. Patrick Camiller (London, 1989).

WARD, CHRISTOPHER, *The War of the Revolution*, ed. J. R. Alden (2 vols.; New York, 1952).

WELLS, ROGER, *Insurrection: The British Experience 1795–1803* (Gloucester, 1983).

—— *Wretched Faces: Famine in Wartime England 1793–1801* (Gloucester, 1988).

WERKMEISTER, LUCYLE, *A Newspaper History of England, 1792–1793* (Lincoln, Nebr., 1967).

WESTERN, J. R., 'The Volunteer Movement as an Anti-Revolutionary Force, 1793–1801', *English Historical Review*, 71 (1956), 603–14.

—— *The English Militia in the Eighteenth Century; The Story of a Political Issue 1660–1802* (London, 1965).

WHITFELD, HENRY FRANCIS, *Plymouth and Devonport in Times of War and Peace* (Plymouth, 1900).

WILSON, KATHLEEN, 'Empire, Trade and Popular Politics in Mid-Hanoverian Britain: the Case of Admiral Vernon', *Past and Present*, 121 (1988), 74–109.

—— 'Urban Culture and Political Activism in Hanoverian England: The Example of Voluntary Hospitals' in *The Transformation of Political Culture: England and Germany in the Late Eighteenth Century*, ed. Eckhart Hellmuth (London, 1990), 165–84.

WRIGHT, RICHARDSON, *Revels in Jamaica 1682–1838* (New York, 1969).

YARRINGTON, ALISON, *The Commemoration of the Hero 1800–1864: Monuments to the British Victors of the Napoleonic Wars* (New York, 1988).

Index